Reading and Teaching

REFLECTIVE TEACHING AND THE SOCIAL CONDITIONS OF SCHOOLING
A Series for Prospective and Practicing Teachers
Daniel P. Liston and Kenneth M. Zeichner, Series Editors

Zeichner/Liston • Reflective Teaching: An Introduction

Liston/Zeichner • Culture and Teaching

Maher/Ward • Gender and Teaching

Commins/Miramontes • Linguistic Diversity and Teaching

Meyer/Manning • Reading and Teaching

Reading and Teaching

Richard J. Meyer
University of New Mexico

Maryann Manning
University of Alabama-Birmingham

First published 2007 by Lawrence Erlbaum Associates, Inc.

Published 2015 by Routledge
711 Third Avenue, New York, NY 10017, USA
2 Park Square, Milton Park, Abingdon, Oxon OX14 4RN

First issued in hardback 2015

Routledge is an imprint of Taylor & Francis Group, an informa business

Copyright © 2007 by Lawrence Erlbaum Associates, Inc.
All rights reserved. No part of this book may be reproduced in any form, by photostat, microform, retrieval system, or any other means, without prior written permission of the publisher.

Cover design by Kathryn Houghtaling

Library of Congress Cataloging-in-Publication Data

Meyer, Richard J.
 1949-Reading and teaching / Richard J. Meyer, Maryann Manning.
   p. cm. — (Reflective teaching and the social conditions of schooling)
 Includes bibliographical references.
ISBN 978-0-8058-5429-9 0-8058-5429-0 (p : alk. paper)
ISBN 978-1-4106-1605-0 1-4106-1605-3 (e book)
 1. Reading—Case studies. 2. Reflective teaching—Case studies.
 I. Manning, Maryann Murphy. II. Title.

LB1050.M475 2007
372.4—dc22   2006038475
                                                                                CIP

ISBN 13: 978-1-138-83438-5 (hbk)
ISBN 13: 978-0-8058-5429-9 (pbk)

This book is dedicated to the teachers that helped us write it, their students, and teachers and students around the world struggling for justice in their reading curriculum.

CONTENTS

Series Preface, *ix*

Preface, *xv*

PART I. CASE STUDIES AND REACTIONS　　　　　　1

Introduction to Case 1, *2*
Case 1: Teaching Reading via Direct Systematic Instruction (Penny), *3*
Reader Reactions to Case 1, *15*
Educators' Dialogue About Case 1, *16*
Reader Reactions to the Educators' Dialogue About Case 1, *28*
Summary and Additional Questions, *29*

Introduction to Case 2, *32*
Case 2: A New Teacher Learns About Teaching Reading and Culture (Sylvia), *32*
Reader Reactions to Case 2, *43*
Educators' Dialogue About Case 2, *44*
Reader Reactions to the Educators' Dialogue About Case 2, *53*
Summary and Additional Questions, *54*

Introduction to Case 3, *55*
Case 3: A Teacher-Constructed Whole Language Program (Kendra), *55*

Reader Reactions to Case 3, *69*
Educators' Dialogue About Case 3, *70*
Reader Reactions to the Educators' Dialogue About Case 3, *80*
Summary and Additional Questions, *81*

Introduction to Case 4, *83*
Case 4: Critical Literacy in an Urban Middle School (Janesse), *83*
Reader Reactions to Case 4, *95*
Educators' Dialogue About Case 4, *96*
Reader Reactions to the Educators' Dialogue About Case 4, *106*
Summary and Additional Questions, *107*

PART II. PUBLIC ARGUMENTS: THREE VIEWS OF THE READING PROCESS AND INSTRUCTION   109

Teachers of Reading as Decision Makers, *110*
Direction Instruction View of the Reading Process and Instruction, *112*
Whole Language View of the Reading Process and Instruction, *124*
Critical Literacy View of the Reading Process and Instruction, *138*
Afterthoughts on the Three Views, *154*

PART III: A FINAL ARGUMENT AND SOME SUGGESTIONS AND RESOURCES FOR FURTHER REFLECTION   157

Decision Making and Teacher Development, *157*
Teachers Face Dilemmas and Make Decisions, *159*
Considerations for Reading and Teaching, *161*
Some Suggestions, *172*
Conclusion, *177*

References, *179*

Author Index, *187*

Subject Index, *191*

SERIES PREFACE: AN ESSENTIAL SERIES INTRODUCTION

Whereas many readers rarely read introductory material, we hope you will continue. The success of this book depends, in large part, on how you use it. In what follows, we outline some of our key assumptions and we suggest ways for approaching the material in each book of this series, entitled "Reflective Teaching and the Social Conditions of Schooling." First, we identify some of our reasons for creating this series. We then relate a bit about our dissatisfaction with how teacher education is usually conducted and how it can be changed. Finally, we outline suggestions for ways to best utilize the material in this and subsequent texts.

Some years ago we were asked to develop further the ideas outlined in our book *Teacher Education and the Social Conditions of Schooling* (Liston & Zeichner, 1991). It was suggested that we take our basic approach to teacher reflection and our ideas about teacher education curricula and put them into practice. The proposal was attractive, and the subsequent endeavor proved to be very challenging. It never seems easy to translate educational "shoulds" and possibilities into schooling "cans" and realities. But we think (and we hope) we have made progress in that effort by designing a series of books intended to help prospective, beginning, and experienced teachers to reflect on their profession, their teaching, and their experiences.

We are pleased and delighted to have the opportunity to share this work with you. We hope you find these texts to be engaging and useful.

We are two university teacher educators, both former elementary teachers, who have worked in inner city, small town, and suburban elementary and middle schools. We are committed to public schools as democratic institutions, as places of learning in which people of all walks of life come to learn how to live together in a democratic society. Although we are personally committed to ways of working and living together that are much more collaborative than exist today, we are educators first, realists second, and dreamers third. It is our firm belief that an education that engages prospective and practicing teachers' heads and hearts, their beliefs and passions, needs to be fair and honest. We have neither written nor encouraged others to write these texts to convince you to see schools and society in a particular light, but rather to engage you in a consideration of crucial issues that all teachers need to address. Once engaged, we hope that you will be better able to articulate your views, responses, and responsibilities to students and parents, and come to better understand aspects of your role as a teacher in a democratic society.

IMPACTS OF THE SOCIAL CONDITIONS OF SCHOOLING

Prospective teachers need to be prepared for the problems and challenges of public schooling. Sometimes the focus of teacher preparation remains strictly on the processes that occur within the classroom and inside the school walls. At times, teacher education programs emphasize instructional methodology and the psychology of the learner in university course work and underscore survival strategies for student teaching. These are certainly important elements in any teacher's preparation and ones that cannot be ignored. But classrooms and schools are not insulated environments. What goes on inside schools is greatly influenced by what occurs outside of schools. The students who attend and the teachers and administrators who work within those walls bring into the school building all sorts of cultural assumptions, social influences, and contextual dynamics. Unless some concerted attention is given to those assumptions, influences, and dynamics, to the reality of school life and to the social conditions of schooling, our future teachers will be ill prepared.

Over the last 10 years, teacher educators have paid greater attention to the social conditions of schooling. But a consensus of opinion on this issue does not exist. The professional aspects of teacher education, including attention to the social conditions of schooling, have been criticized by some scholars and politicians who believe that content knowledge alone is sufficient to teach. Although we recognize the importance of teachers' content knowledge, this view is, we believe, a gross and politically motivated mistake that will do harm to the students in our public schools and their teachers. Students need teachers who have the professional preparation necessary to teach a diverse student population to achieve high academic standards. We hope that the books in this series will contribute to this end.

We are living in a time of remarkable change, a time of social and political transformation. In an era that is rife with social controversies and political difficulties, in which public schooling has increasingly come under attack, during which we are seeing marked changes in this country's cultural demographic make-up, in which there are great pressures to transform public schools into private, for-profit enterprises, we must educate well our teaching workforce. Future teachers cannot, on their own, solve the many societal issues confronting the schools, but they should certainly know what those issues are, have a sense of their own beliefs about those issues, and understand the many ways in which those issues will come alive within their school's walls. Poverty and wealth, our culture of consumerism, what seems to be an increasing amount of violent behavior, and the work pressures of modern life affect the children who attend our public schools. Public attitudes about competition and excellence, race and ethnicity, gender roles and homosexuality, and the environment affect students inside and outside of schools. One can be certain that the issues that affect all of our lives outside of schools will certainly influence students inside their schools.

EXAMINING THE SOCIAL CONDITIONS OF SCHOOLING

Probably the best way to begin to examine contextual issues such as these is to be "attentive" early on in one's professional preparation, to experience features of the social conditions of schooling, and then to examine the experience and what we know about the social and cultural context of schooling. We encourage prospective and practicing teachers to do this. But teacher preparation programs often are not organized in a fashion that would encourage the discussion and examination of these sorts of shared experiences. What traditionally are called social foundations courses are typically not school-based, but set apart from some of the more realistic, practical, and engaged dilemmas of schooling. In schools of education, we frequently teach what the sociology or philosophy of education has to say about schools, but we tend to teach it as sociologists or philosophers, not as teachers struggling with crucial and highly controversial issues. Thus, in our own work with prospective and practicing teachers, we have developed ways to examine contextual issues of schooling and to enable ourselves and our students to articulate our ideas, beliefs, theories, and feelings about those issues. The books in this series attempt to utilize some of these insights and to pass along to others the content and the processes we have found useful.

When students and faculty engage in discussions of the social and political conditions of schooling and the effects of these conditions on students and schools, it is likely that the talk will be lively and controversies will emerge. In this arena, there are no absolutely "right" or "wrong" answers. There are choices, frequently difficult ones, choices that require considerable discussion, deliberation, and justification. In order for these discussions to occur, we need to create classroom settings that are conducive to conversations about difficult and controversial issues. The best format for such discussion is not the debate, the (in)formal argument, or dispassionate and aloof analysis. Instead, the most conducive environment is a classroom designed to create dialogue and conversation among participants with differing points of view. There isn't a recipe or formula that will ensure this type of environment, but we think the following suggestions are worth considering.

It is important for individuals using these texts to engage in discussions that are sensitive and respectful toward others, and at the same time challenge each other's views. This is not an easy task. It requires each participant to come to the class sessions prepared, to listen attentively to other people's views, and to address one another with a tone and attitude of respect. This means that when disagreements between individuals occur, and they inevitably will, each participant should find a way to express that disagreement without diminishing or attacking the other individual. Participants in these professional discussions need to be able to voice their views freely and to be sensitive toward others. Frequently, this is difficult to do. In discussions of controversial issues, ones that strike emotional chords, we are prone to argue in a way that belittles or disregards another person and his or her point of view. At times, we try to dismiss both the claim and the person. But if the discussions that these books help to initiate are carried on in that demeaning fashion, the potential power of these works will not be realized. A discussion of this paragraph should occur before discussing the substance raised by this particular text. It is our conviction that when a class keeps both substance and pedagogy in the forefront, it has a way of engaging individuals in a much more positive manner. From our own past experiences, we have found that during the course of a class's use of this material, it may be quite helpful to pause and focus on substantive and pedagogical issues in a conscious and forthright manner. Such time is generally well spent.

UNDERSTANDING AND EXAMINING PERSONAL BELIEFS ABOUT TEACHING AND SCHOOLING

It is also our belief that many educational issues engage and affect our heads and our hearts. Teaching is work that entails both thinking and feeling; those who can reflectively think and feel will find their work more rewarding and their efforts more successful. Good teachers find ways to listen to and integrate their passions, beliefs, and judgments. And so we encourage not only the type of group deliberation just outlined, but also an approach to reading that is attentive to an individual's felt sense or what some might call "gut-level" reactions. In the books in this series that contain case material and written reactions to that material, along with the public arguments that pertain to the issues raised, we believe it is essential that you, the reader, attend to your felt reactions, and attempt to sort out what those reactions tell you. At times it seems we can predict our reactions to the readings and discussions of this material, whereas at other times it can invoke reactions and feelings that surprise us. Attending to those issues in a heartfelt manner, one that is honest and forthright, gives us a better sense of ourselves as teachers and our understandings of the world. Not only do students walk into schools with expectations and assumptions formed as a result of life experiences, but so do their teachers. Practicing and prospective teachers can benefit from thinking about their expectations and assumptions. Hopefully, our work will facilitate this sort of reflection.

ABOUT THE BOOKS IN THIS SERIES

The first work in this series, *Reflective Teaching*, introduces the notion of teacher reflection and develops it in relation to the social conditions of schooling. Building on this concept, the second work in the series, *Culture and Teaching*, encourages a reflection on and examination of diverse cultures and schooling. In *Gender and Teaching*, the third work in the series, Frinde Maher and Janie Ward examine the central role of gender in both teaching and schooling. In the fourth volume in this series, *Linguistic Diversity and Teaching*, Nancy Commins and Ofelia Miramontes focus on issues of linguistic diversity, instructional practices, and public schooling. And in this volume, Rick Meyer and Maryann Manning offer a fruitful and illuminating introduction to beginning reading instruction. These two well-known experts in reading education have created a powerful format to explore literacy issues. We are fortunate to have these two individuals as guides.

SERIES ACKNOWLEDGMENTS

Two individuals have been essential to the conception and execution of this series. Kathleen Keller, our first editor at St. Martin's Press (where the series originated), initially suggested that we further develop the ideas outlined in *Teacher Education and the Social Conditions of Schooling* (Liston & Zeichner, 1991). Kathleen was very helpful in the initial stages of this effort and we wish to thank her for that. Naomi Silverman, our current and beloved editor at Lawrence Erlbaum Associates, has patiently and skillfully prodded us along attending to both the "big picture" and the small details. She has been remarkably supportive and capably informative. We are very thankful and indebted to Naomi.

—Daniel P. Liston
—Kenneth M. Zeichner

PREFACE

The teaching of reading seems to grow increasingly controversial as teachers, legislators, researchers, and community members all seem to know the best way for children to learn to read. Yet, many of them disagree with each other. Historically, arguments about the best way to teach reading reach far back into the last millennium when, early in the 1900s, Edmund Huey (1908) challenged popular notions of the time that focused on sounds and letter names. Huey wanted teachers and researchers to make the study and teaching of reading more complex, suggesting that the making of meaning was at the heart of the reading process and so it should be at the heart of the instructional process. Later, other theorists, claiming that "Johnnie can't read" (Flesch, 1955), called for systematic phonics instruction with less of a focus on comprehension because they argued that children will understand elementary texts if they simply decode the words. In the current political climate, the federal government has for the first time taken an assertive stance on reading instruction and research through the No Child Left Behind Act (NCLB). In addition to sweeping changes in areas such as assessment, bilingual education, and the achievement gap, the Act impacts reading instruction through Reading First, which is the section having to do with funding for reading programs. Reading First schools are those with histories of chronic poor performance and, typically, high levels of poverty and high percentages of non-White students.

The federal government demands that all reading programs in such schools be based on reliable replicable research. This has led to an aggressive push to incorporate intense systematic phonics instruction into all Reading First schools because some researchers argue that this approach to teaching reading is the only method for which there is reliable replicable research (Moats, 2000; Shanahan, 2005). Other researchers claim that "reliable replicable research" is narrowly defined because it does not include qualitative research, thus eliminating thousands of classroom-based studies of reading instruction and the reading process. The first group counters that reading instruction needs to be consistent across all settings because of the persistent history of poor student performance, which, they claim, must be a direct result of poor teaching. The second group rejoinders that the performance measures used are biased against poor and diverse children. The first group responds that there have been too many excuses for too long and that only reading can bring children out of poverty. The second group retorts that the reading crisis is manufactured (Berliner & Biddle, 1995) and that reading performance does not solve poverty because social conditions must be improved in order for teachers to be able to teach children and for children to be prepared to learn (Street, 1995). The arguments go back and forth, and teachers and their students are pulled in one direction and then another. For a time, teachers were told that they were professionals and should make decisions about reading instruction based on their knowledge of the children, the materials, the reading process, and ongoing assessment. Then, there was a change in direction and teachers were told that they were not to make decisions about reading instruction; rather, they must adhere rigidly to the programs that their schools are adopting, programs that are often carefully scripted so that teachers deliver a consistent and carefully crafted curriculum to all students, regardless of culture, location, language, and social issues.

The publishers of reading assessments and tests are making money—big money. The publishers of reading programs, often the same as the ones designing and selling the tests, are also making a lot of money. There are arguments over whether the NCLB act is intended to privatize education so that publishers and other entrepreneurs can make even more money (Altwerger, 2005). The anger escalates, teachers are held up as incompetent teachers of reading, children are held up as being left behind and failing at reading, and the solutions seem as unclear as ever.

Within all the layers of the debates—including the many perspectives argued by researchers, the screams of legislators, the demands of families, and the claims of publishers about their programs—there are, in classrooms, every school day of the year, children and their teachers. They face each other in a climate in which many are demoralized and worried about their schools going into corrective action or being taken over by their state, as NCLB demands if progress is inadequate. They face sanctions that include curricula being forced on them and funds being cut. And within all of that noise and stress, teachers are expected to teach children to read. Some rely on the mandated programs being forced on them. Others argue and then comply. Still others argue and then exert as much energy as possible to ignore and teach around the mandated programs. And some teachers decide to leave the profession rather than force children to do things that they, as teachers, do not find acceptable in meeting the needs of their students' learning to read.

Many teachers—especially novices—are confused to the point of dizziness. The purpose of this book is to help teachers make informed choices about their teaching of reading. We do this by presenting real teachers of reading in their classrooms, dialogues about that teaching, and exercises for further clarification. Consistent with the other books in this series, this volume focuses on teachers as decision makers. We consider the different types of decisions teachers might make in the teaching of reading and the knowledge on which they rely in making those decisions. Their knowledge is not simply factual information about using certain materials to teach. It also includes knowledge about the mind, the political climate, demands on their students and school, and the communities in which they teach.

Teachers love to hear about other teachers' lives in classrooms. Such stories teach us, and we take those lessons back to our own classrooms. In this book, we introduce you to four teachers of reading as a way of helping you decide how to best teach reading in your own classroom. We analyze, with you and other educators, what transpires in their reading programs, and we address the underlying question that supports the ideas presented in this book: How are children served by their reading program? That ultimate question is what must drive reading instruction. If researchers, special interest groups, and politicians are screaming so loudly at us that we cannot hear the voices of children reading in our own classroom, then our students are not being served well. If threats of financial and programmatic sanctions pervade our schools and force us to do things that appease the sanctions but do not help our children as literate souls, we are all left behind. It is our hope that as you read this book, you will clarify your understanding of how readers read, how they learn to read, and what teachers need to know and do to ensure that learning takes place.

CONTENT AND STRUCTURE

There are three parts to this book. The first section contains the cases of four teachers, with each case followed by a dialogue among other educators about the case. All the teachers, like teachers across the United States, are teaching in schools that are at risk of facing sanctions from NCLB and they all feel under the spotlight.

The second section of the book focuses on views (referred to as public arguments) of the reading process and instruction. There is so much discussion and argument about what reading is (the processes that occurs in the mind) and how to best teach it (instructional practices) that teachers need a vehicle to clarify their beliefs. We present the Direct Instruction (DI), Whole Language (WL), and Critical Literacy (CL) views of reading.

The final section of the book is about teachers' development as teachers of reading and as decision makers. In that section, we offer different ideas for you to consider as you clarify your view of reading. We help you consider your understanding of how children learn, the essence of what it means to teach, the politics that we all feel exerted on us, how to deal with the loneliness that teachers face, and more. We also offer some specific activities for you to try, hopefully with colleagues so that you may have conversations about your experiences.

The Case Studies

The four case studies are presented as scenarios of life within the four teachers' classrooms. We provide readers with a sense of what occurs in the classrooms on a daily basis and each teacher's thinking about her reading program. We also provide some theoretical information to help contextualize each case. Immediately following each case, we've left a page for you to write your thoughts about what you've read. On the pages following your reflection, we've placed the responses of groups of educators that met to discuss the case. We suggest that you read these and also consider acting them out with colleagues so that the discussions in the book seem more like the discussions that actually took place in our homes the evenings we met in small groups to listen to, read, and converse about the teachers' reading programs. We've left room at the end of each dialogue for you to think and write further about your response to each case.

One of the most difficult facets of teacher decision making is the reality of loneliness that many teachers face. Living in classrooms with children all day is a wonderful way of expressing love and caring for them, but it does not completely satisfy the intellectual stimulation and professional development that many teachers want. Those are often ignored, and such ignoring may lead to frustration and an increased sense of isolation. One of our intentions in presenting cases and discussions about the cases is for you to feel included in and connected to professional discussions about the teaching and learning of reading.

Public Arguments About the Reading Process and Instruction

The purpose of Part II is to help you understand the three main factions in the debates on reading process and reading instruction. Throughout this book, we make a distinction between two components of the word *reading* as it is used in schools and in research. One component is the reading **process**. Reading process refers to our understanding of what we believe occurs in the human mind when we read. The other component, reading **instruction**, refers to the way in which we believe reading should be taught. When we write the word *reading*, we are referring to both of these, process and instruction; however, when specificity is required, we add either *process* or *instruction* for clarity. As readers will see, the differences in beliefs about the reading process result in significant differences in reading instruction between DI and WL classrooms.

Direct Instruction (DI) is one faction, view, or public argument about reading (both process and instruction). The DI view of the reading process is that readers learn sounds, the ways those sounds are represented in print, and the ways in which those printed letters are used to represent words. The words, when mastered fluently as independent units, will also be read fluently in texts in which they are encountered. The young reader's mind is viewed as learning parts and then moving from parts (sounds and words) to the whole (meaning a whole sustained text, such as a storybook). If something unfamiliar is encountered in a text, the reader is expected to use the small parts (sounds, syllables, prefixes, etc.) to decode the new word. DI programs are often scripted, meaning they provide teachers with exact language to use during instruction.

The Whole Language (WL) view, faction, or public argument of the reading process is that learning to read is as natural as learning to speak. The "whole" in Whole Language refers to the idea that language exists to make meaning, first and foremost, and in order for a reader to construct meaning, he or she must use phonics, grammar (syntax), and semantics—the whole set of cueing systems that compose a language. Readers learn sounds and words because those elements of language are the surface features that allow meaning to be constructed. Whole Language teachers develop reading programs specific to the students in their classrooms and with the understanding that language is learned from whole (referring to the meaning) to part (referring to the sounds, words, and grammar that are parts of a language).

The Critical Literacy (CL) view, faction, or public argument of reading is sometimes referred to as an extension of the Whole Language view, asserting that language (oral or written) is about the making of meaning, first and foremost, because humans are meaning makers. CL teachers and researchers assert that every language or literacy event is steeped in cultural issues, relationships, and power dynamics. CL teachers work to remain keenly aware of and responsive to groups that are marginalized or disenfranchised. They include consideration of such groups in their teaching from the earliest grades. For example, a kindergarten class learned to understand the ways in which packaging entices young children to purchase certain products Vasquez (2000). Young children studied the ways in which beliefs about gender are perpetuated in advertising (Wilson, 2002). CL teachers involve students of any age in studies of war, peace, gay and lesbian issues, fairness, and equity. Social justice is the theme that underlies all CL classrooms as teachers and students work together to raise consciousness about issues and make decisions about how they might act on those issues as individuals, small groups, or a whole class.

A Final Argument

Most of us did not think about becoming teachers as a way to express or engage in political activity. We didn't want our teaching nested in such complexities as federal legislation, the interests of businesses, or the fear of funding cuts and imposed programs. Yet, here we are in the midst of a much more complex field than we ever imagined teaching reading to be. Our final section focuses on some of the facets of teaching and learning that real teachers in real schools and classrooms face each day. We present these issues as a series of *considerations* so that readers might reflect further on their own practice. We ask that you consider, as a teacher of reading: (a) what you see as your professional responsibilities when you make decisions about reading; (b) the importance of understanding how children learn; (c) the idea that isolation and loneliness may influence the decisions that teachers make; (d) the depth of knowledge that you need about the reading process and instructional options; (e) the relevance of students' cultures to the teaching and learning of reading; (f) the political nature of teaching acts; (g) how you will create a space for literacy learning; and (h) how you might find colleagues with whom you can safely think about your reading program.

Most reading lessons in which teachers are engaged are contextualized in a classroom, in a school, in a district, in a state, and in many more layers of context. Each student's home culture, language, and social issues are present in some form during each reading lesson. As we near the end of this book, we offer readers ideas for enhancing their understanding of these many layers. We suggest ways for readers to engage in studies of family and community literacy. We offer ideas for learning more about how decisions about money and materials are made and suggest the importance of a study of our own literacy lives as a way of understanding beliefs about and expectations we have for our students.

In the final argument, we do take a stance on reading process and instruction, but we do not offer simplistic resolutions to the conflicts about reading in which we seem so deeply embroiled. Rather, we look at all teachers as decision makers and suggest that some make the decision to use programs that organize their reading program, provide a detailed scope and sequence, and provide most of the materials needed to teach reading. Others decide to develop a reading curriculum more locally, using resources they locate while making decisions about scope and sequence. Some decide to adhere strictly to state standards, others decide to use standards as one point of reference, and others view standards as minimalist or limiting. Some argue that they, as professionals, rely on themselves and their knowledge base to inform their teaching; some subscribe to the knowledge of others; some seek common ground or useful ideas regardless of the source. We also suggest that learning to teach is developmental in that one facet of professional decision making involves composing our identity as a teacher, a process that takes time and reflection.

Our goals are to invite you to look deeply at your understanding of the reading process and instruction and to consider the decisions in which that understanding rests. It is our hope that through reflection, other educators' voices, conversations with colleagues, consideration of research, and experiences with children in classrooms, you will become articulate about your views and enter the larger discussions that are influencing what happens in our classrooms. Reflective, informed, and articulate teachers can explain and justify their practice and thus claim the classroom as a space rich in professional decision making in the teaching of reading.

ACKNOWLEDGMENTS

Four teachers let us into their classrooms and their lives. Without them, the cases in this book would not exist. We thank them for their time, energy, thoughtfulness, and honesty. The educators' dialogues involved teachers and an assistant principal taking time to listen to the cases, study them, and engage in conversation about them. We appreciate their time and reflective responses. They added a dimension to this book that gives it warmth and depth and invites others to engage in similar conversations.

We also thank our families and friends for their support as we put hours into this endeavor at the expense of time with them.

Dan Liston and Ken Zeichner conceived of this series, and we find it an essential part of our thinking with teachers in classrooms and study groups. We are grateful for their work in and dedication to the importance of reflection in teaching.

Lawrence Erlbaum is a beacon of hope in hard times for teachers and students. We thank him for his support. Naomi Silverman is a friend and editor whose care and genuineness provided encouragement throughout the composing of this book. Erica Kica helped with many of the details that needed attending.

We also acknowledge the teachers we don't know, whose voices we hear at conferences and other professional development settings. We see and hear your struggle and appreciate the work you are doing with our children and grandchildren.

I

CASE STUDIES AND REACTIONS

There are four cases in this section. Each case is about a teacher engaged in teaching her students how to read. Two teachers are first-year teachers and two are experienced teachers. We have provided space after each case for you to write what you noticed, your concerns, your questions, and your overall reactions to the case. Each case was also presented to groups of educators who met with the authors to discuss the cases. As you read, think about the questions we asked these groups and consider addressing some of these questions in your reactions to each case. We asked them:

1. What did you notice about the way that the teacher teaches reading?
2. What strengths did you notice in the teacher's teaching of reading?
3. What concerns did you have about the teacher's teaching of reading?
4. What strategies did the teacher use?
5. What strategies would you use that the teacher did not? Why would you use those?
6. Based on the case that you heard, what might you expect the students to be learning?
7. What else do you want to discuss with the others in the room about this teacher's teaching of reading?

After you write your reactions to the case, you can read what our groups thought about it. The reaction sessions are *blended* transcriptions of the sessions we held; blended means that we edited for space and to make them flow a bit more fluently than oral language. We discuss some of the themes that emerged during these sessions before presenting the transcripts. We hope that the themes help to guide your reading of the transcripts. We've also left space following the reaction sessions so that you might add your reactions at that point as well. All teachers', schools', and students' names are pseudonyms.

INTRODUCTION TO CASE 1

Penny teaches second grade at a school that seems quite middle class as one approaches the building along any of the four quiet suburban streets that lead to it. However, Penny's school serves just over 25% children of poverty, as determined by the percentage of children who receive free or reduced-price lunches. The school is located in a part of the city dominated by Whites; there are about 25% Latino/a, 3% Native American, 2% Black, and 2% Asian students attending the school. The school resembles the school in which Penny student taught one year ago. Overall, in the city in which she teaches, half of the students are Latino/a, over 10% are Native American, and about 30% are White.

This is Penny's first year of teaching and she's very excited about it. She loves her students and works very hard to ensure that they all meet with success. Her concerns about being a good teacher led her to enroll in an intense master's degree program that includes course work in the summer prior to the start of the school year, two nights each week during the school year, and in the summer following her first year. She particularly likes the part of the program that involves observations of her teaching by support staff.

Rick met Penny when she was an undergraduate in a reading methods course he taught, and he offered to visit her in her classroom as part of his study of first-year teachers. She participated in interviews and monthly study group sessions with other first-year teachers as part of the research project. Her master's degree program and her participation in the study keep Penny busy, but she likes that because, as she explains, "I learn so much from other teachers. I love talking to them and hearing what they're doing in their classrooms. I want my students to succeed and I'm willing to do as much as I can to make sure that happens."

Penny's cooperating teacher in student teaching used a basal reading program. Penny found the teacher's guides very useful because they explained what to teach and when to teach it (the sequence of skill work), and directed teachers to use certain practice activities and worksheets. Penny's cooperating teacher helped Penny understand how to use the various assessment tools that the publishers provided in order to place students in groups. Penny learned how to organize her literacy instructional time so that she could meet with small groups while the other students in the class engaged in independent work that was planned and graded by the teacher. Penny was very impressed with the effectiveness of the supplementary phonics program that her cooperating teacher used. As a condition of her employment at her first teaching job, Penny requested that the school order the phonics program for her before she accepted the position. The school agreed, and Penny arrived feeling confident that she would serve her students well in the teaching of reading and writing. Her confidence was borne out as her students scored well on the standardized tests that the district administered at the end of the school year.

CASE 1: TEACHING READING VIA DIRECT SYSTEMATIC INSTRUCTION

Meet Penny

Penny grew up in an upper middle class section of the city in which she is now teaching. She went to high school at her neighborhood school and lived at home while attending the local university to earn her teaching degree. She wanted to teach ever since she can remember and says, "My mother taught me to love reading and learning. That's the feeling I want to give to my students." Growing up in a very diverse southwestern U.S. city, in a state that guarantees bilingualism in its constitution, sensitized Penny, an Anglo, to the needs of the diverse students that form the fabric of the public school system in which she is thrilled to teach. "Our neighbors spoke Spanish as their first language and I'm comfortable around Spanish speakers," she explains. "I don't speak it well, but I did take it in high school. I also think that it's very important to honor children's home languages and parents' choices about their children's schooling."

Penny has always been successful in school. Knowing that she wanted to be a teacher led her to volunteer at her local elementary school while she was in high school and college, as her work schedule permitted. She loved helping her former teachers and their students and was observant of the strategies and materials they used. "I remember so many of the things we did in school and many of them are good ideas that I'll use with my own students," she told the study group one evening at Rick's house. She has high expectations for her students, demanding that they do the work she assigns. But she doesn't think that she's overly strict with students and loves to smile and laugh with them at appropriate times.

Penny's Class at Adams Elementary School

The district in which Penny teaches has over 140 schools, including elementary, middle, and high schools. Some of the schools have bilingual programs, but Adams does not because of its location in a mostly non-Spanish-speaking section of the city. Adams does have an English language learners program that involves children being taken out of the classroom for extra help in learning English. Penny has one child who is learning English as her second language, but the rest of her 19 students have English as their first language.

Penny expected to be welcomed warmly by her new colleagues and was excited to attend grade-level meetings with the other second-grade teachers. She was disappointed that they weren't eager to help her learn about the school's schedule, reading and math programs, and other facets of life in the building. She'd hoped that one of the more experienced teachers would "take me under their wings and be my informal mentor at the site, but that didn't happen," she reported to the study group one evening at Rick's house. "Not only that, " she continues, "my classroom is not near all the other second-grade classrooms. I'm two hallways over because they decided they needed another second-grade room and put me into a space that was left when they reduced the number of fifth-grade classrooms."

Penny learned that the teachers at the school were expected to use the basal as the main part of their reading program. She liked this idea because she felt that her students and the other second graders would have very similar experiences in reading as they all read the same stories and were taught the same skills. She was also very pleased that she found time each day to do the phonics program that was ordered for her students. As the year progressed, Penny's confidence grew and she reported that her students were growing as readers and writers. She also found a positive side to the isolation she originally disliked: She could do activities independently of the other second-grade teachers. For example, as Valentine's Day approached, the other second-grade classrooms all displayed the identical art project in their hallway. Penny saw it but decided not to do that particular project because she had a different one in mind. She remained cordial to the other second-grade teachers, but rarely met with them. "This worked out okay for my first year because I had so much other support from Rick and the master's program mentors," she explained in an interview at the end of her first year of teaching.

Time

Penny's students experience an organized and consistent daily schedule because she believes that routines help her students to learn. "They know the routines of day and the week and they know what's coming next," she explained to her colleagues in the study group at Rick's house. "It's not boring, though, because we do different art projects, have challenging math, and they get to write many different things during our writing time... I do think it helps them to concentrate when they don't have to worry or wonder about what's coming next."

A typical day in Penny's classroom follows the schedule shown next. Time slots marked with an asterisk (*) denote what Penny considers to be the reading instruction portions of her schedule and are elaborated on more fully after this overview of the day.

> 9:00 (often earlier): Penny is in the classroom getting materials ready for the day.
>
> 9:15: Students arrive, greet, and chat with each other and Penny, and find books they'll read that morning. This reading time is called DEAR (for "drop everything and read").
>
> 9:30: Penny passes out second silent-reading books to children who have completed the first; the second book is usually nonfiction and based on an area of study the class is pursuing (science, social studies). She starts her reading groups with lowest performing student (this is usually a group of just one child) as other students continue to read.
>
> 9:35*: The struggling reader works with Penny at the reading table, where she conducts all reading groups in sequence from lowest to highest performing because highest performing readers seem to be able to handle greater amounts of independent work time. Students usually receive an assignment from the basal (worksheets or work-

book pages) at the end of their time at the table. Penny intersperses reading groups with phonics lessons and other whole group activities so that children aren't independent for too long.

9:50: Students record morning independent reading in their reading logs (a columned sheet with the left column used for the date and the right column used for writing the title of the book and number of pages read).

10:00*: Phonics lesson to the entire class.

10:45*: Introduction of tasks (independent work).

10:50: Recess (all second graders go at the same time).

11:05: Recess ends.

11:05-12:00*: Penny meets with more reading groups as other students do tasks.

12:00: Writing. Penny and her students love this time and as the year progresses, their stories become more elaborate and include various genres.

12:40: Lunch/Recess

1:30: Teacher Read Aloud, when children return to the classroom. 1:40: Spelling. This includes a weekly list of words from the spelling textbook, assignments throughout the week, and a test on Friday.

2:00: Math

2:30: Science or social studies using district-provided materials.

3:10 Finish the work from the day, play a game, or do an art project.

3:40 Dismissal

The Basal Reading Program

Penny uses the basal reader for reading instruction. Many readers of this book learned to read using basal reading programs. The term *basal* refers to an organized system for teaching that is produced by a publisher. The basal program (sometimes referred to as a system) includes texts for the children, guides with instructions for the teacher, workbooks and worksheets for skills instruction and practice, and supplementary reading books that are typically multiple copies of paperback stories. Many basal programs include assessments given at regular times as children progress through the program. The guide helps teachers by explaining grouping strategies, providing teaching strategies, and giving ways to help children practice reading. The programs are referred to as direct and systematic instruction because teachers teach specific vocabulary words, phonics concepts, comprehension strategies, and fluency strategies by following the specific order and explanations within the guide. The children's text is an anthology of readings bound into a single volume, although some basal programs have more than one volume per grade level. The younger grades have anthologies containing complete stories and the older children have books containing excerpts from full-length novels. Most grade levels also include self-contained selections such as poems, short nonfiction pieces, plays, and short stories. The focus in recent years has been to include stories children could find in a library or bookstore, including common and popular reading with high-quality illustrations.

Penny has three groups in different parts of the second-grade basal, a struggling reader in the first-grade basal, and one group in the third-grade basal. Although the other second-grade teachers teach the same basal lesson to their entire classes, Penny explains to the study group at Rick's house that she wants her students to be in homogenous groups that meet their skill and performance levels and needs. "These groups allow me to give the children the time they need... everyone gets to read aloud everyday and we all start the work on the worksheets and workbook together in the small group. I just don't understand why they [the other second-grade teachers] would put all of the students in one group. Too many kids fall through the cracks when you do that."

The basal publishing company provides the texts that the children read. "It's a good collection of stories you could find in the library," Penny says to Rick one day when he is visiting her classroom. "You'd have a hard time buying or finding multiple copies of these books so the children could each have one on their lap when we read. But with this program, the stories are all here." The program also comes with charts that Penny uses for the skills lessons. The sequence of skills makes sense to Penny and the workbook and worksheets provide the practice the children need with the skills. "It's not all phonics," Penny says. "There are many lessons on comprehension, writing, grammar, prefixes, suffixes, and other important things that the kids need to know." The program has a scope and sequence chart that shows teachers how it is organized from simple skills to much more complex ones. This makes sense to Penny because she views reading development as sequential and she trusts that the publishers have researched the program thoroughly.

The program that Penny uses is also specific in the language that teachers are expected to use in the teaching of reading. Sample specific wordings of instructions are provided on many pages of the teachers guides, and Penny usually follows that wording. She explains, "I worry about saying things or teaching things in ways that the children won't understand. I pretty much trust that the authors of the program have tested the language and they know it works best to teach kids to read."

Working With a Struggling Reader (9:35)

Penny has one student in her class who is performing well below the district's expected performance level for second-grade readers. She works with this child individually every morning, sometimes bringing a few of her other lower performing students into the group, too. They work on a story from the basal reader, and Penny also teaches skills lessons from the first-grade teacher's guide. When the child complained that he read the book last year, Penny asked him how well he could read it now. He told her, "Not that good." "That's why we're reading it together, now. So you can read it good," she explained, smiling at him. Her warmth and her belief in teaching children at the level that they truly need for instruction convince the child that this is a good plan.

Penny believes that struggling readers need a lot of practice and repetition, so they read stories two or three or even four times. They practice being fluent and reading with expression; she often laughs with them, gives "high fives," and offers other encouragement. "They really have to master one story before moving to the next," she explains. She usually asks comprehension questions that the teacher's guide lists and sometimes asks her students to find the specific sentence that answers the questions she asks. "I like the way the book asks the children to think of their own experiences, like if we're reading about a farm, there are questions about whether or not they've ever been to a farm and what they know about life on a farm." Working closely with this student helps Penny monitor progress and make decisions about which supplementary materials (worksheets and soft cover books) to use with the student.

Phonics (10:00)

The phonics lesson is given to the whole group at the same time. Each page of the teacher's guide offers specific instructions, which Penny used at the beginning of the year, but she relies on them less and less as the year progresses as she understands the expected sequence of each lesson. "I didn't know what a digraph was and I wasn't sure how to divide words into syllables. So I really had to use the guide exactly because I was learning these things as I was teaching them to the kids," she explains to Rick in an interview. "I knew about prefixes and suffixes, but I didn't know a lot of the other rules that I teach the kids. I think it's really important for them to know those rules."

The children typically sit at their desks or on the rug in a circle for phonics lessons, sometimes beginning at the rug and then moving to their desks to work on worksheets. The desks in the room are in a horseshoe, leaving a circle large enough for the entire class to sit. The phonics lesson begins the same way each day, and the children know the routine. They start by watching Penny present a stack of about 40 cards to them. Each card has a picture and a letter on it; the children say the name of the picture and the sound. For example, when she holds up the card with a pencil and the letter <p> on it, they all say, "pencil, puh." Penny thanks the class and smiles at them when they're done. "You're so good at these," she beams at them. Many children smile.

The second part of the lesson involves another set of cards each with a word on it. Penny holds up the cards, one at a time, and the children say the words in unison. Some days she has individuals say the words, going quickly around the circle. The words on the card are referred to as *sight words*, words that the children are expected to say instantly upon presentation by the teacher. The idea of children being fluent in reciting sight word cards is part of the phonics program and the basal, too. The deck numbers almost 150 cards, and the children read them quickly. As soon as they've finished reading the cards, Penny stands and goes to the chalkboard. She writes "return" on the board. One student reads the word, but she ignores him. She turns to the class and reminds them that they are *coding* the word before they say what it is. Coding means using rules that they know to figure the word out. Among the things they'll do are: look for consonant digraphs (two consonants making a unique sound, like <ch>), look for vowel digraphs (two vowels making one sound, like the <ea> in *read*), look for common syllables, and more. The following is a transcript of the class working on the word *return*. P stands for Penny and S stands for student (various ones); notes in brackets [ ] are for clarification so readers know what happens during the lesson.

P: 5-4-3-2-1-0 [counting down is how she gets attention; the students are usually very quiet by zero]. Let's have our attention on the board and our hands in listening position.
P: [writes *return* on the board].
S: Return! [She ignores him.]
P: What's the first thing we do when we're going to code this word?
S: Digraph? [meaning that they say the sounds of two neighboring vowels or consonants, but this word does not have those]
P: Not digraph; but good try.
S: Final stable syllable [meaning that they are to look for a word with a consonant + <le> at the end, like *stable* or *mumble*).
P: What would be our final stable syllable? [No students respond, silence.]
P: Hmmm, so no final stable syllable, what's next?
S: Suffix or vowels? [Student is asking if there are suffixes to consider or if the focus should be just on the vowels because consonant sounds are fairly reliable, but vowels are very unpredictable.]
P: Vowels [a hint that they aren't going to find a suffix in the word.] How many vowels in this word?
S: Two.
P: If the word has more than one vowel, it has…
S: Suffixes?
P: Not quite. Not quite. But you're thinking about language. Two vowels mean it has two what?
S: Vowel suffix?
P: No, but you're thinking about language [She wants the children to think about the structure and sounds of language and saying "you're thinking about language" is how she does this.] Two vowels means we have what?
S: Two vowels come together…a digraph?
P: No.
S: Two syllables.
P: Yes. Great…code this word to show two syllables…vcv rule. [Penny wants them to use the rule that they've learned, finding the first vowel in *return* (<e>) and putting a <v> under it (for *vowel*), then putting a <c> under the consonant (<t>) that comes after that vowel, and putting another <v> (for *vowel*) under the <u>. The vcv rule tells students to draw a line up between the first <v> and

CASE 1: PENNY

<c> so that *re* and *turn* will be divided. The rule also says that the first vowel will be long.]

10:12: The kids discuss and tell Penny about putting a v under the first vowel, <c> under the consonant, and <v> under the vowel to draw a line between <e> and <t> in *return*. They also tell her to put in the breve (the diacritical mark for a short vowel) and the line between the two syllables. [NOTE: the children have made a slight error here because the coding should be a macron, which indicates the vowel is long. They are using diacritical marks, similar to ones found in a dictionary.]

P: Read it the way it's coded, with the <e> short.
S: Return. [Says the word properly.]
P: That's not the way it's coded.
S: Ret [rhymes with 'pet'] urn. [Says it with short e, as it's coded.]
P: Does it sound right?
S: No.
S: It should be a macron.
P: Boys and girls, if you remember when we have the vcv rule, we have a long vowel. It's hard to read this word with a short vowel.
S: It sure is.
P: What if we did this instead [she moves the line so it is after the <t> in *return*]? Somebody read that word for me.
S: [Reads it with a short <e>.]
P: Do we know a word like that?
Students say: Noooo.

The students are then dismissed to their desks one at a time as Penny hands each one a worksheet that has five words that they must code and a short story that uses those words. Penny calls three students to the board to code the first word; she's already written that word on the board three times (spread out so each child can stand at one word to code it) and children begin writing <c> for consonant and <v> for vowel under the letters of the word. The rest of the children are doing the same thing at their desks. One student at the board looks at the written word, *release*, and begins writing the little letters below it. She draws a line between the first <e> and the <l> and puts a macron above the first <e>. The student also puts a diagonal line through the <a> and the final <e>, indicating that they are not heard. This is correctly coded.

Penny asks the student what she did, and the student explains, "I used the vcv rule, found the first vowel, drew the line, crossed out the silent letters, and put in the macron."

"Excellent!" Penny exclaims. "What's the word?"

"Release," the student says.

"What does it mean?"

"Like... to set something free."

"One more thing...," Penny begins, but the student anticipates what's coming.

"The accent goes on the second syllable," the child suggests and puts an accent mark after that syllable. "Outstanding," Penny beams. The student smiles broadly.

"Make sure yours looks like this one," Penny says, pointing to the child's work on the board. Then they move to the word *fairly* and one child immediately notices the suffix. Another points out that the <r> may change the sound we expect to hear from the two vowels together. They continue this way with the list of words, children explaining the rules they'd use to make the sounds of the words.

The children will work the rest of the words in the same way. Then they'll read the story silently and out loud. Penny will ask some questions about the story. "The publisher doesn't say to ask questions, but I always do. I want to make sure they know what the story is about," she explains to me after I observe the lesson. This particular story was about Greenland and after Penny asks a final question about it, she writes a student's response on the board and tells the children to copy that answer.

Introduction of Tasks (10:45)

The children are introduced to the tasks they'll need to complete while Penny works with her other reading groups. She spends about 15 minutes per group and some days needs to extend reading groups into the afternoon, in place of science or social studies, in order to get to each group every day. Occasionally, she meets with reading groups during their writing time in the morning. Reading always is at the top of her list of things to complete.

The tasks are much more than the children can complete in a morning, so Penny prioritizes them for her students. They know which items she expects them to complete and which are optional. The children move around the room getting supplies as they need them, sharpening pencils, and filling the water bottles many keep on their desks. If the room becomes too busy with activities not focused on the tasks, Penny tells them that no one may move about until she gives them permission. The children know not to interrupt her reading group instruction unless something occurs that is extremely urgent. Samples of tasks include: (a) putting spelling words into sentences; (b) writing a story that begins with the prompt, "I'm lucky because"; (c) making a leprechaun and writing a story about it; (d) reading a story for 20 minutes; (e) putting a list of words (provided by the teacher) into alphabetical order; (f) making rows of specific letters of the alphabet to practice handwriting; (g) using clay snakes to spell out the spelling words; (h) going to one of the centers Penny has designed (with math games, reading games, or listening to a story on tape). The centers option is only available to children who have completed all their other tasks.

Reading Groups (11:05)

The basal reading program provides a 1-week format for each new story. On the first day, Penny is required to read the story to the children. She engages them in discussions to access and assess their prior knowledge about the topic of the story before reading it to them. On the second day, the children read the story to themselves or aloud, whichever Penny decides. They read a few pages at a time and respond to comprehension questions that are listed in the teachers guide. On the third day and fourth day, the children work on skills that the program recommends, often using the charts that are part of the program. The charts are in a large flipbook that allows Penny to set it on an easel or on the reading table. There are also charts that introduce new words that the children will meet in their reading of the next section of the story. The teacher's guide has sections on enrichment and remediation from which Penny gets ideas to meet the needs of her students. Readers who are struggling might read the story again, either alone or in pairs referred to as "buddy reading." The program comes with supplemental books for reading. These are soft-cover books containing one story per book. There are multiple copies of these, and the children often read them together in pairs or in round robin fashion.

    The skills portions of the program can be covered quite quickly with the two stronger groups. Penny tries to juxtapose skills days with those groups and reading days with the slower moving groups in order to complete each week's work. She knows that five groups is probably too many, but says, "I like the smallness of these groups. Some days, I just ask the stronger group to read the next story to themselves at their desks. Then, when we meet, they are ready to answer the questions and read aloud." Although the basal offers some really good supplemental ideas, Penny rarely has time for them. For example, after one story about a bear and his shadow, there are suggestions for science activities with light. Penny doesn't have the time to do this with the whole class, but she does set it up as one of the centers for the following week. She reads the guides carefully and decides what she can and will do each week (reflective of her time and her understanding of her students' abilities).

In Closing

Penny teaches reading throughout the rest of the day as well. "When I teach science or social studies or even an art project, we read and write. I ask the children what sounds letters make, we code new or difficult words, I ask about prefixes and suffixes, and I'm always checking for their understanding of what they've read." The basal and the phonics program are the heart of her reading program. She's comfortable with that and confident that the programs provide just about everything she needs to teach reading. "And there's more," she tells the study group one evening. "I don't spend my whole life planning lessons, like we did as undergraduates. I don't feel like I'm having to make everything up or invent the wheel all over again. I follow the programs and I can still have a life outside of school." At the end of a very successful year (as measured by reading inventories administered to her class), Penny decides to seek a position in a more diverse school. "I love the kids here, but I want to work with children from a more diverse neighborhood. I think I want to work where the poverty rate is higher. I just seem to think that there's more need there for me." Penny gets a job in a school much like the one she explained that she was seeking and will start a new school year at that location.

CASE 1: PENNY

READER REACTIONS TO CASE 1

EDUCATORS' DIALOGUE ABOUT CASE 1

Two first-year teachers and two second-year teachers gathered at Rick's house to discuss the case of Penny. Monica, who describes herself as a Chicana, and Sandy, who describes herself as Hispanic, are the teachers with 2 years of experience. Monica teaches second grade and was an educational assistant in the district for 20 years prior to returning to school to earn her degree as a teacher. Sandy is a third-grade teacher who felt that she had to "grow up fast" (her words) when she got her own classroom. Pam, a sixth-grade teacher and Annie, a fourth-grade teacher, both White, are in their first year of teaching. We met in February and each teacher arrived anxious to hear what others have to say about the case and, at the same time, wanting to hear about the other teachers' lives. Each also wanted to share her own experiences as a way of thinking about, questioning, and validating her practice.

Each of the teachers received a copy of the case when they arrived and Rick read it aloud as they read along, making notes of things they wanted to discuss after the reading. They ate pizza, drank soft drinks, and worked to understand Penny's teaching of reading and her students' experiences in becoming increasingly literate first graders.

After Rick read the case, he asked for general responses and offered the guiding questions on page 1 to help frame the discussion. "The questions," Rick explained to the teachers, "are not meant to confine you. You're free to take this discussion where you want it to go as you connect Penny's and her students' experiences to your understanding of the teaching and learning of reading." The teachers discussed some important points about being a new teacher. Overall, the teachers agreed with many of the things that Penny does and the reading and phonics programs on which she relies. They brought out their concerns about management and discipline, an area about which many new teachers have nightmares. They discussed the importance of a good schedule, one that the children and the teacher know and understand. These new teachers are keenly aware of the influences of No Child Left Behind. They also discussed the positive and negative aspects of using a basal reading program and a phonics program in addition to the basal. They have questions about the use of scripted lessons, but they also rely on them to some degree. They all resonate with Penny's use of grouping and worry about addressing individual students' needs. There are specific areas of reading instruction, such as the use of diacritical marks, about which

CASE 1: PENNY   17

they're unsure in terms of usefulness to children. As you read, consider your response to the case and these teachers' thoughts.

The following transcription is a fairly accurate representation of the teachers' responses to the case of Penny's teaching. Some of the language was edited for length and clarity. An ellipsis (…) is used to show that someone's speaking turn didn't seem completely finished, but another speaker initiated talk. Most often, the second speaker picked up as the first seemed to be ending her turn (indicated by an ellipsis at the beginning of the second speaker's turn). We used brackets [ ] to insert information that readers may need for clarity or understanding.

Pam: I hate to sound too much like a teacher, but could we follow the questions in order? I have so much to say and I wrote so many notes to myself next to the questions that I think it would be helpful to go in order.

Sandy: If we did, we'd make sure we got to all these things. And the last question really would help us get to some of the other issues we might have.

Monica: That's fine with me.

Annie: Yeah, me too.

Pam: Thanks, I know it's a bit obsessive compulsive [teachers all laugh], but I really appreciate it.

Rick: OK, so let's begin with the first question. I'll state it for the tape: What did you notice about the way that the teacher teaches reading?

Pam: She's very organized. She knows what's coming next and so do her kids. She has a routine going.

Monica: I agree. I think that kids of all ages really need to know the routine. It's almost a form of security for them.

Sandy: In my first year of teaching, I think I was just too friendly with the kids. I wanted them to like me and like each other and I imagined some kind of community that I couldn't seem to get with them. I'm not blaming them, but I kept trying different things. We have to use a basal program at our school, too, and I use it. My first year I did what the program said and kept the class in one large group for most of the days of the week and did smaller groups other days. Things got out of hand on the days they met in smaller groups because they didn't work well independently. I wonder how Penny got them to work quietly and get things done.

Monica: I've seen so many classrooms as an EA [educational assistant] in my 20 years in school that I knew I had to be really organized and strict with the kids. We use a basal, too, but I don't read the guide that much. It's just too much for me to read and follow. I check out what skills are supposed to be taught and I teach them.

Annie: I think that it's a lot easier your second year when you know what things are supposed to look like because you've already had a full year's experience. I feel like I'm hanging on by a thread some days, staying just one day ahead of my kids. Some days, some groups are ahead of where I've read in the guide and I have to follow the guide really closely to stay on top of things. It's stressful.

Sandy: I think that's true, Annie. If I didn't have that guide the first year, I would have not known what to do. When I got to my own classroom a week before my first year of teaching, I looked around and thought, "I don't know what I'm doing. I don't know how to teach. I haven't learned a thing at [the university]."

Rick: I'm sorry.

Sandy: It's not you. It's that I just didn't know how to shift to being a teacher and to really think like a teacher. Penny's organization and her use of the guides for reading and phonics really saved her. I wonder if she had discipline problems.

Annie: I'm sure this sounds a bit sick, but I hope she did. I mean I just can't imagine a first-year teacher not having to deal with discipline.

Monica: I know I said I'm really strict and I think Penny was, too. There should have been more about that in the case.

Rick: Well, I observed there and Penny definitely had her bad days. Sometimes we'd sit and only talk about management. But she had very supportive families [of her students]. She'd call them in the evening and report unacceptable behaviors. Those kinds of parents help a teacher feel supported and successful.

Monica: That helps a lot. At my school, parents...well, I almost said they don't care. But that's not true. They care, but they're so busy working and just making ends meet. My school is a high poverty school and we haven't made adequate yearly progress [part of No Child Left Behind] in 2 years. All the teachers are worried.

Sandy: And I bet they're stressed, too.

Pam: My school is about like Penny's. I do get parent support. I even have grandparents coming in to volunteer because they're retired and want to do something. They help some of the struggling kids and give them individual attention.

Annie: I know...it's so hard to ask for help. It's like we're supposed to be experts at every part of teaching even though it's only our first year.

Monica: And we just can't be. We're just beginning in our own classrooms. We have ideas, but we have to test them out.

Sandy: That's where the guide from the basal is helping me. Third graders know a lot and can be very independent in some ways, lots more than Penny's second graders. I also want my kids to read more than the basal so we do SSR [sustained silent reading] every day. Penny called it DEAR. Some days it's only for a few minutes, but other days they get a full 20 minutes. And I don't let them fool around, either.

Pam: I like that Penny started the day with her kids reading books. That's a great way to begin a day. It tells kids that reading books is important. Our basal doesn't tell us to do that, I don't think, but I want to do it a lot more.

Rick: I think we're moving into some of the other questions, so I'll state the next question here, but you can jump back to the first question if you want: What were some strengths you noticed?

Pam: Well, we already said that she's organized and that she's having her kids read from the basal and from other places, too.

Annie: And we talked a little about sequence. I really don't remember much about my own fourth-grade experience and so now that I'm teaching that grade, I just am not sure what to teach. I think Penny feels the same way. She's not sure what to teach and she relies on the basal program to make sure she's doing what's appropriate to that grade level.

Sandy: If her basal is like ours, it has some good stories. These are books that you'd find in the library. They're great stories and they're by some of the authors that we studied in our children's lit class on campus.

Monica: I like Penny's tone with her students. She seems really warm and that's so important. Our kids have to know that we care about them and their learning. We can't just get up there and teach like it doesn't matter who they are.

Sandy: That's what I found so hard my first year and I think Penny is doing a better job of it than me. She's being somewhat strict, it seems, so the kids are expected to do a lot and get as much done as they can. She doesn't want them fooling around.

Pam: She also seems to be doing the lessons each week that she's supposed to do. The basal is pretty demanding and you've got to move through it at the rate they suggest or you won't get everything done by the end of the year. Then, you'll be stuck because the tests are coming along and you haven't got things done that are on it.

Annie: I think five is a huge number of groups to have in one classroom. I don't know how she could get to all of those each day. She really uses time well if she actually does that.

Pam: I couldn't do that. My groups take longer, maybe because older kids do more complicated skills work and it takes them longer to read the passages.

Monica: Our school is looking at more whole group instruction, and the way they want to do it is by having children move from class to class during reading to have homogenous groups. So I wouldn't have all of my own students for reading. Some of them would be down the hall with another teacher. That takes the pressure off for having so many groups, though.

Sandy: I think it's good that Penny has all of her children for reading. Then she knows where they are, what they are doing, and what they can do. She's really accountable for their learning and her teaching.

Annie: I do think it's sad that she's isolated from the other teachers. Teaching is stressful and to be isolated like that can be lonely. So it's lonely and stressful. I can see why she left. I think that's a strength, to get out of a situation where you feel that way.

Sandy: I don't want to look like I don't know what I'm doing. That's why I like the language the basal gives us. As new teachers, we need to know the words to say. It helps a lot.

Annie: She also got major support from the families of her students. That makes so much of a difference. She knows that her kids will pay attention or she could call their parents and their parents will do something about it. Getting kids to pay attention is not always easy and that kind of support, well, it's really wonderful when you can get it.

Rick: What about the next question. What concerns did you have about the strategies she used in teaching reading?

Monica: I'm glad we're on this question because, well, I have some questions about her phonics program and marking the sounds of vowels. They were crossing out the silent vowels and marking the long and short vowels. And even the accented syllables. I didn't understand that.

Pam: I think it helps them read the words. When my kids go to the dictionary to check out how a word is pronounced, many of them don't know what those marks mean. Penny's second graders understand the use of accents, what they mean, and the use of those vowel markings. I wish my kids had that coming in; they'd be much better at saying those new words.

Sandy: Here's what I don't get about it. The way that they're teaching it, in that phonics program, the kids have to know the word before they can mark the sounds of the vowels or put in the accent.

Monica: Ohhhh, I hate that stuff.

Sandy: But do you see what I'm saying? Knowing how to code means you already know the word, so why are you spending your time coding?

Monica: Maybe you shouldn't be spending time coding, especially if the basal has phonics in it.

Pam: Or maybe it helps with words you don't know. Like when you learn prefixes and see them in words you know, then you recognize them in words that you don't know. I think she's brave for asking for that program as a condition of her employment. She knows what she wants to teach with.

Annie: This really makes me want to teach kindergarten. [Laughter]

Annie: No, I mean it. It really does. We don't have a phonics program that I have to use, but sometimes I teach things to my kids and I don't know the concept. But I'm expected to teach it and they're supposed to master it. I thought I was a good

	reader, but I didn't know what a schwa sound was when we were doing syllables one day. So I'm reading ahead of the kids and working on the words that were already divided in the guide and I'm wondering "Why am I teaching this?"
Pam:	Why are you?
Annie:	Because I am terrified of what might be on the test they have to take. If we don't make AYP [adequate yearly progress, part of the No Child Left Behind law], it gets personal at my school. They look at which teachers' students did poorly.
Monica:	This is a real problem because you know how to read but you don't use schwa sounds to figure out new words, but it's on the test…or it might be on the test. It feels like a trap.
Annie:	I have another concern about the reading program that Penny uses. Maybe she's already addressing this by having them read in the mornings and maybe second graders are too young for this, but shouldn't kids be reading chapter books in fourth grade? I love to read and loved to read in fourth grade, too. I read so many books, like the *Little House on the Prairie* books and more, in fourth grade. But my kids are only reading selected chapters that are in the basal. And it seems like a lot of them don't want to read the whole book when I suggest they get it as a library book.
Pam:	The sixth-grade basal is like that, too. We have chapters in there from some really great books and a variety of genres. There are biographies, autobiographies, science fiction, historical fiction, and much more. The kids have to learn the genre and answer all the questions in the basal, and by the time we're done, I'm not sure they want to read the whole book. So this year, now that I've been through this once, I am doing some novel studies. Our school has a book room with multiple copies and we're going to read at least two novels this year.
Sandy:	That sounds great. I wish I were brave enough to do that. Maybe next year we will. Or maybe when the test is done and things lighten up a little.
Monica:	I'm pretty sure we use the same basal as Penny, but I noticed that she didn't talk about guided reading. The basal talks about guided reading as the way that instruction takes place. Maybe that's what Penny does when she's in the smaller groups with her students.

CASE 1: PENNY 23

Rick: That's exactly what she does. The basal is pretty specific about what Penny has to do with the stories the children read. The idea of guided reading is that kids read at their instructional level and the teacher guides them through it by focusing on what the story is about, the specifics of new words, and using skills to identify new words or concepts.

Monica: I guess that's what I thought. It just struck me that it wasn't described that way in the case.

Sandy: I think that this is because this is my second year, but I'm concerned about struggling readers. My first year, I wanted to be loved by the kids, well, and survive. [Laughter] But this year, I see struggling kids and I don't know what to do.

Monica: Penny goes back and has them redo some of what they've already done.

Sandy: Yeah, I saw that. I even did that. It doesn't feel like enough. What are we supposed to do with the kids that aren't getting it? I feel so sorry for that one struggling reader, isolated in a group alone.

Pam: They really get lost by sixth grade. We do so much of our work as a whole group.

Annie: Fourth graders, too. They have social studies textbooks, science textbooks, health, English, and the basal reader. They feel behind in all of these because they're struggling as readers.

Monica: I think many of them wind up getting referred for special help from reading teachers...at least we do that in our school. We have a team that meets to help the teacher, that's the first step. Then, if the interventions that group plans are not successful, the child is referred for further testing.

Pam: We need more help knowing what to do with them on a daily basis.

Sandy: I know the basal has some suggestions and even has some easier-to-read little books for the struggling readers. But they're the ones we worry about most. They're the ones that Penny worries about most.

Annie: I know we're doing concerns, but I just realized that I didn't mention how great it was that Penny reads aloud to her students.

Pam: Oh yeah, I think so too. [Others nod their heads in agreement.] My students, in sixth grade, still love to hear things read aloud. Anyway, sorry to take us back...

Sandy: ...I'm sure I've taken this a little too far, but one part of read alouds that I love is the discussions I have with the students. I read *Just Call Me Stupid* to them and we'd stop after each chapter and just talk. I'm not sure how deep Penny goes into discussions, but my kids love it. Maybe second graders can't do that...

Monica: Sure they can. If we give them the chance...

Annie: But there's not always time for such discussions. I think that Penny's schedule is really packed because of what she wanted in the room, that phonics program, and what she has to do, the basal. It's just not always easy to find time for discussions.

Sandy: That's one shortcoming of a basal if it takes a lot of time. But Penny did make a lot of decisions that affected time, like choosing to have five reading groups. She might have had more time if she did share kids with the other second grade teachers and have some homogenous groups across classrooms.

Rick: Well, we're overflowing to the next question. What strategies would you use that Penny did not?

Pam: Yeah, I think we really have sort of gotten into that one quite a bit.

Rick: Anything else anyone wants to add about that? Are you doing things or would you like to do things that Penny is not doing?

Monica: Penny is pretty locked into what her school has adopted and it's a good lock because it's keeping her organized and she's getting the instruction done in a way she's confident about. There's just not much room or time for her to get into other things. I know a lot of songs and my students are learning them. I give them song sheets and some of the songs are on charts hung around the classroom. I think a lot is learned from singing songs, especially when the words are right there for us to study.

Annie: You're so brave. I don't know if I'd sing in front of my class, but I wish I could. I think that using things we're good at, like singing, is an important part of teaching. It makes the year feel special to the children if they're getting something from their teacher, something that their teacher is an expert at. For

	me, I love poetry and want to do more of that in my class. I'm just not sure yet exactly how I will do that.
Pam:	One more thing to try…after the tests are over for the year.
Sandy:	But what about this…is it fair for some kids to get singing from a teacher and others to get poetry, when the rest of the group doesn't get those things? I mean, I'd want those things for my own children as well as my students, but, I don't know. Is it fair? I just wondered if all classrooms were supposed to look the same. Is that what they want from us?
Monica:	I don't think I want all classrooms to look the same. Penny, in her classroom, does art and decides what tasks she wants to assign her kids. That's how she meets individual interests and needs, I think. It's also how she makes decisions about what's important and what should be taught. We do have state standards and that's what the tests are supposed to be based on. I think teachers need some freedom in deciding how to meet those standards.
Annie:	In our district, we have so many different types of children with so many different needs. My school is also a lower class school if you look at poverty level. We also have a large number of English language learners. There's no way my kids need the same program as the one that Penny's kids get, and the basal accounts for this. There are ideas for English language learners, other ideas for struggling readers, and ideas for more advanced readers. Teachers need to take the time to read the basal guides closely so they can use it to meet the kids' needs…
Monica:	…And you can meet kids needs by looking at the standards. We ignore the standards because we have the basal…
Pam:	…I ignore the standards because I assume that the basal that the district chose meets the standards. It's just too much to keep up with the standards and the basal and all the kids in my class and that's just reading. I also have language arts, math, spelling, science, well, you get the idea. It's a lot for a first-year teacher.
Rick:	We're really getting into the complexity of teaching and all the decisions a teacher has to make about curriculum so that the needs of her students are met. Are there other strategies that you'd use that you didn't notice in Penny's classroom?

Annie: When we were in methods classes at the university, a really big thing was the use of thematic units. We had to develop theme-based units that we would teach in our student teaching. I loved mine. It was a unit on war and peace that I used in student teaching. The kids read lots of different books and then took one part of the theme for closer study. Some boys looked at all the kinds of weapons that are used. A group studied the Holocaust and another looked at the treatment of Japanese soldiers here. We also studied the ways different people responded to the situation in Iraq, although that made me a little nervous because we had students whose parents are in the military where I student taught.

Sandy: I don't think Penny had time for that as part of her formal reading program, but maybe she worked it in through her social studies and science units. But science is mostly the science kits and social studies topics are pretty firm in third grade, so I'm thinking Penny faced the same problem in second.

Annie: I really get that and haven't done any themed units in my classroom. I'm just saying that it was so good for the kids, they learned so much. I just think it's too bad we can't or don't do more of that.

Pam: I don't want us to think we're criticizing Penny's teaching because I think she's doing a good job. We said a lot of good things about her classroom and her teaching.

Sandy: I don't think we're criticizing. We're just thinking about ways to enhance or even wondering about our own teaching.

Pam: What about assessment? I wonder what she does about assessment.

Rick: This really seems like we're into the last question, so let me state it here: What were your reactions to her teaching? It's a very general question and can let us get at any loose ends you might feel we still need to address. Pam's question about assessment fits here, I think.

Pam: Okay. I remember being told so much in methods courses that assessment should guide instruction, but I don't think I always do that.

Annie: I think Penny does. She has five reading groups. That's a huge amount. And it seems like she makes decisions to move children in and out of groups, like when she takes other struggling readers with her lowest reader. That's a lot of assessment.

Sandy: Doing phonics lessons to the whole class probably doesn't look like it fits with the model of teaching from assessments. Penny is following the program in the order it comes. I think her phonics program is meeting needs for different children differently. Some are learning to read the words, others are learning the sounds, and others might be learning to spell the word. It sort of makes sense to me that different kids learn different things from what seems to be one experience.

Pam: That's a good point. I never thought of that. It actually makes me feel a little better about what I do when I do whole group lessons. I mean, we know about individual differences but we don't always have to assume that it means that each child receives different instruction. They each experience instruction differently.

Monica: That's true. And we have to balance that to make sure that specific needs are being met. That's where five reading groups, which is tough to balance, seems to make some sense. Although, I'd sure like her to get it down to three so she has time to breathe and maybe make the groups a little longer.

Rick: How about we go around the table and each of you offer any final thoughts.

Pam: This has been great. Thanks for sort of going in order with the questions [laughter]. I think Penny moved quickly, as a first-year teacher, from seeing a sea of faces to seeing individuals with individual needs.

Sandy: I wish I could visit her classroom and talk with her. Or talk more with everyone here. I miss talking about teaching.

Monica: Between new laws and the pressure to do well on tests, teachers and kids are really in the spotlight. I think Penny is doing great with all that pressure and I admire her for moving to a school like the one she's going to. She likes challenges and that would make her an interesting colleague.

Annie: I'm glad I came tonight. There's a lot of pressure to blindly get rid of the basal and I'm glad to be with a group that sees the ways in which it supports teachers in making decisions and making sure children get the instruction that is appropriate for them.

READER REACTIONS TO THE EDUCATORS' DIALOGUE ABOUT CASE 1

SUMMARY AND ADDITIONAL QUESTIONS

Penny survived her first year of teaching by being organized and following the program that the school was using. She supplemented that program with a phonics program that she selected and requested that her school order for her, which they did. Her success in teaching reading was also reflective of her well-organized classroom and her kind and caring nature. She had expectations that her students would succeed, worked hard to have them meet those expectations, and enlisted the help of families if children's behaviors were not appropriate. Despite the rather cold reception from her colleagues and a sense of isolation throughout the year, Penny remained clear in her visions of success for her students. Although that success was realized, as evidenced by the students' performance on tests at the end of the year, Penny sought a more challenging position for her second year of teaching. She did not demand that the phonics program be purchased as a condition of her employment at her new school. She visited the school prior to signing her contract and found that the reading program in use there had a sufficiently robust phonics program. Although the phonics program that she would be teaching at her new school did not require that children code words, she was convinced that it would be equally as effective in helping children learn the phonics elements that she considers essential to the teaching and learning of reading.

The educators in the dialogue about Penny's classroom were disappointed in the way that she was received at the school. They found Penny's response to her isolation remarkable, noting her organizational strategies, her use of a tight schedule, and her reliance on the teacher's guides as important facets of her success. The educators concurred with Penny that the guides are well-conceived and articulated and have a research base that supports using them. There was some question about the use of coding as a way of teaching phonics and, interestingly, it is a piece of Penny's reading program that would not be present during her second year of teaching.

The educators also noted her warm nature as an important part of her success. Penny's warmth did not simply reside in her smile, high fives, and willingness to laugh with her students. It was reflected in her commitment to their success in ways such as having five reading groups. The educators mentioned the difficulty of balancing so many groups. They also noted that they, and perhaps Penny as well, didn't feel equipped to deal with struggling readers. They wanted, for themselves and for Penny, a greater repertoire of strategies for helping struggling readers than the ones listed in the basal program guides. Many first-year teachers see their students as a sea of faces that they must manage, but Penny saw individuals and their needs quite early in her first year of teaching. Her sensitivity to them and her willingness to adjust the number of reading groups in her classroom to meet their needs are noteworthy.

After reading this case, we suggest readers discuss the following lingering questions as a vehicle for deepening understanding about the complexity of teaching and learning reading:

1. The use of basal readers is controversial among some teachers and teacher educators. Some feel they provide organization and structure, something Penny found useful. Others find them too rigid. What do you see as the pros and cons for using basal readers? How would you feel about using a program that has a specific script that you are expected to follow? How much would you rely on the script, verbatim? If you would not rely on it (like Monica), what issues might be part of that decision? You may also consider the questions to which the educators responded in their dialogue.

2. The phonics lessons that Penny taught were also part of a basal program. Remember that *basal* means that the program is sequential and contains pretty much everything that one should need to teach a subject or area (such as phonics). Some of the educators suggested that coding words (putting in diacritical marks and accents) might not be helpful in reading and writing. How important is it for children to be able to code words? How important is it for children to be able to recite rules that should be used in figuring out new words? What purposes do coding and reciting rules serve? Think of the rules you would use to read a new-to-you word.

3. Penny's reception at her school was cold. How might such a reception affect the way you teach and your students' learning?

4. The educators in the dialogue and Penny did not seem adequately prepared to deal with struggling readers beyond offering them the same program as the more developmental children, only in a slower or more repetitive fashion. What are other ways for struggling readers to learn to read?

5. What information would you want about struggling readers that you might not request of children that are not struggling? For example, you might want their vision and/or hearing screened. You might want to

know about their language history, such as home language if it's not English.

6. What do you see as the relationships between poverty and learning to read? What factors that support reading might poor children not experience that more privileged children do? How might a teacher deal with these differences between more and less privileged children?

7. What factors, aside from economic ones, seem to predispose children to learn to read? How can or should or do schools compensate for these factors if some children seem deficient in them?

8. What roles do parents play in teaching children to read and supporting their learning more generally?

INTRODUCTION TO CASE 2

In this case, we meet Sylvia as she goes through her student teaching experiences and into her first year of teaching. Most student teachers expect to finish student teaching having accomplished the immense tasks of learning to manage a classroom, understanding pedagogy, and ensuring that children will learn, especially the all-important skills of reading and writing. Sylvia defers to her cooperating teacher as the expert in all of these areas, a very legitimate expectation, but one that ultimately postpones her deeper understandings about how children learn to read and write. Her first year is extremely emotional and culminates in January when she is close to breaking down from physical exhaustion, mental anguish, and the tensions and feelings she lives with vicariously through her students' lives. She makes it through her first year by (finally) honoring her own identity and the identities of her students, including their language and cultural practices.

CASE 2: A NEW TEACHER LEARNS ABOUT TEACHING READING AND CULTURE

Meet Sylvia

When Sylvia was a student in her undergraduate reading methods class at a university in the southwest United States, she often arrived at class very tired. She had big bags under her eyes and she struggled to stay awake during some class sessions. Her tongue was pierced just before the semester started and when she talked, we often heard the sound of the lead-colored ball affixed to her tongue as it hit her front teeth. She slumped in her chair and listened to her colleagues in the class as they struggled to understand the reading process, miscue analysis, and worked with case studies. Sylvia always handed her assignments in on time; they were reflective, and demonstrated a high level of understanding of the content. Although her reading methods instructor, Rick, was disappointed in her classroom "presence," her assignments and occasional comments suggested that she was engaged in the class.

The reading methods students learned about culturally relevant (Au, 1993) and responsive (Ladson-Billings, 1994) pedagogy through reading, discussions, and presentations during the course. They also read and wrote responses to the idea of community or family funds of knowledge (Moll,

Amanti, Neff, & Gonzalez, 1992). Sylvia wrote thoughtful responses to these pieces but also commented that she wasn't sure what teaching looked like when it was culturally responsive and included funds of knowledge as part of the foundation of pedagogy. "Where," she asked during one class session, "are the examples that we can go and look at?" Rick provided the class with names of practicing teachers who, he knew, were sensitive and responsive to their students' cultures. He knew such teachers from a study group he was in and from graduate courses he taught, but not one preservice teacher accepted the invitation to visit those teachers' classrooms.

Sylvia's preservice teacher education program was two professional semesters long. During the first semester, the students took reading and language arts (both from Rick), special education, social studies methods courses, and a seminar related to their student teaching placement; they also were required to be at their student teaching site for 2 days each week. During the second semester, they took math methods, science methods, a seminar, and were required to be at their student teaching site 4 days each week. They student taught with the same cooperating teacher for the entire year. Sylvia also had a job for 20 hours a week for most of the year.

Sylvia told Rick that she was miserable during her student teaching. The roots of her unhappiness were not uncovered until she completed her student teaching assignment and was well into her first year of teaching in her own first-grade classroom. She would find that the unhappiness she felt was directly related to her identity as a Hispanic woman and the fact that she had not paid significant attention to her Hispanic roots.

During the methods course, Rick stressed the importance of student and teacher identity in the teaching and learning of reading. The students in the reading/language arts methods course were required to study their culture and explain the connections between their culture and their literacy lives in a literacy autobiography. In her literacy autobiography, Sylvia revealed that her mother was from a northern European country and came to the United States having learned some English in her home country. She learned to speak, read, and write English fluently upon arriving in the United States. She did not learn Spanish, even though she fell in love with and married a man whose first language is Spanish. He, too, reads and writes fluently in English, the language in which they fell in love. Sylvia's father grew up in a Spanish-speaking family in the southwest United States. Sylvia attended many family functions and listened as her grandparents, aunts, uncles, cousins, and father—all of whom she saw very regularly—spoke Spanish. She admits that she aligned herself with her mother at these family events, knowing her mother did not speak Spanish. Sylvia described herself sitting with her mom, speaking English with and to her, and only playing with Spanish-speaking relatives at her mother's insistence. Sylvia wrote in her autobiography that she learned to understand Spanish, but she thought that her level of understanding was not sufficient to support interactions with her family or to play a role in her teaching life.

Sylvia's Student Teaching

Sylvia's cooperating teacher was a White woman who taught her mostly Hispanic first-grade class in a traditional way. The cooperating teacher, Ms. Stringer, used the *Four Blocks* (www.wfu.edu/fourblocks) approach to teaching reading to her first grade because that was the program selected by the school. Ms. Stringer did not respond to the children in her class through culturally responsive lenses, but Sylvia did not know that this was a problem. The children in Ms. Stringer's class were compliant; they followed the rules and did what they were told when Ms. Stringer taught. But when Sylvia taught, lessons typically became unruly and disorganized. Sylvia carefully planned each of her lessons, but as she lived them out, her face lost its color, her eyes did not focus on the children, and she almost robotically proceeded through her plans, paying little or no attention to the children. Although Ms. Stringer had considerably more control over the students, Sylvia said that her cooperating teacher wasn't "nice to the children." Rick asked Sylvia if she (Sylvia) was nice to the children. "I can't be," she said. "It's not my classroom. I have to do what she tells me to do. I want to learn to do this [teach]." Rick asked Sylvia if she wanted to change her student teaching placement. "No, I have to do this. I have to do this here." Rick didn't understand why she had to do it there, but his hope was that as he followed Sylvia into her first years of teaching he'd find out. Sylvia and Rick would eventually learn that Sylvia felt more than some of the traditional discomfort that student teachers feel because they believe they are guests in their cooperating classroom and are unsure of what to do and how to do it. She felt what many of the Hispanic children in the class were feeling; she felt like an outsider.

Sylvia's cooperating teacher focused on following the *Four Block* program. The name *Four Blocks* refers to the four equal time periods, usually 15 to 20 minutes each, during which reading is taught. The blocks are: guided reading, sustained silent reading (SSR), working with words, and writing. The equal distribution of time between instruction, reading practice, phonics, and writing led to the program being called a "balanced literacy program." The teachers' guide offers specific suggestions for the way time is used during each block. The children were used to the routine of the program, and Sylvia eventually completed lessons successfully because she emulated the very strict demands the cooperating teacher placed on the children. Although Sylvia explained to Rick that she didn't agree with the management program in the classroom, she used that program systematically during her student teaching. She deprived children of recess, isolated them by demanding they leave the group, and talked to them very sternly if their behaviors deviated from the cooperating teacher's expectations. All the children were expected to work alone, not help each other, and not converse with each other during instructional and work times.

Her First Teaching Job

Sylvia got a job at a school that had a population very similar to the one at which she student taught. She was somewhat relieved to be teaching first grade and to find that her new school also used *Four Blocks* as their reading program. Sylvia allotted 20 minutes per block at the beginning of the year and increased it to over 30 minutes as the year progressed. Her schedule filled out to the entire day when she taught math, chose from science, social studies, art, or an occasional health project, and followed the lunch, recess, and special class schedules (music, art, etc.). She was familiar with the program, and she was determined to use it the way her cooperating teacher did. She was also familiar with first graders. Sylvia was very strict with the children and used as much teacher power as she could muster to keep them in order. She insisted that the children look at her when she taught, write what they were instructed to write, and follow her directions. Failure to do so resulted in the offending child being separated from the group and sitting alone until Sylvia decided the child could return. She typically asked them if they would follow directions before allowing them to return to the group. She demanded that students who continued to misbehave stay indoors during recess. She was living the lessons of her student teaching experience.

Still, Sylvia felt unsure of the overall direction of her teaching. She wrote this in an e-mail to Rick in November of that first year:

> Although I try to be the "prepared teacher" and plan for months ahead, I often find myself saying, "Why am I doing this?" I have no idea where my students will be in one month. I don't know if they are going to master this one topic and be ready and willing to be on the topic that I have planned for the next month. I just believe that it is important to have a guide or skeleton of ideas on

what you would like to accomplish for the coming months, but to completely plan out everything is nonsensical. Maybe I am just a new teacher who doesn't know all the tricks of the trade (which is true) and I am not ready, or rather [don't] have the ability to plan for months or even years in advance. But, you know what Rick? I don't think I would ever really want to be that kind of teacher. The teacher who has everything planned, scheduled, and set before my class walks in the door in August. Yuck! I am a teacher who is GETTING very comfortable with days being, well...chaotic and very unpredictable. It keeps me coming back for more...

Rick visited Sylvia's classroom once a week during the first year of her teaching, and she was part of a first-year teacher study group that met at Rick's home once each month. Rick also interviewed her during lunch or after the school day when he visited. The chaos she described did not seem apparent during these visits. She had the day timed almost to the minute as the children were led from activity to activity with little tolerance for misbehavior. In reality, the chaos she described was an internal state reflective of Sylvia's stress level.

Increasingly, Sylvia knew about her students' lives outside of school. Although she liked the idea that school is a "safe harbor" (Paley, 1995), she was also becoming confused about what to do with all the information about home and community life that her students volunteered to her in the tiny open spaces of time around the official curriculum. These unofficial times included when they arrived in the morning, walked to recess or lunch, or were dismissed at the end of the day. Sylvia explained to the first-year teachers study group one evening at Rick's house:

> I've found out more stuff this way that I just don't, I didn't want to know, you know. I mean I sent a note home two days ago just because.... It, it never even occurred to me that something could happen and I sent this note home just because this little boy, J——'s been kind of running around attacking me and doing all this stuff. It just was kind of weird, you know. And I sent this note home and so his [grandmother] ended up calling me and said, "Well about three days ago, J——'s mom, in essence, was doing all these drugs in a hotel room with the kids and left the kids in there... So, we're in the process of trying to get custody and the reason why he was probably acting rude like three days ago is cuz he was left in the hotel room before." [Pause] So you go, "Oh." (Sylvia, transcribed from 10/19/00 study group)

Sylvia cries about her children's lives and doesn't understand how they could learn to read when they are in constant states of trauma because of what is going on in their lives at home. She's an inner city teacher dealing with the many complexities of their lives. She feels somewhat paralyzed by her students' experiences. Monica, another teacher in the study group, suggests that Sylvia listen to J—— when he talks about things that scare him. Both of these first-year teachers are convinced that J—— is scared and they want to support him. Monica suggests asking the child, "What scared you, do you know? What scared you, babe?" Sylvia wasn't sure she wanted to do that because it would require hearing even more about situations that she felt were overwhelming for her and unbearable for her students. She did, however, find herself listening in another way.

Sylvia's understanding of Spanish seemed to rush back into her life when she listened to her students. Reflecting on her first graders' discussions in Spanish, she says, "I understand a lot. They know that, I think. They know they can talk to me in Spanish and I'll talk back in English. I do that a lot. I listen to conversations a lot. And at first, they didn't know, [and they] thought I had no clue as to what was going on."

Still, the more Sylvia's knowledge of her students' lives increased, the less she felt able to teach. One day, one of her students arrived at school and announced that her baby brother died. Sylvia explains:

> So she came in and she wanted to talk about it and the day that her baby brother died was also the day that my aunt died. And I had just found out [about my aunt] at school and I was an emotional wreck and I was crying as it was. And I'm sitting there trying to do attendance and I can't leave because I didn't have my stupid sub plans ready, so I'm having to do attendance and having to start my whole morning before I can sit and do sub plans and I'm crying as it is and [she] comes up to me and tells me her little baby brother died yesterday. And she wants to talk about it and I couldn't do it. (from 10/19/00 study group)

Platica

Each day her children arrived with stories to tell, and each day Sylvia felt the pressure to do the *Four Block* activities that the first-grade team had planned together. Just after winter break of her first year, Sylvia was exhausted in spite of the 2 weeks she spent at home. One day early in January, as the children gathered on the rug to start their day, a child told a story about something that happened at home. As usual, there was silence and the children all looked at Sylvia expecting her to comment or explain, which she rarely did in any depth because of the instructional time she feared losing. She glanced at the clock to see how soon the morning announcements would begin. She checked the board where she had written five new words for the week. Exasperated at having another home story hanging in the air,

Sylvia asked, "OK, who else?" There was silence. The children didn't know what she meant because these stories usually seemed more bothersome than interesting to their teacher. She asked again, "Who else wants to tell what happened at home?"

This might sound like show and tell in the most traditional first-grade sense, but it is not. This was Sylvia's cultural consciousness and competence coming into play. In the Hispanic culture, stories are very important on a few different levels. Platicas (Guerra, 1998) are almost like coffee klatches, where groups sit and tell stories. These occur in communities when small groups of people gather to share the stories of their families and the neighborhood. It's not quite gossiping because of the negative connotation of gossiping. It's more like informing each other, although sometimes judgments are implied and lessons are learned. Sylvia, as she asked the children, "What else?" was essentially inviting into her classroom a cultural norm of the Hispanic culture of the neighborhood in which she teaches. Now, she had created a space for her students' stories.

Sylvia incorporated this time for sharing life's events into her daily schedule. Each day the children arrived, hung up backpacks, and sat huddled together around the chair where Sylvia sat in one corner of the room. "Who has something?" she asked. Someone told about a puppy that got away. Someone else told that it was run over. Someone else told that her cousin saw it first and ran home to tell her aunt, who knew the owner. There was some discussion about how to care for puppies so this does not happen. This was one of the few times during the day that the children talk to each other as part of the official curriculum (Dyson, 1993). Sylvia listened and sometimes contributed her thoughts and questions. Sometimes, she tried to resolve an issue or feeling, but most of the time she let the children process the issue through cross talk. Many of the social connections of the neighborhood were now legitimate within the classroom. The children relived, with their teacher and each other, the stories of life outside of school while perpetuating one of the social practices of their neighborhood.

Gradually, the classroom began to change as a result of these daily sessions, even though they took less than 15 minutes. Sylvia explained that letting the children vent helped them focus more on their *Four Block* work and they also treated each other in a more neighborly way. Some even joked about the ways that their families did not get along with each other outside of school. Yet, in the classroom they were living together more cooperatively because of the ways in which platicas supported social activity and relationships.

Sylvia's rediscovery of platica is rooted in her past. Her family engaged in this cultural activity at every family gathering she attended as a child. In her weariness and exasperation, she drew on her past by allowing the students to do something she intuitively sensed they needed. This intuitive sense was a social and cultural act based on what Sylvia knew of herself, her students, and the cultural practices they shared. Sylvia did not call this time platica; rather, her students lived platica within the context of her classroom each day. She didn't know the name for what they were engaging in. She did understand the need.

Consejos

One day, Sylvia added another facet of Hispanic culture to her classroom. Rather spontaneously, during a *Four Blocks* lesson, she told a very brief story about one of the children in the class. "Oh, we all know that your work is always neat," she announced so that the whole class could hear. "Yours is just so neat. You are the neat one." Later, she added, "I want everyone to be like his. Neat neat neat." Many Hispanic families, indeed many families of many different cultural groups, tell stories about individuals within their families. These stories teach and preserve family history and they also position family members in certain ways. One child might be the one who finds humor in everything, another might be a bit of a prankster (or even referred to as an outlaw). Still other children might be considered the artist, the historian, the thoughtful one, and so on. Sylvia began to tell stories of her students to them, just as some of their families did when they were at family gatherings. She asked, "Who will draw a picture in their journal today? [Hands go up.] Well, we'll all try to be as good an artist as..." and Sylvia would talk about the child whose artistic abilities were now becoming part of the official funds of knowledge within the classroom. Sylvia began to talk about "our classroom" as though she was discussing a family, telling them about themselves and even telling them what she expected. "My first graders," she explained to them, "are neat and careful." When she did this, sometimes some of the children would glance at each other and nod their heads in agreement. This was as much like being at their aunt's house as being at school. The children were positioned, by Sylvia, as different because they were in her class and with each other. The difference they felt had to do with their culture, their language, and the legitimacy of the uses, functions, and structures of those within the classroom. The use of story "to influence behaviors and attitudes" is referred to as *consejos* by Valdés (1996, p. 125).

Sylvia had intuitively drawn on another culturally relevant practice that helped to support her students' engagement in the schoolwork she asked them to do.

Committed to Three of the *Four Blocks*

The overall theme in Sylvia's classroom, echoing the work of Valdés (1996), was respect. She cultivated a mutual respect that the children were expected to appropriate and live daily. She, as a teacher, respected their identities and the stories of their lives, and they, as students, engaged in the prescribed curriculum. They did the three reading blocks of the *Four Blocks* program carefully, followed the recommended procedures, and used the suggested lists of words for the *working with words* (phonics) portion of the program.

Sylvia took no risks in her use of the reading portions of the program. The three blocks that focused specifically on reading (working with words, guided reading, and SSR) she did as the program and the advisers from the district office and within the school building suggested. During guided reading and working with words, every child did the same thing. They all said the words and wrote the words together. They played various *Four Blocks* games with the five or more target words of the week. They all read the same text for the guided reading piece together, following a student as he or she read or reading chorally. They were allowed to choose a book for silent reading from a plastic tub of books that were selected by Sylvia as she tried to ensure that the children chose books they could read independently. This was supposed to be the time that children read at different levels, but the books in the tubs had a very limited range. For example, even though Sylvia had two students who could read quite complex texts, there were no chapter-length books in the tubs. Some children selected the same book to read for weeks at a time. During her second year of teaching, Sylvia circulated the room more as children read. She also kept track of books the students read and eventually let them keep track on a form she designed. That second year, she encouraged students to read different books, and she also kept track of their reading strategies by using running records (which she learned in a graduate course).

In her first year, Sylvia remained true to the recommended time periods for each of the three reading blocks. Throughout the reading blocks, she used *consejos* to talk about how the children were doing, who was doing what they were known for, and who was surprising her. She laughed at silly things she did and reminded the children to focus on the words, be neat, and always think hard about what they were doing. Although she knew that her students were at very different points in their reading development (from nonreaders to children who could read quite sustained and complex texts), she delivered these three blocks by adhering to the *Four Blocks* guides for teachers.

It was in the writing part of the *Four Block* program that Sylvia departed from the recommended activities. She allowed the children to write in journals, compose stories, publish books, make posters, and other activities not specifically prescribed by the program as she understood it. She allowed the students to approximate spellings on first drafts, consult with each other about ideas, and share their writing daily in small groups or at an author's chair where the whole class listened to a finished piece. She conferenced with them individually and often let the block extend beyond the required time allotment.

At the end of her first year of teaching, Sylvia's students did very well on reading tests that she was required to administer. First graders do not take standardized tests in her district, but teachers did need to demonstrate students' growth through an informal reading inventory that yielded a grade-level score on performance. Her students showed such remarkable growth that her principal mentioned her teaching at various administrative meetings (including those attended by the principal of the school in which Sylvia student taught).

Connecting to Families

Sylvia's classroom was orderly, predictable, and safe. Children could bring their identities to this classroom and were happy to have a teacher who understood Spanish. Sylvia admits that knowing Spanish influenced how she was perceived by families and how she was probably discussed at home. She said:

> Well, you know, you know right away the parents who just speak Spanish. They walk in right away and that's the very first thing they ask you. They ask you if you speak Spanish. So then I'll usually just say, you know I speak a little bit and I can understand better than I can talk it. So then they'll talk and then I'll [understand].

Sylvia wanted parents to speak Spanish if they could articulate their concerns, thoughts, and responses about their children's learning more effectively in that language. She wasn't sure she would understand every word they said, so she invited her father to be part of the conferences that she held with families. She preferred that her father, someone she knew, translate rather than request a district-supplied translator. The idea that their child's teacher's father was present at the conferences influenced Sylvia's relationship with the families. They confirmed that Sylvia was Hispanic, and they saw that she cared enough about them to bring her father for linguistic support.

In Closing

At the end of her first year of teaching, Sylvia asked to move to second grade with her class and her principal allowed her to do this. At the beginning of her second year of teaching, her cooperating teacher (from her student-teaching semester) contacted her and asked to visit Sylvia's classroom. Word of Sylvia's successful teaching of reading had reached her cooperating teacher after their principals met. Sylvia said, "I'll talk to her, but I can't say that I'm doing *Four Blocks* the way she did it." Sylvia understands that culturally based relationships with students influence their learning.

READER REACTIONS TO CASE 2

EDUCATORS' DIALOGUE ABOUT CASE 2

Similar to the first group of teachers who discussed Penny, a group congregated at Rick's house to listen to and analyze the case of Sylvia. Luisa is a Chicana who teaches a multiage first and second grade at a middle and upper class school; this is her 8th year of teaching, her 7th at this school. Donald, an Anglo, teaches third grade at a middle class school; this is his 4th year in third grade, having taught fifth grade for 4 years before that. Leanne, an Anglo, is in her 11th year of teaching. She taught special education for 7 years and presently teaches a multiage K–3 at one of the district's alternative schools that focuses on families teaching their own children for half of each school day. Anita, a Chicana in her 11th year of teaching, is at the same alternative school as Leanne. This is Leanne's and Anita's first year at the school; previously they taught in bilingual or dual language schools. Anita spent 3 years as a mentor for teachers in a master's program for experienced teachers before returning to her own classroom this year.

As you read and reread the educators' responses to Sylvia's first year of teaching, look for the ways in which they address some overarching themes that may apply to many new teachers who teach reading. You'll notice concerns about Sylvia's student teaching experience as her vehicle for entering the field and understanding what a teacher's role might be in teaching reading. There is much empathy expressed for Sylvia in her first year in her own classroom, particularly concerning her identity, the identities of her students, and the roles that language and culture play in teaching reading. A few of the educators mention Sylvia's choices about her writing program and wonder why she has not questioned her reading program with the same intensity. Rooted in their concern about how all teachers are treated, these experienced educators offer Sylvia some advice as the session nears its end. Think about the ways in which you agree or disagree or might even elaborate on some of the suggestions they offer her. Again, we encourage you to perform the following as a play in order to more easily get a sense of how the conversation flowed and the points that specific individuals make.

Luisa: Wow. I have so many thoughts, so I'll just spill them and we'll see where we go, okay? I feel empathy for her because she's hanging on. It's not easy being a first-year teacher. Before she let the children talk about their lives, they were kind of isolated from each other. I hope that Sylvia will speak in Spanish more to the children, have Spanish literature in the classroom, and encourage the writing of Spanish. When I think of the reading program she is required to do, it's hard to understand because I've never had to teach in a strict program like that. When she finally tapped in to the children's funds of knowledge and let them bring in their own sense of community and family, I think it really helped a lot. And so did the writing component of her program. I wonder if their lives were brought into the writing part of her program. That may have helped with their reading achievement at the end. I've read about *Four Blocks*. Reading levels were not differentiated by Sylvia for her children. That was a concern.

Donald: She was doing guided reading as shared reading. Guided reading is usually in groups, when I do it, and shared reading is a text that we do as a whole group and that everyone can learn something from. So we might do a poem for shared reading; some kids learn about the sounds of some letters or about, say, alliteration, while others notice things they want to use in their writing. Everyone has access to the text on some level. With guided reading, I group my kids, often homogenously. But I'm even moving away from that as I rethink grouping.

Anita: I taught in a *Four Blocks* school and was trained in it. Teachers are supposed to choose books that are at the class average reading level for 3 days each week, 1 day above the class average, and 1 day that is below the class average. During guided reading, they read the same text except that not everybody reads it the same way. I read it with some, some children buddy read it, others read it in a group. Some kids do it by themselves. They come back for closure.

Rick: Sylvia did it whole class.

Leanne: I'm concerned about the children's individual needs not being met the way Sylvia is teaching.

Luisa: It could be related to management. First-year teachers don't want to let children go as you did, Anita. They want to keep things tight, management-wise. I think Sylvia was afraid to let go because of the experience she had student teaching. It also seems like the mentor did it this way to help with management.

Anita: I have a concern about her finding a place for herself and her students in the class; it's a strength but it's also a concern.

She was fortunate to break that mold and find a space. I'm not convinced that teachers with more years of experience than Sylvia could break the mold and bring a personal element into their teaching. Most teachers just follow the routine at their school. It's a strength that she was able to accomplish the changes she made. I wonder if on some level the preservice teachers were really angry because their culture was not responded to when they were students. Maybe it seems too huge to consider, "How can I relearn how to embrace who I am and what I love and invite that into the classroom?"

Donald: I was real puzzled…the way I understood it, this was her last year of training to become a teacher and you're trying to implement by learning from an experienced teacher. I don't understand why she disregarded her own instincts or was holding them back or almost disregarding her own cultural experiences. It wasn't until experiences in the classroom caused her to surrender and start making the experience with the kids more personal and allowing that personal aspect to come in to her teaching day, that's when her teaching began to get more substantive and her kids attached more meaning to the discussions they were having. There was a personal relationship and it was the beginning of better teaching for her. It was almost like once she brought her own funds of knowledge into the classroom, that is when it was permissible for the kids to bring theirs in. And that's when the whole situation got more real. I also noticed that the one area that she allowed to go out of bounds was writing and she seemed to somehow consciously say, "We're not going to do it that way. We're not going to stick to the time frame." She really accessed reading through writing because you can read without writing, but you cannot write without reading.

Leanne: One of my concerns is that she may not have made the connection between reading and writing in her thinking as a teacher. Children being allowed the space, even when you're doing the writing part well, need to see the connection between reading and writing. So if she's doing the reading component as separate and different, then the kids see reading and writing as separate. Reading is this work that they have to do. Writing is where they can truly express themselves. And they're reading that writing, but my guess is that they don't think of the reading of their writing as the same kind of reading they do during the other blocks. The tubs of books did not seem to be organized in any way in terms of children's literature or the children's reading performance. And I think the undergraduate experience needs to teach teachers to think about our profession...

Donald: This case also shows how important the match between the student teacher and cooperating teacher is. You don't have a lot of confidence during student teaching to go against what your cooperating teacher is modeling for you. You are in the room with a teacher who is supposed to be an expert. Unless you're specifically given freedom, you are not necessarily given that much leeway to find yourself as a teacher unless you're really lucky.

Leanne: I agree and that is really complicated. It speaks to the need to teach future teachers how to look at children. A student teacher could go into someone's classroom who is doing a really wonderful job of teaching reading or writing but not understand what they are seeing because they don't know how to look and no one's talked to them about how to look. If a district is trying to promote a given program, student teachers are going to those classrooms and may not be getting the best experiences. They're learning how to do a specific program. Sylvia realized very quickly that the program wasn't working for the population of children she was working with. How do we educate other new teachers to look this closely and feel confident in acting on what they see?

Anita: Speaking from my own experience, I am a teacher who does many culturally responsive approaches to reading, writing, and math, but at [my previous school] I approached it differently than the program that my school was using. My principal wasn't going to give me a student teacher. Our principal picked the cooperating teachers and only program-dedicated teachers got the student teachers. Now I'm in a different school and we have students from a methods course observe 4 hours each week. I tell them that I need them to talk to me about what I'm doing, even to say they don't agree with me or that they never thought to do something a certain way. Their questions help me. But they've never heard anyone tell that them that it's ok to disagree with me.

Donald: At both schools I've worked at, if you want to be a cooperating teacher you have to respond to a memo that goes around. It's possible that a principal might ask new teachers to wait, but it's really up to the teachers to volunteer.

My school uses balanced literacy because it allows for flexibility. In balanced literacy, the teacher makes many decisions about teaching reading. Some might choose a basal; others might use a literature-based approach. We're treated like professionals who know kids and understand reading; we make the decisions about instruction.

Leanne: So you're at a school where each teacher's approach to teaching reading is valued, so student teachers will get a thoughtful approach. But in a school where a specific program is valued, the teachers chosen as cooperating teachers are the ones who do that particular program and do it without asking any questions.

Luisa: When I student taught, I was carefully matched.

Anita: Student teaching could be about learning to build relationships with children and colleagues in order to teach reading more effectively. Sylvia learned to build those relationships in her own classroom, after which more real teaching and learning occurred in her classroom community.

Luisa: Well, do others think that she really used her own funds of knowledge in her teaching?

Donald: There was a change and I don't think it was even conscious on her part when she began drawing on her own experiences, like when she invited the children to share their experiences. She had accessed something that was genuine in her own life and that was the first step in her bringing her own funds of knowledge into her classroom. At the very least, it seemed that was a stepping stone to allowing the kids to actually interact more as peers and talk to each other. I think she also sensed or knew that those real experiences, outside of school, affected learning to read and write.

Luisa: I think it was when her aunt died that the urgency for some changes really surfaced...

CASE 2: SYLVIA 49

Anita: ...And she also invited her students' parents to use the Spanish language if it felt more comfortable and even invited her own father to be a translator at conferences.

Luisa: I couldn't imagine going into my classroom and not telling my children that I'm having a hard day, like if my aunt passed away. I would share that with them.

Donald: It's almost like she went into the classroom being an authentic person but she felt like she needed to check that at the door and approach teaching as a clinician. Teaching has to be personal and based on relationships; it's about relationships with all kids all the way through school.

Luisa: Wow, that helps me clarify something about why I didn't become a speech pathologist. I didn't want to be a clinician. I wanted to have more personal experiences with the children.

Anita: Sylvia felt like a guest. That ties into that clinical approach and to my teaching last year. I was told by my administrator that I was a guest and that when you are a guest at someone's house you are not expected to move the furniture. And the furniture meant that I was not supposed to come in and question and try to make changes to a school that had adopted a specific program. And still to this day, I wonder how many teachers feel like they are coming home when they are coming to their classroom or if they feel this it is just a place for them to be for a part of their day and they're just a guest there and can't suggest changes or question things.

Donald: I can't imagine not being able to arrange the learning environment, choose the curriculum, make decisions about teaching...

Anita: ...That principal meant I had no business changing *Four Blocks* and letting children do different things within that program. He said I must do the program. But I said that the families of my students expected something different from what was in the program. He once told our staff that our parents are our consumers and I reminded him of that, but he said that's not what he meant and that I was moving the furniture. "That was not ok," he said.

Rick: Anita's experiences make me wonder about Sylvia. What advice would you give Sylvia as she goes forward in her teaching of reading in light of what we've said so far?

Leanne: Part of that goes back to knowing yourself and finding out what you've lost in the process of being formally educated. I think looking at her literacy autobiography means honoring who she is as a literate person and then looking at her teaching of reading through that lens.

Rick: What does that mean, to teach reading through that lens of autobiography?

Leanne: For me it's meant that I learn about the reading process and I also learn about how children live that out. I use what I know to make teaching decisions, and what I know is more than a program. It includes knowledge of children's language, culture, and experiences.

Donald: I would tell her that teaching reading takes more time and energy than you think when you're learning how to become a teacher. I think that at the grades I've taught, the teaching of reading is most successful when the kids' interests are honored. Having a variety of reading materials and motivating kids from their own interests will engage them with the written word in a way that has something to do with them. They want to read and write when it's important to them.

Anita: My advice would be if you can't see yourself or your students' lives in what you're reading, then ask what's the purpose in reading this. I'm not saying that everything that you read has to be about you or them, but if it's not, you really should know the purpose behind it, and the kids should know too. If you're talking about teaching in a more culturally responsive way, you must always be cautious that it doesn't turn into teaching the dominant curriculum. If you're teaching in another language, you have to understand what is culturally responsive and what is just language. If you're reading something that kids don't respond to, you have to ask why you're asking kids to read this. If you can't say a good reason, you're just wasting everybody's time. Culturally responsive also involves personally responsive; you want the children to engage.

Leanne: I think that it has to be apparent to you as the teacher and to the children as to why you're doing something. Otherwise, you're just perpetuating the experiences you had at school and then kids just sit and listen and just guess the purpose or don't care what the purpose is.

CASE 2: SYLVIA 51

Anita: I was brought up in a family that spoke both English and Spanish, but I was taught in a way that only valued one part of me, the English part. It took many years for me to find a space for my language and a space for my culture in classrooms when I taught; it wasn't easy. I didn't have good models and I butted up against a lot of walls. For me, teaching is emotional, and if I don't feel emotional about it then I'm concerned. I want children to read and write with and from those emotional parts.

Luisa: It's about being authentic and putting yourself out there for the children. I can't imagine teaching without being me. I put that out there and my kids know me. I have to ask myself why I'm doing this. I'd advise Sylvia to ask herself if what she's doing is meaningful for her children. She's struggling with the program she's using because she is asking herself "Is this meaningful for my students?" With the writing she did, that was meaningful for the children. She needs to keep building on that in all of her curriculum.

Anita: Last year, in my classroom, I taught almost all day in Spanish and Leanne and I team taught. In her classroom, the children had to have 10% of the day in Spanish and my students needed 10% of the day in English. We found ways to mix groups. We really moved the furniture by putting our children together throughout the day. We made the curriculum more powerful. And, I had a majority of the Mexican immigrant children and she had the second, third, fourth, fifth generations who called themselves Chicanos. There was tension between the two groups of children. When we took this on, it was actually a healing process for the children and even for some of the families. This year, I'm not teaching in Spanish. Hearing about Sylvia's children made me miss who I am and where I grew up.

Luisa: I wanted to teach at a very diverse school, but my school is not that diverse. And I bring my background into my teaching and it's been a good experience for my students and their families.

Anita: I'm realizing that the schools that I would love to teach in, the diverse schools and especially the poor and diverse schools, are where I can best use my gifts and identity. Teaching is so relational for me and even passionate, but if

> I'm not in the right place I feel like my time is being wasted and it's not where I'm needed.

Leanne: Maybe her reading program was reflecting the isolation she was feeling as a teacher. Now that she's connecting to the children more, she will have to make choices about their reading and writing instruction.

Luisa: She's a young teacher and now that I'm in my 30s I'd want Sylvia to know that time makes it easier to know who she is. Confidence in who she is will be the strength she can draw on in teaching reading.

READER REACTIONS TO THE EDUCATORS' DIALOGUE ABOUT CASE 2

SUMMARY AND ADDITIONAL QUESTIONS

Sylvia's growth as a teacher is remarkable and, at the same time, leaves us wondering about the decisions a new teacher faces. It is also important to consider her knowledge of reading and writing instruction and her understanding of the roles that language, culture, child identity, and teacher identity play in that instruction. Sylvia's sensitivity to her students' neighborhood and the issues in their lives within that neighborhood led her to create an oral classroom community that reflected the cultural practices of the neighborhood, at least for part of the school day. That sensitivity was also reflected in her writing program. Sylvia remained committed to the prescribed reading program for the remainder of her literacy program. One idea that was noticed by the educators who responded to her reading program was that all of her children may not have been served well by the way Sylvia was teaching reading. Delivering what appears to be a "one size fits all" (Ohanian, 1999) program seems to treat all of the students as having very similar needs as emerging readers, but recall Penny's experience (and some of the teachers in the dialogue about her teaching). Penny and some of the teachers felt that children learn different things regardless of what we might deliver as the goal or objective in a lesson. This suggests that sometimes we must dig deeper than our beliefs to uncover what children are truly learning. Consider the following questions as a way of clarifying your understanding of appropriate reading instruction:

1. What could or should have been done to ensure that Sylvia left student teaching feeling more competent as a teacher of reading?
2. What adjustments or changes might Sylvia make in her reading program based on what she knows and sees each day in her classroom?
3. How important is it for a reading program to include culturally relevant material and what does the use of such material demand of the teacher?
4. How can teachers become more aware of their own and their students' cultural practices? How important is it to integrate those practices into a reading program?
5. How can a teacher make decisions specific to the reading needs of her classroom and also address the requirements for the reading program as articulated by the school or district in which she teaches?
6. You might respond to the questions on page 1, as these teachers did, to help in your thinking and discussion about this case.
7. Under what conditions and how much should a teacher be allowed to depart from the school's reading program?

INTRODUCTION TO CASE 3

Kendra teaches first grade at a very diverse school in which over 15 different language groups are represented, and the poverty rate is quite high. With so many different language groups present in the school and community, Kendra and her students rely on English as the language of school learning. Kendra composes a reading program specific to the needs of her students and reflective of their interests. She is extremely informed about the reading process and reading instruction, takes courses regularly to stay current in the reading knowledge base, and participated in a study group with Rick and her colleagues at her school. Kendra views teaching as child-specific and only groups children with common needs; she also develops whole-class reading lessons that are broadly focused, allowing the many different performance levels within her classroom to benefit. She is fortunate to work at a school in which the principal trusts teachers to make informed decisions about their students. Her systematic collection of children's growth serves as a strong and articulate evidentiary base for her teaching and her students' learning.

CASE 3: A TEACHER-CONSTRUCTED WHOLE LANGUAGE PROGRAM

Meet Kendra

Kendra is a first-grade teacher at Ridgeway Elementary School. She participated in a study group with Rick and other teachers at Ridgeway. The study group began as a course in a master's program, but Kendra and others wanted to continue the conversations about reading that began in the class. The group met weekly at Ridgeway on Wednesday afternoons. Kendra credits this group of thinkers as critical in helping to shape her reading program. She regularly brought her thinking to the group and made decisions about how to organize, keep records, use time, and teach individually, in small groups, and to the whole class. Although the term is politically loaded, Kendra describes herself as a whole language teacher. She's articulate about what that means, explaining that "I understand what it means when a child reads something other than what is on the page. I analyze the way they read and make decisions about teaching based upon what I see and hear."

Kendra's Class at Ridgeway Elementary School

Ridgeway is one of over 30 elementary schools in a medium-sized Midwestern U.S. city. It is unique in that it is one of only three schools with an English as a Second Language (ESL) program. There were 17 different languages represented in the school during the years that our study group met regularly. The reason for so many languages is that various humanitarian and church groups worked to help families find refuge in this city as a way of removing them from war-torn regions of the world. There were students at Ridgeway from Southeast Asia, the former Yugoslavia, Spanish-speaking countries, Arabic countries, and more. An English as a second language (ESL) program (rather than a bilingual program) was the only viable option because of the large number of different languages. Seventy-five percent of the children at the school received free or reduced lunch. We include this statistic as a measure of the poverty level of the school. Since her arrival at Ridgeway, Kendra befriended another first-grade teacher (also named Kendra), and the two planned and taught together as much as possible. They share similar philosophies about the teaching and learning of reading. During the year discussed in this case, Kendra and Kendra taught in one large classroom that was intended for 30 kindergarten students. They had 45 first graders in this space. The quarters were crowded, but their students gained in the richness of having two teachers with similar beliefs as close-working colleagues. The focus in this case is on the first Kendra and Maria, one of the first graders in that Kendra's charge.

Time

The following typical daily schedule demonstrates the ways in which Kendra's knowledge about reading is enacted each day in her classroom. This case focuses almost exclusively on reading, but the entire day's schedule is included to give a sense of the overall picture of days in the classroom. Each of the time slots is described in greater depth with a focus on Maria, one of Kendra's students, as a way of seeing what one child experiences, as well as to demonstrate how teaching and learning occur in this classroom.

8:15–8:45 Planned Activity Time (centers)

8:45–9:15 Group Time

9:15–9:30 Personal Reading

9:30–9:45 Recess

9:50–10:30 Literacy Centers
10:30–11:00 Writing
11:00–11:30 Literature Circle
11:30–12:05 Lunch
12:05–12:50 Math
12:50–1:40 Special Classes
1:45–2:00 Read Aloud
2:00–2:40 Explorers' Club
2:45 Dismiss

Literacy Teaching and Learning (Meet Maria)

Maria is one of the many bilingual students in Kendra's classroom. There is one other Spanish speaker with whom Maria occasionally speaks in Spanish. Maria arrived at Ridgeway on the first day of kindergarten speaking mostly Spanish and understanding some English. She was enrolled in the ESL program and graduated from ESL by the end of first grade. Maria has a brother in an upper grade and a sister in high school. They are a transnational family (Guerra, 1998), making trips to Mexico at least once each year. Maria missed school for 6 weeks around the winter holidays when her family visited relatives in Mexico.

It's almost 8:15 and children are entering the classroom. After they hang up their backpacks and jackets in the hallway, they enter the room. Kendra is waiting in a chair near the door and has the daily quote on a marker board near her. Children must read the phrase, title, short poem, or other text on the marker board before they choose a center for Personal Activity Time. Kendra selects a text that's interesting, hoping to generate teachable moments based on what she knows and notices about her students. On one day she has "And in that dark, dark house there is a dark, dark room" on the marker board. Most of the children recognize this from *In a Dark, Dark Room* (Schwartz, 1984), a book they'd read at literacy circle the previous day. Kendra asks different children different questions once they've read the sentence. "Where's a period?" she asks one child. "Find the word 'dark'…Tell me another word that has a <d> in it," she asks others. Some do as she asks and move into the room, others linger to hear what their colleagues are asked and sometimes to help them respond.

Maria enters the room and Kendra asks her to read the marker board. Maria says, "I don't know."

Kendra reminds her, "It's from the book we read yesterday." Kendra points to the book on a table near the marker board. Maria is silent.

Kendra picks up the book and reads the title to Maria. Kendra opens the book and begins reading the first page aloud. She hesitates, waiting for Maria to join in the reading. Maria joins in and they read a few pages, with the children around them joining in. When Kendra reaches the lines that are on the marker board, she says, "Look, I took these same words, didn't I?"

"Yes," Maria answers.

"So now read it from the marker board." Kendra and Maria both smile because they know that she can read it.

Maria reads the marker board, smiles, and goes to one of the centers that is not yet filled with other children. Kendra's commitment to teaching that reading is meaning making is always at the surface of literacy activity in her classroom. She recontextualized the text for Maria by providing the source text and reminding Maria of what they'd read the day before. This single teachable moment in the classroom is one of many in which Kendra will value and revalue readers. As Maria leaves the marker board, Kendra says to her, "I thought you could read that."

Over her shoulder, Maria responds, "Oh yeah, I thought so too. I like reading it out of the book better."

Jumping ahead for just a moment to the next morning, Kendra has another excerpt on the marker board from the same book. Maria bounds into the room, clearly excited. Kendra asks her to read the marker board, but before Maria focuses on the board, she says to Kendra, "Read this!" Maria has a shoebox wrapped in aluminum foil and held closed by layers of duct tape. There are holes punched in the top of the box and all the children around her are excited. On a piece of paper that she taped to the box, Maria wrote in marker, "in that dark dark box there was" without putting a period at the end. She had a second piece of paper taped over the end of the sentence so that no one could see the last word. Kendra read the box sign and asked, "Ohhh, Maria, is there something alive in there?"

"You have to guess," is her reply.

More children gather around, and one says, "I know what it is." Maria had apparently revealed the contents to this child and Maria admonishes her, "Don't tell." Then she announces, "I will tell you all at group time."

Later, at group time, Kendra helps Maria cut through the layers of duct tape, peel back the foil, and before opening the lid Kendra asks Maria once more, "Is it alive?" "Noooo, " Maria almost howls with laughter, loving the attention from everyone.

"Wait," Kendra says. "Before we open the lid, let's have people guess."

When Kendra asks if they think it's an elephant, she is playing with predictions and possibilities. The children analyze what might be in the box and eventually ask for clues, but Maria can no longer contain herself. She holds up the paper with her sentence on it, peels back the covered piece of the paper, and reveals the word "klay" to her classmates. Some read it, a few mention that it really begins with <c>, and Maria triumphantly holds up a big blob of green clay.

Kendra knows that she has just witnessed an evaluation moment and later explains to Rick, "Maria understood the 'dark dark' part of the book, the mystery of not knowing how something will end, and then she made a connection to her world at home. She constructed a dark dark *something* to bring to school. This is meaning-making at its best."

Kendra has a class list on her lap as the children enter each morning. She makes notes about what she learns from each child as they read from the marker board. These notes eventually find their way to a three-ring binder in which each child has a section where Kendra notes their progress in reading.

Planned Activity Time

This is a social learning time when children interact with each other and with texts at the various centers around the room. At the Discovery Center, there are sets of rubber stamps and stamp pads. Some of the rubber stamps have animals on them and the name of the animal is written on the wooden handle of the stamp. Maria gets writing paper from the writing center and stamps three insects on her paper. Then she builds sentences around what she stamped by writing "I love" before each stamp. Her paper then says "I love" followed by a picture of a butterfly. The next sentence says "I love" followed by a ladybug, and the last one says "I love" followed by the grasshopper stamp. Then she goes back to the stamp and carefully copies the words from the stamps so that it reads "I love" followed by the stamped picture followed by the word "butterfly" for the first sentence, "ladybug" for the next, and "grasshopper" for the third. She rereads each sentence and then goes back to each and adds an <s> onto each insect word.

At this point, Kendra comes over and asks Maria to read what she wrote. Quickly, Maria says, "I love butterflies. I love ladybugs. I love grasshoppers."

"How do you know that isn't 'silkworm?'" Kendra asks Maria.

She laughs and says, "It looks like a grasshopper."

"That makes sense," Kendra says. "How else would you know, if there wasn't a picture?"

Maria says the sound of the letter <g> three times, "guh, guh, guh," and looks up at Kendra.

"Oh, the sound of <g> helps you know, too, doesn't it?"

"Yes," Maria says.

"So it looks like a grasshopper and the letters tell you that you're right, too, huh?"

"Yes," Maria affirms.

Group Time

When the children transition into Group Time, Kendra's focus is on extending the individualized teachable moments that occurred during Planned Activity Time to lessons for the entire group. During these whole group lessons, Kendra uses texts that can meet multiple agendas that she has as a teacher. While some children might focus on letter–sound relationships, others focus on the conventions of written texts, and still others are learning that reading is always supposed to make sense.

The first part of group time typically involves the presentation or review of a whole text. That text might be a book, a poem, a story, a song, or just about any other text you might imagine appropriate for first graders. When they are working on learning a new song, they sing it first and then again. They might hear it on a tape or CD if such a recording is available. Aside from being on a chart, each student gets a copy of any song or poem that they are learning. The focus is always on making meaning, and the lessons always originate in a text that is meaningful or has the potential to be meaningful to the children. Maria's text that accompanied her box was honored at Group Time. Other important and child-generated texts are also honored.

One day a child brings a family photo with some cursive writing on the back. Kendra asks, "What might this say on the back of the picture. It's cursive and most of us don't read that kind of writing yet."

A child answers, "It says who's in the picture."

Kendra says, "It might...what else might it say?" "Maybe it says where they are," another child volunteers.

"It could," says Kendra.

Other guesses are welcome. Kendra asks, "How did you make such good guesses about what it might say?"

A child responds, "Well, it's a picture so there isn't a lot of room on the back."

"That's true," Kendra says. "What else helps you predict what it might say?"

"It has to be about the picture," another says.

Kendra reads the back of the picture, "Grandma and grandpa at the zoo, February, 1996."

One day Kendra reads *Peanut Butter and Jelly* (Westcott, n.d.) to the class. It's a "play rhyme" (according to the cover of the book) that explains and shows the making of bread, jelly, peanut butter, and then the putting of all those on bread. It also repeats "peanut butter, peanut butter, jelly, jelly" on every page. Kendra reads the book, discusses it with the children, encourages them to make connections and tell what they notice, rereads it, and eventually moves to very specific parts of the illustrations and verbal text in order to make some points and push the children's understanding of reading and themselves as readers. Taking words out of the text to discuss onsets and rimes, looking for patterns in the text, asking how children might figure out challenging words, asking what to do if part of the story doesn't make sense, and discussing the joys of rereading a text that you love are all parts of Kendra's teaching of strategies.

One page in the book reads:

Glop it on the bread and

Smear it, smear it. (no page numbers)

Kendra reads to the class, intentionally making a miscue. "Listen to how I read this page and tell me what you think. Glop it on the bread and spread it, spread it." She pauses. One child raises his hand and says, "You mean *smear it, smear it.*"

"I see what you mean, I think," Kendra responds. "You wanted me to say *smear* and not *spread*, right?"

"Yes."

"But what if I was reading along and I said, *'spread'* and I didn't even notice that I said something different? I didn't even stop! Would that be so bad?"

By this time of the year, the children have appropriated the answer that is cultivated in this community of readers. One says, "It sounds good."

"Anything else?" Kendra asks.

"It sounds good and it makes sense."

Kendra says, "OK, now let me be a little strange and read that part of the book again." She has the book opened to the page where elephants are helping to pat down the sandwich as a baker pours in some jelly. "What if I read it this way?" she asks. "Glop it on the bread and smile it, smile it. What would you think?"

"Some of the people are smiling and the elephants are, too," one child notes.

"Yes, that's true. That's maybe why I might say *smile*, isn't it? I looked at the picture and I might have said that. So maybe it's a good guess in that way. But does it really make sense to you?"

"Nooo," comes a chorus from most of the group.

"I don't think so either," Kendra says. "Look closely at the lines of print. Look right here." She is pointing to the <sm> in *smear*. "You see these letters? What do they say?"

"Smmm," say some kids.

"Yes, so I might have seen those letters and seen the smiles on those faces, but it still does not make as much sense as it should. So, I need to go back and think some more about that word so it makes sense."

"It's smear," Maria says.

"If I was sitting next to Maria reading this book, I'd have some help to make sure it makes sense, wouldn't I?" Kendra asks the class.

They smile.

It's a quick lesson, and similar lessons occur each day at group time. Through their discussions, the children inform Kendra of their emerging understanding of reading and Kendra makes decisions about what to demonstrate. They conclude this particular lesson by listening, at first, and then singing along with a taped version of the story in which it is sung almost like a rap.

After the lesson, Kendra makes notes about what she introduced and what specific children said in response to her and each other. She uses class lists for this, to ensure that she pays attention to each child. She puts notes next to the names of children until each has at least one notation; then she gets a new list and begins again.

Personal Reading

This brief period of time prior to recess will extend as the year progresses and children can sustain their reading of longer and more complex texts. Maria grabs a book and starts to read. As soon as Kendra or I sit next to a child, that child typically begins reading aloud. They know that Kendra and I are there to listen to them. Maria is reading *The Hungry Giant* (Cowley, 1990), about a grouchy giant who has a huge club, called a "bommy-knocker" with which he intimidates people in the village. Maria reads on page 4, "Get me some butter," and then she stops. "I thought it was bread, but it's butter," she says to me.

"Oh, how come?"

"Well, it would make sense you know. And it has the <b>."

"Wow, you know a lot. So why did you say butter?" I ask.

"Because it's *butter!*" she says.

Later in the same book, on page 5, Maria reads, "and got the giant" and then she pauses. "Got," she whispers. "Oh," I say. Yesterday, they worked with *got* and found other words that end with <ot>. They generated a list of rhyming words. At the end of that lesson, Kendra said, "Got," with amazement. "All these words from *got!*" she announced remarkably. There was spontaneous applause that apparently left a mark on Maria's reading life. When Maria reaches the place in the book where the townspeople are frantically searching for honey to feed the giant, she reads, "They looked everywhere for honey," (p. 11). She looks at me wide-eyed and points to a person bent over a trash can looking for honey. "People looked in the garbage cans for honey," she tells me. "I drew that in my literature log."

"Oh, you've read this before?" I ask.

"A lot!" she says. "I like it."

She sticks with this book for 3 weeks and then decides to read a different book during this time, one that one of her friends has had for about the same amount of time.

Literacy Centers

The children go right to literacy centers on returning from recess. The centers are delivered to the children in the form of a thick, two-pocket folder for each child. In it, they have a record sheet for keeping track of the date and what they've read, the book they are reading this particular week, and any project about the book that they are developing. The books were selected with Kendra's input and are challenging ones that are interesting enough to the children so that they will read and reread them for at least 1 week. This focused study of one text is Kendra's way of supporting the children in "intensive reading" (Peterson & Eeds, 1990). The very strong readers are reading chapter books that may take more than 1 week. We'll follow Maria during this week.

As she was completing last week's book, Maria met with Kendra to select the book Maria will master this week. Kendra knows the book is challenging for Maria so they read the book together during last week's reading conference. It was a sort of choral reading in which Maria sometimes lagged behind Kendra and sometimes Kendra slowed to lag behind Maria. They talked about the book a little bit, and Maria slipped it into her Literacy Center folder.

Now it is Monday and the children are expected to spend the week becoming experts on reading their books and developing a project on the book. Each child in the room has a different book. Eventually, Maria will make puppets and glue them to tongue depressors as her project for the book. Other weeks she's made posters, clay figures, bookmarks, and paintings about books she's read. The Literacy Center time always begins with children reading their books. If they rush too quickly into their project, Kendra brings them back to the book.

I sit next to Maria as she begins reading, *I Like Me* (Carlson, 1988). Mondays are always difficult for Maria because the challenging texts with which she is faced seem to frustrate her quickly. She reads the title and skips the author. "Nancy Carlson," I say.

"Oh, Nancy Carlson," she repeats and smiles.

Then Maria moves her thumb across the edge of the book as she bends it in half so the pages flip by quickly. She says, "Neh neh neh neh the end." I look at her and wait. She turns back to the first page of the book. The first five pages of the book are as follows (the first two numbers are the page, the second two are the line):

0101 I have a best friend.

02—[Illustration, no written text]

0301 That best friend is me.

0401 I do fun things with me.

0501 I draw beautiful pictures.

The book continues with things that the main character likes to do. On 0101 Maria reads, "I" and then elongates the sound of that letter for about 10 seconds (Iyyyyyy). Then she pauses for 15 seconds. Then she says, "I have a bend," and looks at me for help, but I offer none. She regresses, "I have a picture? Play? Play." She sighs a deep sigh and says, "I don't know." She folds her arms and waits for 24 seconds, an eternity for anyone working with a struggling reader. I wait. The children learn not to interrupt or volunteer help too soon when someone is quiet. "Shhh, she's thinking," is a response often heard when Kendra is silent with a text after she's begun reading it. The children wait in anxious anticipation for the explanation she'll offer. Kendra will do the same for a child, offering, "Shhh, she's thinking," as a signifier that we let readers be with text to make sense.

Maria regresses, using a strategy she has heard Kendra use. "I have a something friend," she reads, emphasizing *something* in order to make it clear that it's a placeholder. Maria looks at me. I smile. She smiles. She sits up, unfolds her arms and reads, "I have a best friend." She turns the page and begins 0301, "This, this, that this," and then she spells the letters, "t-h-i..."

I say, "Yes, *that*, it's *that*."

She ignores me. Then she says, "this...that...ohhhhh, it's the same word," referring to the word *best* on 0101. Although struggling with this/that, Maria is already looking ahead and noticing *best* as a word from the previous page she read. She looks at the text, looks at me, and reads, "That best friend is me," with no miscues.

Reading 0401, Maria begins, "I do," repeats it ("I do") and then pauses for 8 seconds. Then she says, "you, I do pictures...paint...I do fun stuff with me." Maria points to *things* and says, "ing! ing!" They have done so much with "ing" that one day a child called out, "ing alert!" while reading and coming across a word with that rime. Now the whole class is on the lookout for such words. Maria does not correct the stuff/things miscue, probably because *stuff* makes good sense. She moves on to the next line and reads, "Iyyyyyy" [elongating the sound of that word] and then looks at me and says, "Please, Rick, ohhh, please, what is that word?"

I respond, "Do what you do when I'm not here."

Maria says, "I ask H——."

I say, "Oh," as H——leans over and tells her, "draw."

Maria will read the entire book every day of the week. She'll ask friends, one of the teachers, or me for help with some words. She'll make different miscues each day she reads and studies this text seriously. Maria and Kendra decide Maria would work on this book for 2 weeks because Maria wants to read it with the same flow that she's heard others read it. By the end of the second week, she read it with almost no miscues and with much expression. She especially liked 1301 and 1302 and would reread them with much expression: "When I get up in the morning I say, 'Hi, good-looking!'"

When Kendra calls Maria to conference about the book, Kendra uses a form (Figure 3.1) to keep track of Maria's miscues. She offers strategies and chooses one or two miscues to discuss with Maria. For example, Maria reads, "I eat good fish," and regresses to correct it to "I eat good food." Kendra asks Maria, "How come when you read this you said *fish* and then went back and read *food?*"

"Because it's food," Maria responds.

"How'd you know?" Kendra asks.

Maria makes the sound of <d> a few times.

"Ohhh," Kendra says, "so you knew because of the letter <d>."

"Yes."

Kendra suggests, "But fish makes sense. It's a good guess."

Maria points out that fish are in the picture, but that food is the best word to use because, "that's the word *food.*"

Kendra talks about one or two miscues and also engages in a retelling discussion. The conference takes 6 minutes and Kendra moves on to the next child.

Writing

The focus on this case is reading and reading instruction, so I will not explain Kendra's writers workshop. Many of the lessons from reading extend into writing.

Literature Circle

The Literature Circle is a time for introduction of new texts and sometimes the rereading of old favorites. Culturally relevant (Au, 1993) and responsive (Ladson-Billings, 1994) texts are often used and discussions often take place (Peterson & Eeds, 1990). Poems, newspaper articles, songs, books, and other texts are brought by Kendra to share with the children.

Chapter Book

Kendra finds books that are intriguing and exciting so that the children will see the book in their minds. Kendra explains, "The Literature Circle and Chapter Book segments of the day round out the children's reading experiences in school because these times are demonstrations of proficiency." If Kendra miscues or something does not make sense to her, she demonstrates how a reader stops and makes sense of text by regressing, questioning, and thinking aloud. If she comes across a fascinating word, she'll mark it with a

Reading Conference Form

Name:_____

Date:_____

Title of Book:_____

Author:_____

Retelling: "Tell me what the story is about."

[Kendra puts notes here. Her focus on meaning is clear because the retelling is at the top of the form. She asks the children questions as part of the retelling. Then she moves to considering strategies they've used (below) and values those by telling them that they made good decisions as a reader and by asking more questions about their choices. She also offers them other strategies for proficiency.]

In Process Reading Strategies

Looks back	Rereads
Skips	Substitutes word
Asks for help	Uses graphophonic cues
Uses pictures/visual cues	Uses context
Uses background information	Self-corrects miscues
Recognizes miscue	Other_____

Regressions: Are there many regressions in the same line?   Yes   No

Was the child taped while reading?   Yes   No

Did the child write in their literature log?   Yes   No

Did the child complete a book project?   Yes   No

Book Project_____

Comments: _____

Figure 3.1. Reading conference form Kendra designed and uses.

sticky note and return to it after the reading. She'll put the word on the board and invite conversation about it. When she regresses because meaning falls apart due to a miscue, she explains to the children what happened and that good readers sometimes reread or even stop reading to think about the text at hand.

Explorers' Club

This is the inquiry portion of the children's day. The first graders do research through interviews, investigations, conversations, Web searches, library searches, experiments, and more of their own devising. This is another time in the day when reading and writing overflow into each other. The children are expected to journal about their learning each day and eventually to produce a product of some kind. Kendra helps the children as she asks: "What do you think that word is? What might make sense? Do the letters look right to spell it that way? How did you know that word was ____ and not ____?" She also teaches strategies for reading and writing within this context of the children pursuing their interests.

In Closing

Kendra and her first graders ask questions, gain confidence, and view challenging texts as part of living the lives of readers and writers. They celebrate their learning, read many different texts and genres, and feel that they are doing important work. They know that they are valued as learners and as thinkers when Kendra constantly asks, "What do you think?" in relation to world events, texts, sentences, words, and letters and the sounds they make. These questions cover important areas in the standards to which Kendra will answer, including phonics, grammar, and comprehension.

READER REACTIONS TO CASE 3

EDUCATORS' DIALOGUE ABOUT CASE 3

The four teachers who discussed Sylvia were invited to discuss the case of Kendra. They were joined by Tina, a first-year teacher at a lower to middle class school. The five teachers gathered around Rick's kitchen table and ate homemade lasagna while considering and discussing Kendra's teaching of reading. The teachers listened to the case as they followed along on their own copies and took notes as Rick read. They discussed the case using the questions on page 1 as a guide. This group of teachers pointed out that reading instruction lies within many layers of life in school. One of the layers is the relational one, in which teachers cultivate relationships with their students. Such relationships involve teacher knowledge of children's homes, communities, and cultures. Other layers have to do with teachers as knowledgeable about the reading process, materials to use for appropriate instruction, and knowledge of the children's reading performance. Reading is further complicated by the idea that, even though we may read alone, reading and meaning making are socially rooted processes. Readers need time to talk and interact about the texts they read, and classrooms need to reflect that need. A crucial layer is that reading instruction is contextualized within a school and district. Kendra's principal is the link between her classroom and the broader contexts of the school and district (contexts in which many demands lie). His support is demonstrated by his trust in the curricular decisions she makes.

Rick: We can follow the questions in order or we can jump around and discuss your responses to her teaching. [They chose to jump around.]

Donald: I think she teaches reading as a peer process. As she works with her students, she is interacting with them in a way that allows them to believe that she's working through the same processes as they are. She's very artful about it.

Tina: I think she makes them own it, where they have to create projects about the books that they're reading.

Luisa: They're [the children] always talking about what it is they are thinking about and Kendra asks them more questions or discusses in ways that push that thinking even more. That really stood out for me. She's always sharing her thinking and encouraging the kids to do that, too.

Leanne: I think that she gives them enough time to understand that reading and exploring literacy take time. It's not something that you just do for a small portion of the day and set aside. When you look at that morning time and see 3 hours, well, that lets them value that time and they have a lot of opportunities to explore.

Anita: She revealed the value and insights she was having and sometimes that is not valued when we teach kids to read. She's trying to get them to understand the process of reading by reading to them and with them; and she's allowing them to read in multiple ways. It stands out that she spends and her kids spend so much time on literacy. The entire day is literacy, except for 45 minutes of math. I'm sure she approaches math as literacy, too. We want kids to read but don't always give them time to really engage; she gave the kids time to read, time to talk about reading. They were thinking and talking about their thinking. When I first looked at her schedule, the chunks of time were separate, but as I heard about the day, it was clear that the times flowed. The expectation is that the kids read a lot during the day.

Leanne: Kendra really shapes children's value of reading by giving them time to read. She shows that she values reading.

Donald: She seemed to approach the classroom culture of reading in a thoroughly integrated way. In balanced literacy, when you do a think-aloud, it's like a separate lesson. Kendra thinks aloud as opportunities arise for her to do that. Even when Maria is focusing on the difference between *fish* and *food*, she makes the sound of consonants but the meaning is always right there, always part of the process. That was a phonics lesson, but it was also focused on what the sounds and word meant in the story.

Luisa: The heart of Kendra's reading program is that she emphasizes strategies and not skills. That goes back to what she says about being a whole language teacher. She analyzes what the kids are doing all the time. Her kids have a lot of strategies for reading: making connections, keeping it meaningful, having it be purposeful. The "ing" alert was interesting. They understood the use of "ing" and it was a powerful lesson for them. It is a great strategy because the children are reading and thinking about reading. It's clear they are learning to read and reading to learn. Those two ideas are not separated by Kendra or her students.

Donald: She's really good at making Maria an insider. Kendra gives Maria the insider glance. You got the sense that Maria was hanging back and Kendra gave her that insider glance that means Maria could contribute and be part of the class. It's that look you exchange with an individual child and it encourages her and lets her know she is part of things. This is the subtle use of her body, her eyes, to send a message to Maria. It's like a private message, but Maria gets it; she's part of the reading life of the classroom.

Luisa: It made her feel like a reader. She was part of the reading club. She makes Maria an insider when Maria became more involved with the literacy of the whole class. Kendra tells kids to sit next to Maria because she [Maria] knows certain words. That was really powerful.

Tina: I was impressed when Maria brought that box in and it turned into a whole class lesson. Kendra has to always be thinking about what the children bring in, either a real box or an experience, and she works to show the kids that there are literacy lessons to be learned in all those things.

Luisa: That book had layers because readers go deeper and deeper. Maria made the layers, like in the book. You had to go through tape and the box to finally see what was inside. The book did that, too, as Kendra read about the house and the room and cabinet and so on. Maria got that idea of layers; I'm not sure she could express it as such, but she built into her box the layers reflective of the layers in the book.

Rick: Do you have concerns about Kendra's teaching of reading?

Luisa: I had a question. When she talked about giving the children a book for the week, and wanting a book the children can read for a whole week, I find it hard to find those kinds of books. Especially as a first-grade teacher, with emerging readers, I find it hard to find books that they'll want to read for a week. I would be interested to see what the criteria were, why these books were engaging…so many of the books we have for emerging readers won't engage them for a week. What were these texts?

Anita: I think when kids are first starting to read, we look for books with a familiar pattern or rhythm or rhyme. The kids were reading at different levels. She is finding engaging material and not belittling the act of reading. Some of the texts that we

	give beginning readers don't give them the feeling that they're real readers. Kendra found books that would engage the children. She wants them to have a meaningful experience. Kendra provided so much background for the book that if Maria chose to read it, she [Maria] would have the prior knowledge she needs because of all she did with it. She heard her teacher read it and she made a project about it.
Luisa:	We want kids to use what they know. Like in one book I had my first graders read, the text said, "Up went the zebra, up went the elephant, up went the giraffe" as those animals were climbing into a tree house. The giraffe's neck was all bent and the kids looked at me and said, "Giraffe's don't climb trees." If we want to activate what they know, their schema, it almost hurts their understanding when we give them some of these books. That was a big *aha* for me this year. Some of them even had trouble reading the word giraffe because its neck was so bent and they couldn't really tell what it was. I tried, like Kendra, to teach them strategies to think. I asked, "What do you think that could be?" They talked to each other about it. They looked at the pattern on the animal, but looking at the back and bent neck of the giraffe, they couldn't tell what it was. Anyway, I'd really like to see what texts she had and used with her first graders.
Anita:	There's something I want to address. My fear with this case is that I think there's a lot to learn from Kendra. Right now, this practice seems almost extinct, a precious animal that we have to work to keep alive. If we pick it apart, it might give someone permission to say that it's not good teaching.
Tina:	I feel the same way, too. I'm a first-year teacher, and instructional coaches or administrators come into my classroom and I get criticized for what my children are not doing. They want to see the children choral reading but not think or talk about the text, just read it and move on. It's just phonics-based choral reading, everybody reading out loud together. It's really hard to do it that way because I see the frustration with the kids. They think it's just a pointless waste of their time. They act up. When I do teach anything like this, where the kids get to think and discuss, I have to do it in secret.

Anita: That's the reality of it.

Leanne: It's a policing mentality. You can't tell the police what you're doing. This keeps you afraid that the police will come in and see you doing something that you're not supposed to be doing.

Donald: It's like you have to teach underground.

Leanne: That speaks back to what Anita was saying. We, as articulate teachers, are trying to teach like Kendra. We're trying to be thoughtful about what children know and what we see...to build our teaching on that. But there's that level of discomfort, of knowing someone might come in and disapprove.

Anita: I think that she's doing some phenomenal things, but I think that just to say that, to put that "good job" sticker is not enough. My fear is that by analyzing it, we run the risk of having someone else come in and take our words and say "see, this is not good teaching." Good teachers may have something to say about Kendra's teaching, but I am just afraid it will be used against good teaching, against Kendra's teaching. The climate right now is not a climate of trust about teaching and learning. To put this under the microscope feels risky, but to not look at it feels fake.

Rick: How do we take lessons from what Kendra does and put that into the larger commentary in a way that is useful to teachers' thinking about teaching reading? How do we do that in the current political climate?

Anita: I wonder if Kendra is still teaching. We're in awe of her teaching and we can learn from it and take a part of it with us.

Donald: This is risky teaching because of the political climate. If this kind of teaching isn't illustrated and detailed as the kind of alternative to what we keep hearing about in the press and what some teachers are doing everyday, then the public's awareness is not going to be raised enough to know that there are meaningful alternatives. The fact is that there are myths about some ways of teaching reading, like whole language or literature-based instruction. This case sheds some light on the myths. I also see that Kendra is doing some things better than I am. I look at Maria and I reflect on situations that are similar where I might have copped out because of fears and pressures. One example is just letting a child take a book and spend a lot of time with it...like *My Father's Dragon* (Gannett, 1948) is a silly book that I did as a read-aloud and there are three copies in the room and they are always in use, always someone in line to take it for quiet reading time. There's something in our classroom culture or their lives that makes this book valuable to them. They already heard the book in its entirety as a read-aloud, and many of them have already read it individually, and they're talking about it with each other. It's an informal, spontaneous, unassigned book club. The process of looking at a case, like Kendra, and thinking about our own teaching helps me a lot. It helps me feel a little more confident in doing certain things.

Luisa: I understand where you all are coming from. I have a really supportive principal so I've never felt the way you're describing. I never felt that kind of pressure; I know it exists. Nobody ever comes to watch us teach at our school. No one ever comes to make sure that I'm teaching what I'm supposed to be teaching. I'm spoiled.

Donald: Well, it's a continuum. And it sounds like you feel pretty free to teach the way that you believe in teaching.

Luisa: We have teachers at our school who are teaching skills from a textbook and nothing else in reading. Nothing like Kendra did in her classroom. Then we have others who are doing all inquiry-based teaching and a lot of engaged children in their classroom.

Donald: I have a fair amount of freedom. My principal acts out of fear and with no real educational vision. But this is relatively benign in many ways except for the fact that because there's no vision and no proaction, you end up spending a lot of energy doing things you wouldn't have to do if the principal had some educational vision. My principal would go to a principals' meeting and return to say things to the staff about some other school using some program so we should be doing it too, to get on that program train or get off at the next station. Even with that, there's a certain fear that you have to do things a certain way. So we have to be ready to put on a show to show that we are doing what they expect.

Leanne: What is it about teachers that we feel "I should be cautious about what I say?" I'm wondering what it is about the climate of teaching that causes that. There's either the idea of policing and we're going to monitor what you do in your teaching. Or, there's this notion of it's a free-for-all and you can do what you want to do and nobody's going to come in or ask you about your practice. I think the policing part of it is a problem because it's about controlling what we do and our decision making. But just letting us go seems problematic, too, because that means teachers aren't coming together and having conversations. Either way, we're not talking to each other. And, either way, we become cautious about talking to each other.

Donald: It's like talking about teaching as a muscle that we don't get to exercise enough.

Leanne: When we come together around the table, we sometimes come with this hesitancy about talking about teaching reading. There is almost this fear about who will know what I said and where will it go? There's this fear of putting things out there and being seen as an incompetent teacher. I think this is caused by both ends of that spectrum. I've been at a school where no one ever talks to you. I've also been at a school where they come in and make sure of what we are doing. Both of those things lead to stilted conversations when we get together because in both of those places, there were no ongoing conversations about teaching and learning. So we are hesitant to talk about our teaching of reading, someone else's teaching of reading, and even the climate in which we teach reading.

Anita: Maybe someone who doesn't understand what's going on in Kendra's classroom has no right coming in to ask her.

Luisa: Hmmmm...I think the amazing thing is that she wouldn't have to explain it to visitors. The children could. They knew what they were doing and why they were doing it. And they knew that it was important. These kids are 6 years old and they are very articulate about what they are doing. Look at Maria and how she could talk about what she was doing.

Rick: One of the themes here seems to be leadership at the school. You all have very different principals. Is that a very important piece of the picture of reading instruction at your schools?

Luisa: In my case, the reason is the socioeconomic issues. My school is a very high SES [socioeconomic status]; our kids get the [high] test scores and no one's going to be putting their nose into my classroom. My principal cares about the kids in the school, but there's no policing. We're not all having to teach the same way.

Anita: How come we, as teachers, aren't having conversations like Kendra's kids? Why don't we have a climate of learning from each other as part of our ongoing professional development?

Donald: We, as teachers, need to get to the point where we can disagree with each other. Why can't we have conversations as a collaborative process, where I question your practice, rather than have it viewed as an indication that you're not a good teacher? We need to embrace the idea of true discourse around the profession. The profession needs to provide space for that. I think there's a concerted effort to make teachers feel isolated.

Luisa: My first reaction to hearing about Kendra was to wish that my classroom were like hers. When I visit other classrooms, I find myself wishing my classroom were like the one I'm visiting.

Rick: I wonder if that's because of that sense of isolation. Who does benefit by teachers being isolated? If there's a concerted effort, it's usually because someone is served.

Donald: I think there's a lot of insecurity within a lot of levels of administration. I worked at a school once where the counselor told me that the principal had trained in the "management by chaos" school. The place was constantly in crisis. It's a management style that is a way to avoid having serious conversations about what's going on...

Anita: ...to keep us chasing our tails. If we were really learning about our profession and making an impact on it, what would that do to their world?

Leanne: Or having teachers realize that they, teachers, can be leaders.

Tina: As a first-year teacher, I really have to go out and find people to really give me feedback. I feel I know so little and I'm expecting to learn from other teachers. I student taught at a school where everyone was involved in learning from everyone else. But here I have to seek it myself. I ask my mentor teachers to come in and give me feedback. The principals won't, and I don't know how I'm doing.

Donald: It would be nice if there were a way to go around and observe teachers that you would like to observe. If I'm good at something, in the right teaching culture, people would invite themselves to observe good teaching. It needs to be part of the process.

Tina: At times, I think that my school could be different with different leadership. A lot of the teachers who have been there a long time just do what he says to do and they get their checks and go home. It seems like the mindset of the school, not all but most of the teachers are afraid to speak out, and they've had other principals there and it's been the same thing.

Anita: I only stay in a school for 3 years or so. The first year I learn about the school. The second year, I try new things based on what I've learned. The third year is when they say, "Remember the first year you were here. Teach that way, not the way you did it last year." So that's the year I look for another place to teach. It's like I said last time we met. If a principal tells me that I am not allowed to move the furniture [her metaphor for making changes in curriculum], then I get ready to move to a different school. I want to find a place where I'm supported in moving the furniture.

Luisa: I always thought I'd move around, but I don't want to leave my school after talking to everybody else here. But now my principal is retiring, so maybe I'll be on the other side of all this. Faculty will be involved in hiring the new person.

Rick: Do you have any advice for Kendra and also, based on the conversation tonight, do you have advice for people who are interested in teaching reading this way in the present climate?

Anita: Keep talking about your practice. Leanne and I have conversations all the time. We teach at the same school now and were at the same school last year. I really enjoy learning from her. I think if you can't find someone to talk to at your own school to get insights into teaching this way, then find someone at another school. You get to see someone else's reality and appreciate what you have or ask questions like, "why does it have to be this way?" And to ask yourself if you're going to be a change agent, how are you going to start that? I get so much value out of talking to people I don't see on a regular basis. I put my whining and my dreaming in perspective and find the reality.

Donald: I agree with what Anita said about finding ways to speak with people that you respect. Finding ways to exchange ideas and staying true to that. And teaching true. In this culture of fear, it's easy to become a compliant teacher. There's nothing rewarding about that. It's a lot better to teach true to your values about teaching than to sell your soul.

Leanne: Kendra's teaching showed how smart she is about teaching reading. We also have to be smart about how we teach reading. We also have to know the culture of the school, the leadership, and the other teachers to understand how much we can teach the way we want. We have to know how the furniture is arranged, and we have to understand whether we can move that furniture and how much we can move it.

Tina: Teaching reading is about a lot more than just a program. I know that. It's very complex.

Luisa: I'm really glad we got together to talk about these two cases.

Anita: I enjoyed this small group. It's so important to get our voices heard, and we don't get lost in a group this size.

READER REACTIONS TO THE EDUCATORS' DIALOGUE
ABOUT CASE 3

SUMMARY AND ADDITIONAL QUESTIONS

Luisa makes a distinction that is important in discussions of teaching reading. She suggests that Kendra teaches strategies, not skills. Teaching reading *strategies* involves the teacher in selecting what a reader needs to learn based on what the reader is doing and focusing on the making of meaning. Strategies-based teaching requires that the teacher know a lot about the reading process and options for instruction. Luisa's reference to the teaching of reading *skills* has to do with Direct Instruction; DI teaching involves a predetermined sequence of teaching reading, as Penny does in her classroom. Whole language teachers, like Kendra and Luisa, are concerned that in some reading programs, the teaching of skills takes precedence over reading a variety of interesting texts.

Kendra also relies on her colleagues as sources of encouragement, challenge, and ongoing professional conversations. Her view of teaching reading is rooted in the necessity to constantly discuss what her children are doing, the instructional decisions she is making, and the evidence of their learning. The educators that responded to the case of Kendra felt protective of her. They wanted Kendra's decision making about her students to remain at the center of their instructional day.

Here, we provide some questions to help you consider what you think teachers need in the teaching of reading as they seek to serve their students well. Again, consider the questions on page 1, as well, as you reflect on this discussion.

1. What do teachers need to do to create a climate in their classrooms in which reading is seen as an important activity?

2. How important is administrative support for teachers in a school? We often hear teachers say, "I just close my door and teach the way I want." Do you think this is possible?

3. Kendra actively sought out a community of colleagues with whom she could discuss reading instruction. This type of interaction is important because the specifics of a local school can be addressed through a professional development agenda created by the teachers. How might you initiate such a group? What does such a group need to sustain itself over years?

4. Both Kendra and the educators that responded to the case about her discussed ways in which teaching is about relationships and knowledge of the reading process and instruction. How have relationships with

teachers (including teachers not in the school setting) influenced your life as a reader? How might those relationships inform the relationships you have with students in your own class? How would those relationships influence or affect the teaching and learning of reading in your classroom?

INTRODUCTION TO CASE 4

Janesse is an African American woman with a strong sense of her cultural identity, which she applies to her teaching in an inner city school with a mostly Black student population. The school is dilapidated and materials are scarce, yet Janesse strives to create what she considers to be an engaging reading program for her middle school students in what seems to be an impossible situation. Janesse describes herself as, "well informed about the reading process." She works to find ways that she can integrate reading and writing in her classroom, sometimes having students write about what they've read and other times having them compose original work that they read to the class. Janesse has sought out theorists and researchers who discuss the relationships between culture and the teaching and learning of reading and writing (Ladson-Billings, 2001). She works to use culturally relevant curriculum, which she designs through ongoing decision making informed by her students' interests and needs. Janesse and her students face constant pressure to prepare for and perform well on standardized tests. She knows that these pressures can influence curriculum in ways that do not always serve children well (Ohanian, 2001), but Janesse is vigilant in her efforts to have school be an important and productive learning place for her students.

CASE 4: CRITICAL LITERACY IN AN URBAN MIDDLE SCHOOL

Meet Janesse

Janesse has taught middle school for 9 years, the past 4 years in an inner city school in the southeastern United States. Prior to that, she taught for 5 years in a rural county in western Alabama. She grew up in a rural Alabama town near the Florida border. She is the mother of 5-year-old twins, a girl and a boy who are vivacious and active, demanding Janesse's attention during their waking hours. Her husband works at a large health care company and is very helpful with the twins and the house. Janesse is a sports fanatic, explaining that her love of sports reflects her position in her family while she was growing up. She calls herself a "daddy's girl" because her father raised her. Her daily talks with her students about sports increase her popularity, especially with the males. She thoroughly enjoys every sport but is particularly fond of football. Currently, she is finishing her master's degree and will eventually complete Alabama's state reading certification. Coworkers, friends, and central office administrators are encouraging her to pursue a doctorate and complete her administrative certification in order to have a greater influence on reading instruction in the district.

Janesse was a student in some of the graduate courses that Maryann taught. Maryann was impressed with Janesse's knowledge of literacy in two important ways. First, Janesse was well read in the research on reading, including the various perspectives within the ongoing debates about the reading process and instruction; second, Janesse knew the works of many children's literature authors that her middle school students would come to learn about and love in her classroom. Atwell's *In the Middle* (1998) has been one of the greatest influences on Janesse's teaching. Janesse's understanding of Atwell is something that Janesse mentions in almost every discussion she has about her teaching. Janesse has become a resource for her colleagues and Maryann when they seek someone to discuss issues of literacy teaching and learning in middle school.

Maryann is one of the directors of the Red Mountain Writing Project, one of the National Writing Project (NWP) sites in Alabama. The NWP is a summer program that helps teachers with their own writing and invites them to learn about the research on written language development and instruction. When Janesse participated, Maryann got to know her warm and kind ways with colleagues, her passion for writing, and how thoughtfully she reflects on her practice. She also learned that Janesse's cognizance of her own Blackness and the position of Blacks and other minorities in society is an issue that Janesse does not hesitate to bring into her classroom. Janesse is committed to teaching and engaging her middle students in discussions of equity and social justice.

Kellogg Middle School

Kellogg Middle School is located in an urban area on a busy street near a major highway that feeds into a major interstate. Virtually every street in the vicinity of the school seems to be part of an ever-sprawling strip mall filled with fast food shops, jewelry stores, pawnshops, large car dealerships, and small retail shops. The original Kellogg school, a large two-story brick building built in the 1920s, remains an integral and aged part of the present-day school. The last major renovation of the school was in the 1970s when there were concerns about conservation and fuel efficiency. Subsequent additions include a gymnasium and a lunchroom. Some of the classrooms are below ground level and the office is on the second floor. The property on which the school is located is small, and the configurations of the streets limit further physical growth.

The location of the building and its original architectural design and placement result in significant and periodic flooding. There is a hill located directly behind the building, and heavy rains often result in flooded classrooms as runoff goes directly toward the building. The students in the flooded classrooms have grown accustomed to having their classes moved to the gymnasium or the lunchroom while their classrooms dry out. The lingering dampness creates a problem with mold in classrooms, which has resulted in some students and teachers developing respiratory problems. Classroom materials are also destroyed during floods. Although trenches have been dug around the building and new drains installed, every few years the problem returns. Janesse's classroom is in the flood zone, but she has learned to store things as high as possible, having salvaged most of her books and materials after downpours. She and her students have discussed the state of their school, how funds for public education are distributed in their state, and the ways that poor people get ahead (including the myth of the American dream).

Most of the students who attend the school travel on school buses that pick them up as early as 7:00 a.m. A large percentage of Janesse's students are from working-class families; almost 90% of the students receive free or reduced lunches, a statistic we include as a measure of economic poverty. At the time of this writing, in 2005, the SAT 10 reading scores for the sixth grade were at the 44th percentile, which was very high for the school system; the school made adequate yearly progress (AYP) in the 2003–2004 school year. AYP is the federally required amount of yearly growth a school must make to avoid sanctions and is part of the federal No Child Left Behind (NCLB) law. Kellogg is one of only two middle schools (of 13 in the district) that has not been designated "deficient status" by the state department of education's ranking (also in line with NCLB). In spite of the high poverty rate among the students' families, the school lacks the state and federal support that Janesse thinks it needs for the children to be successful in school.

Many of Janesse's students are considered to be in need of reading intervention (according to achievement test scores), even though the school as a whole made adequate yearly progress. One reason for the need for intervention is the high number of transfer students moving into Kellogg. Under NCLB, students at failing schools may be entitled to move to a nonfailing school. Thus Kellogg and the other nonfailing school receive students from failing schools in other parts of the city. Kellogg accommodates 15% more students than the school is staffed to hold, and a high percentage of those students have special needs. All of the students are mainstreamed into classrooms throughout the school. Janesse has fought hard to keep her students from being pulled out of her reading class. She wants them to read real books and engage in conversations that make them feel as thought they belong to "the literacy club," a phrase that Janesse learned in her professional reading (Smith, 1988). The special education program at Kellogg relies on scripted commercial materials with decodable books, skill sheets, and many drill activities. Decodable books are phonetically regular (Dan can fan. Can Dan fan?), but Janesse's students refer to them as "dumb and boring."

Janesse's Classroom

Janesse teaches five classes of reading to a total of 147 sixth-grade students, all of them African American. One of the effects of 50-minute periods at Kellogg is that reading and language arts are separated as subjects, with students having a different teacher for each. Janesse argues, "You can't separate reading and writing! Now, I don't have time to take my students through the writing process because that is another teacher's job in language arts class." But she finds ways to help them understand that writers are readers because, as she explains, "They read their own writing."

The classroom is crowded with desks large enough to accommodate the class of typical, mostly 12-year-old sixth graders who range in size from less than 5 feet to over 6 feet. There are tiny girls who wear size minus-4 skirts to some who wear large women's sizes. The boys range from small and skinny to football- and basketball-player large. Two walls are chalkboards, one wall is all windows with bookcases built under it (not a safe storage place in light of the floods), and one wall is bulletin board space.

There are books in many bookcases, posters, signs, and student work displayed on virtually every wall space. There are baskets of trade books on the bookcases and on portable carts. The tray of one chalkboard has children's picture books displayed. The students' reading folders and journals are in crates above the bookshelves and are easily accessible to Janesse's students. There are charts that Janesse made hung on the walls so students have access to vocabulary words they are learning.

Janesse's pride in her and her students' African American heritage is quite evident. There are pictures of African American achievers on one very large bulletin board, and books by African American authors, poets, and illustrators saturate the bookshelves and crates of books. Janesse wants her students to read authors whose lives resemble the lives that her students are leading as a way of engaging in discussions about their own lives. There are tips for good writing on one bulletin board, and there are many samples of student writing posted around the room. Janesse's writing is present in her classroom. One of her own pieces of poetry is on a wall for students to see, and Janesse's journal is available for her students to read.

A Period in Janesse's Day

Maryann visited Janesse's classroom often because Maryann enjoys reading the students' writing, hearing their discussions, and engaging them as thinkers. Here, she recounts a typical class period:

> When I entered the classroom, I noticed Janesse talking to a tall male student and saw only boys in the room. Since there were boys and girls in the hall, I was confused at first until I recalled reading in our local newspaper about gender specific classes at Kellogg. The boys were dressed in uniforms that included navy blue slacks and white polo shirts. The strict dress code prohibits earrings and other jewelry and requires that belts be worn. The specific brand of sneakers that the boys wore and the types of watches on their wrists were the only expression of socioeconomic differences. They are required to carry their books in their arms rather than in backpacks from class to class because of security concerns.
>
> The teachers and administration believe they have seen an improvement in behavior as a result of the gender separation. Janesse explains that many of the teachers recall that prior to the move to gender-specific classes, there were frequent situations in which students felt a need to "put on a show" for the opposite sex: boys acted macho and girls gave sassy answers to teachers who questioned them. Janesse thinks that behavior has improved because the audience for these acts has been reduced. She engages the class in conversations about the gendered classes and other issues that they confront both in and out of school. She can be heard asking, "What would a girl say about that? How come? Why does it matter that this author is African American and a woman?"
>
> The 50 minutes that Janesse and her students are together passes quickly. Janesse is articulate in her belief that 50 minutes of reading instruction is inadequate to meet the needs of many of her students, especially if they have special needs. In the past, the school used block scheduling, which afforded teachers 90 minutes per day with their students. Janesse wishes her school would revert to block scheduling, but acknowledges that most teachers in her school didn't like 90-minute blocks. The general complaint was that the teachers didn't know what to do with 90 minutes. "If I had 90 minutes," says Janesse, "I could get in my individual reading conferences and students would have more time for discussions and independent or group projects."

The students sit together in groups of four. Janesse tries to work in small groups so that more students have a turn to speak and so they learn to rely on each other for help. Like many students, Janesse's sixth graders are accustomed to teacher-directed lessons so, from the first day of school, she invests time in helping her students learn to work with peers and in small groups. It takes at least 2 weeks before her students are ready for small group work without being overseen by her. Today, well into the school year, the students understand the possible routines they might experience in Janesse's classroom.

This morning, Janesse is handing out a copy of a one-page sheet of paper that is full of writing and augmented by a picture. She says, "Good morning class. I am handing out an article from a current news magazine I receive at home. Choose one student to read the article aloud to the group, but more than one person can read aloud if you wish. When you have finished listening to the article, begin discussing it in your small groups. When you are listening to the reading of the article, underline all the facts you read so you can bring them up in your discussion." Each group begins discussing the one-page article about unemployment from the popular news magazine. Janesse works to fit self-contained literacy activities into this brief period of time, so she chooses a short article for today. She likes to use texts such as this one because the students consider the topic to be relevant to their lives and will be stimulated to share stories and consider actions in their own lives, both now and in the future. Some of the groups take time deciding who should read and some compromise with two or more reading. As I look around the room, I notice that almost all the students are reading along and have a pen or pencil in one hand doing some underlining.

I pull a chair closer to one small group of students and hear them talk about the ways in which unemployment affects their own families. I am struck not only by the connections they make between the facts in the article and their own lives, but also their willingness to share their feelings. One boy says, "We didn't ever eat at McDonald's when my mom was out of a job." Another boy says, "My shoes were from Payless [a discount shoe chain] and I didn't want anyone to know when everybody at my house was laid off." Another group discusses how people who lose their jobs have to sell their houses and don't have big presents for Christmas. They tell personal stories, refer to the article for clarification, and separate out ideas from the article and thoughts from their lived experiences. They discuss the faces of poverty, noting that the photograph near the article shows a Black family. Some of the students wonder about the family's past asking, "Are they married, you think? Is he her boyfriend?" Others ask about where the family can get food or live if they have no money at all. More stories arise about their own experiences as they make connections to the families discussed in the brief article.

Janesse walks around the room during the discussion, listening in on different groups. She asks questions like, "Does this remind you of anything that has happened in our city?" "Do you think there is unemployment around the world?" "Does losing a job ever help anyone?" "Why have some jobs disappeared?" After she asks the question about whether losing jobs helps some people, one group discusses the better jobs that mothers, fathers, and friends had gotten after being fired or laid off. A few have unemployed parents now and are worried about getting new clothes and food that they like. Janesse stays with each group for enough time to see who is participating, the nature of the discussion, and to get a sense of their understanding of the piece.

The discussions begin to wind down and Janesse transitions her students into the next part of a very packed period. During the last 20 minutes of class, the students write in their journals while Janesse has four quick reading conferences. The students who are writing focus on the ways in which the article touched their lives. Some write about unfairness, others about things they want but cannot afford, and some dream about the future as they imagine jobs they hope to get. Janesse asks the students, during their conferences with her, about their pieces, their immediate goals, and their goals for the future. She tries to meet with each student individually at least every 2 weeks. She feels that she knows her students well and has ideas for each conference specific to her understanding of her students' needs. She asks about their independent reading, their thoughts on the day's reading, and the status of their journal writing. Today is one piece of a larger literacy experience her students will have this year. Some other pieces include reading for a research paper, poetry writing, and novel reading. Janesse works to address what she considers to be the individual needs of her students' unique literacy lives.

As the period ends, Janesse's students seem reluctant to leave the classroom and at one point there are some from the exiting class and some from the entering class squeezing through the doorway at the same time in opposite directions. Janesse continues conferencing with one student until she interrupts herself saying, "You'll be late for your next class but I want to hear more about why the book was so interesting to you. Please tell me tomorrow or after school because I really want to know." The student smiles and leaves. The next class is settling into their seats. As I think about what an exhausting schedule middle school teachers live each day, Janesse seems energized by each group of students. She smiles as she surveys the group, takes attendance, and reaches for a poem that she'll use in opening a whole class discussion of the way poets use images in their writing. "This African American poet...," she begins, as I quietly walk to the door of the classroom. The children's bodies lean toward her as she holds up a book of poems the way I'd imagine one of the students in the class holding up a new CD of a favorite singer as she entered the school bus. All eyes are on the book as I send Janesse a small wave and leave.

Janesse's Curriculum

There has been an ongoing debate over the best way to teach reading to urban African American students (Delpit, 1995; Delpit & Dowdy, 2002;

Perry & Delpit, 1998). The conflicting views about how to close the achievement gap are hotly debated every time the local newspaper prints full-page charts that show just how low the scores are for the inner city schools. There is actually a 70-percentile difference between the reading achievement scores in some city schools and schools in the affluent suburban school district that is only a few miles away. Some educators in the urban system blame families for not sending their children to school already reading like the children they believe affluent suburban parents send to their suburban school. Some teachers, if they are honest, don't believe the children will ever read well because most were born into poverty and seem locked in a cycle that perpetuates the belief that school does not truly offer a path to the American dream. Many teachers see "adequate yearly progress" as a trap in which their school and students are stuck. A few citizens in the community question the court system for allowing 12 school systems to be formed in one county, which has resulted in the segregation of some students by race and socioeconomic level. In the midst of all this turmoil lies Janesse's classroom.

Janesse explains that with each change of superintendent in her district, there is a concomitant change in what teachers are told is the best way to instruct students. Each superintendent and several assistant superintendents for instruction had their own agendas, suggested or required new programs, and abandoned the previous administration's curriculum decisions and directions. Additionally, the federal program and special education coordinators interpreted new legislation, such as NCLB, in different ways—even concerning what could be purchased with federal and state dollars. Because of the differing philosophies, agendas, and interpretations, closets and book rooms are filled with materials that, when purchased, were touted as the panacea for the problem of low achievement among African American students. Some of those materials are gathering dust, but are available to teachers for use with their students.

Janesse knows about those numerous commercial programs available for her use, such as an anthology of stories with accompanying workbooks and worksheets. She prefers to use the literature-based program she developed to be specific and responsive to her students' linguistic, cultural, and social lives. She has some curricular freedom because Kellogg hasn't been taken over by the state or identified as being in serious academic trouble. Janesse is relatively free to select her own curriculum as long as her students continue to do well on the annual high stakes test. She calls these "high stakes" because her freedom to choose curriculum is what is at stake. Schools with less than adequate yearly progress are increasingly being forced to use prescribed and scripted programs in which teachers deliver the same curriculum to all their students.

Janesse approaches her reading curriculum by considering her students. "I think reading should be taught in a way that considers all of the child's needs first and foremost," she says. She tries to help her students connect with the text and understand what the author is intending to do within a particular piece of writing. To do this, she reads aloud a lot to her sixth grade students. Books Janesse read aloud to her classes included: *Bad Boy* by Walter Dean Myers (2005), *Circuit* by Francisco Jiménez (1997), and *I Know Why the Caged Bird Sings* by Maya Angelou (2002). She also shares authors that she is sure her student will love, including Sharon Flake, Sharon Drapper, Christopher Paul Curtis, Sharon Creech, and Cynthia Voight. She has seen students read one book by one of these authors and proceed to read as many of that author's works as can be located.

"All of these books," Janesse says, pointing to the many books in her room, "are about people in their adolescence. My students come to understand that their families are like everyone else's...or they learn about and talk about the differences." By choosing materials her students can identify with, Janesse helps them to form personal connections with the books. She demonstrates how to talk about books when she speaks aloud in response to what she's read. Eventually, her students understand that reading involves a relationship with a text and that each reader is entitled to a view or position about what's been read.

Janesse is committed to discussions of the political issues that run through her students' lives and the texts her students read. The short article they read on the day of Maryann's visit, the intensity of the lives of some of the characters they read in novels, and the reality they confront when they engage in their own research projects are all moments of politicization. In their conversations about privilege, power, money, and position, they also talk about race, gender, language groups, and segregation. In her mind, this type of consciousness raising is an important part of what Janesse does with her students. They explore ideas and events from multiple perspectives as ways of clarifying their own beliefs and making decisions about their own actions, understanding and interpreting the ways in which they and their families are treated, and understanding beliefs held about their communities and other communities.

In keeping with African oral tradition, Janesse often employs storytelling and the retelling of texts. For example, her students sometimes work in pairs, turning to each other and retelling what has just been read aloud and sharing their reactions to a selection. This retelling activity helps the students organize their thoughts and it demonstrates that other students might feel the same way they do about certain passages. It is also a place in which she helps students understand that one text may lead to multiple interpretations and reactions. After such retelling activities, Janesse often asks the students to write their retelling. This helps them understand the ways in which discussions and writing shape thinking.

Janesse believes that a successful reading curriculum supports the use of all the reading cueing systems (phonics, grammar or syntax, and semantics). Each year she has some students who rely heavily on phonics and are good word callers, but who can't make sense of what they've read. She can be heard saying to her students, "Use your power of context," because, she explains, "they can usually figure out meaning when they don't focus exclusively on sounds." For example, during one conference she asks a child to read aloud from the novel he's chosen. When he comes to a word he can't read, she waits. Janesse explains to Maryann, "Children need time to figure the words out. If they're stuck, I remind them of what to do. I'll say 'What can you do?' And if they don't answer, I'll say, 'You could go back and try again...or think of any word that would make sense...or look at the letters and ask yourself what those letters say. But it has to make sense!'" She offers strategies and expects the children to appropriate them. She expects them to talk about their miscues (a word she prefers to *errors* or *mistakes* because those words suggest being wrong, whereas *miscue* suggests information from which a teacher can teach). Even if a reader makes a miscue, she expects the student to participate in discussions about meaning. This process of interrogating meaning making while dealing with miscues is referred to as *retrospective miscue analysis* (Brown, Goodman, & Marek, 1996). "Retrospective miscue is so valuable with my students because I want my students to talk about their own reading processes," she tells Maryann.

Many of the students in each class are categorized as struggling readers in need of intervention. At the beginning of each school year, Janesse receives a list of the intervention students and suggestions on how to teach those students. Janesse disagrees with the rankings of some of the students on the list because she finds students who read well in age-appropriate texts but have scored poorly on the tests. She also finds that there are students who are not on the list who appear to be good readers by some teacher's standards because they say words fluently, even though they don't seem to understand what they've read. She prefers to do her own assessment, but it takes a lot of her free periods and time after school. She considers every reader who doesn't understand what they are reading or isn't reading age-appropriate text to be a personal challenge.

Janesse's teaching reflects her understanding of the reading process and her relationship with her students. She explains, "I'm trying to get many of my students to admit that they don't know how to read well, and by sixth grade they should know how to read. I can't be cold and indifferent and expect for them to open up about their struggles. I want them to have confidence in my ability to help them, but it isn't easy."

Janesse knows that struggling readers don't like to read, so she locates books, stories, articles, songs, and poems that feel familiar, touch their lives, and entice their curiosity. "With struggling readers," she says, "to get hooked on books, the books have to have some immediacy, a place they know, an idea, a concept they are familiar with."

Janesse has read Payne's (1998) work, in which Payne writes about kids from low socioeconomic levels. Although she doesn't agree with everything that Payne has written, she agrees that children must navigate two worlds. They must live in the world outside of school in order to survive, and they must thrive in school in order to, hopefully, enhance their lives. She also uses Payne's notions about speaking in casual and formal registers. She works hard to instill the idea that the students' dialect isn't inferior to Standard English and that there is a place for both registers. Janesse explains her understanding of registers in oral language by noting, "I want my students to know that using casual and formal registers have nothing to do with Black or White. One register isn't better than the other and there is a place for both. What you say at home is for one audience and interviewing for a job is for another audience." Yet she knows that certain registers have greater power and prestige in the mainstream, and she's not shy about explaining that to her students. She uses the examples of casual and formal register when discussing written language, too, explaining that, "If you are writing about the sounds of the city, you write in a casual register, but if you are writing a report you need a formal register."

Janesse wants her students to enjoy reading but says, "I think we do children a disservice when we say there is only one purpose for reading [pleasure]. It is important for teachers to help students read in the school world, but we must also help them apply those same skills to problems they have in their home world." Teaching her students about different language uses across different contexts is a political act. The homework for Janesse's class is reading a self-selected book 20 to 30 minutes independently at home. She knows that the reading doesn't always take place but families are aware of the requirement. She believes the requirement does help some students to read outside of school. Their record of their outside reading in their reading notebook is dated with the name of the book, the number of pages read, and a reaction that the students write. They're asked to react by making connections to themselves, other texts, or things they notice in or know about the world (Keene & Zimmerman, 1997). Although she does not have the time to write lengthy responses to each of her 140+ students, Janesse does read the notebooks one night every 3 weeks and writes brief comments.

Students also have a free writing journal. She doesn't grade the writing journals because it helps her get to know the students; it allows her to use their writing to learn about them and ultimately help them find readings they might enjoy. The journals also increase writing fluency, help them practice new vocabulary words, and, most importantly, are a place in which students can think about their worlds.

In Closing

Janesse will tell you that she still has many professional development goals related to reading. "I want to readily identify what my students are doing. I'm looking forward to learning more about miscue analysis. I'm moving from being a teacher who reads, to being a teacher who thinks about how you learn to read." For this process, she is relying on experts like Weaver (1988), Keene and Zimmerman (1997), and Atwell (1998). When Janesse leaves the school at the end of the day, driving past the now-familiar fast-food shops and various urban bric-a-brac, she hopes she has positively influenced the lives of her students. But like the best teachers, she is already thinking about her plans for tomorrow.

READER REACTIONS TO CASE 4

EDUCATORS' DIALOGUE ABOUT CASE 4

Seven teachers and an assistant principal who read Janesse's case met to discuss it early one evening at Maryann's home. We suggest that if you act out this dialogue, you provide a name tag for each educator because it's a large group. Put the educator's name, position, and years of experience on the name tag so that observers can keep track of who is speaking.

Bea is an Anglo second-year teacher who has taught kindergarten for 1 year and now teaches second grade. Cedrick is an African American teacher who has taught for a total of 11 years and teaches second grade this year. In past years, he looped between fourth and fifth grades, having the same students for 2 years. Danielle, an Anglo, has taught for 13 years in both rural and suburban schools; she currently teaches fifth and sixth grade language arts. Denise, an African American, was a rural fifth-grade teacher in both departmentalized (teaching only language arts) and self-contained classrooms (meaning she taught all subjects to one group of students). This is her first year as an assistant principal. Katrina, an Anglo, has taught for 12 years and presently teaches first grade. She taught for 4 years in a K–2 multiage classroom and also has experience in kindergarten and third grade. Leigh Ann, an Anglo, has 7 years of teaching experience and is also a first-grade teacher this year. She has also taught kindergarten, primary enrichment classes, second grade, and third grade. Linda, an Anglo, is teaching fourth grade this year. She has 12 years of teaching experience including first grade, third grade, and multiage settings. Nara, an African American, is a first-year kindergarten teacher who just completed a fifth year alternative program for teacher education, after being a pharmaceutical representative for 6 years.

The reactions that are raised by the educators in the following dialogue cover a broad range of issues that middle school language arts teachers address if they decide to teach specifically to the needs and interests of their students, rather than to teach the prescribed program. Janesse's decision to teach "against the grain" (Cochran-Smith & Lytle, 2000) is one issue that the educators noticed. She made the conscious decision to not follow the prescribed curriculum. Her decision was rooted in her understanding of her students' academic needs and their cultural identities and probably reflects Janesse's consciousness of her own identity as an African American woman (Liston & Zeichner, 1996).

Janesse feels her success has to do with her decision to use literature that resonates with her students' lives, combined with her knowledge of the reading process and instructional strategies. She also engages her students in ongoing assessments to document their growth and identify areas for instruction. Furthermore, her knowledge of her students' interests in sports is genuine and her willingness to engage with students in conversation about mutual interests (like sports) demonstrates her understanding of teaching as relational work (Goldstein, 1999). She demonstrates through her daily personal interactions and her teaching that being a literate citizen is more complex than saying words or recalling facts from a reading selection. Being literate always involves power, social relationships, gender, class, and other political issues.

The effects of poverty on school morale and performance are well documented. In cases where students perform well in high-poverty schools, intense teacher interactions with students and their families, increased funding for materials and buildings, smaller class size, and well-informed teachers are influencing factors (Kitchen, Valasquez, & Myers, 2000). In the midst of flooding classrooms, mildew, insufficient funds for books, and low expectations from her colleagues, Janesse encourages students and engages them in reading and writing activities that seem to catch their interests, curiosity, and even passion.

Leigh Ann: I felt like I've been in a similar situation to Janesse's because I once had administrators that wanted me to follow a prescribed curriculum. Like me, Janesse has her own teaching philosophy and beliefs about teaching. She doesn't let what the system dictates be the driving force behind her curriculum. She does what is best for her students. She is a learner right along with her students. She knows what her students are up against in life and that's what she brings to the table. That is what is so genuine about her and what makes her an excellent teacher.

She knows it's not about scores, it's not about fluency, but it's about developing readers. She wants readers who understand and love to read and writers who love to write. Every day she brings in situations that are relevant to the students.

One important thing I noticed was that she developed a strong community. She taught them to have respect for each other and how to take responsibility. I believe she

|||has really built within her students a sense of commitment and love for what they are doing. Did you notice that they didn't want to leave at the end of her class? I think that really shows something because she makes her students feel that her classroom is a good place to be.

Bea: I like how Janesse uses a lot of good literature written about things that apply to their lives. The literature isn't just what is in her school's reading program. She chooses readings that her students personally understand because the content relates to their lives, unlike the content often found in prescriptive reading programs.

Danielle: The literature that she uses demonstrates to her students that there are other people who have had their same experiences. They learn that there is a wider world out there and they aren't the only ones who experience their situation. It also makes them want to act on their worlds.

Leigh Ann: She also shows her students that they must transcend their situation. She says to them, "Well, we don't have everything. Yes, the room is flooded, yes, we have mildew." Many of her students may have the same problems at home. She helps her students every day by saying, "Hey, so what if it's flooded? We'll go sit outside." Janesse sends the message to her students that the physical situation doesn't dictate how we learn. She thinks that things like the neighborhood, the school building, the school reading program—even if it's old—that is not what makes a rich program.

Danielle: Her focus is on the bonds she has developed with her students. She has shown that despite the curriculum you are forced to teach, despite the conditions you are in, the floods and the mold, it is the relationships with students that drive learning. The respect that she shows for her students and their experiences are what speaks to them. In a situation that sounds like it is otherwise drab and dreary, Janesse's classroom is a place where they can bloom as people.

Linda: Janesse's teaching shows that she really cares for her students. She has developed rapport with them. She says, "Come talk to me tomorrow and see me after school." She is telling her students that she is willing to make time for them outside of their one period a day. She doesn't say, "When you leave my room, you are gone from my mind." Instead, she is saying, "I really want to hear what you have to say. I value what you are thinking, what you are doing, and what you are writing about."

Bea: I believe that Janesse is more concerned about her students as individuals rather than how the state and federal government judge them on a standardized achievement test. She is concerned if they are understanding and enjoying what they are reading rather than if they are reading on a sixth-grade level. She wants them to learn that they have important ideas that can grow into actions.

Katrina: I wonder what her test scores really are because if you look at the research, you know that the socioeconomic level affects this group of students—the cards are really stacked against inner city students. There are a lot of factors that the students and teachers don't control that affect academic achievement in school. Janesse's teaching demonstrates how powerful constructivism is, and how teachers can use student choice and other strategies with inner city students. Her approach seems superior to Direct Instruction and behaviorist methods with students who don't traditionally achieve at high levels.

Nara: If you have the calling to be a teacher, it doesn't matter what your teaching circumstances or what you are told to teach. She could go in there everyday and say, "I hate this classroom because it floods. My administration is not supportive, and the teachers down the hall think I'm crazy for what I'm doing." She could go on and on with a litany of what's not working, but she chooses to focus on the best practices she knows.

Cedrick: I think the circumstances do matter. Janesse doesn't say, "These children have no experiences." She takes the experiences they have and builds on them. You don't hear Janesse saying, "They just have no prior knowledge." No, they have experiences that are different from mainstream experiences. It's not that they don't have experiences; it's just that their experiences are different.

Katrina: I don't think we can totally relate to Janesse unless we've taught in the inner city. The thing that is so interesting to me is that when you teach inner city students, they are still students; they have their own culture and experiences. All students will do whatever you expect of them so you need to have high expectations. If you believe in your students, the classroom will be a safe place for the majority of them.

Leigh Ann: At my suburban school, I have only a small portion of the problems that Janesse experiences. She has been able to do a lot of good things that work for her students, and she still has positive things to say about her school. She has made personal choices about how she will react to her system's mandates about how to teach reading.

One thing in the case that I found discouraging was how administrators from the central office are always encouraging good teachers to go into administration. I've seen so many good teachers in the inner city eventually pulled from the classroom where they are doing really good and important work.

Denise: I was thinking about that idea also. I hear what you are saying that Janesse won't be working with students if she works toward her principal's certificate. In my case, I believe that as an administrator, I can affect more children because I think you should have a really good teacher leading the school and advocating for what is best for the students. In my job, I want to support teachers to do what is best for students.

I can feel Janesse's passion for her students because regardless of their socioeconomic status, what she is surrounded with in the neighborhood and school, she is fervent about what she knows the children are capable of doing. She wants her students to be good readers and writers, but she also wants to instill a love of literacy and a sense of the purposes literacy can serve. With all the pressure to have students do well on tests, not everyone who is making decisions about students has the best interests of the students in mind.

Leigh Ann: You know that's what is so sad is that the school system that she's in lets test scores drive the curriculum. Inner city schools are desperate for more money because they receive fewer taxes because of new houses and shopping centers built in the suburbs. Because they need money for schools, they often take bad reading programs because they are free [meaning they are funded by federal, not state dollars, through grants]. Those of us who teach in suburbia don't have that much pressure because the students who live there make better test scores. Because our test scores are higher, we're not really impacted with the same pressures that inner city teachers face.

My admiration for Janesse goes up each time I think about her situation. She wants the children to be surrounded by books. She wants the resources that suburban schools have for their students. It is a shame that as educators we have to talk about tax dollars, but if we are honest, the money doesn't always go where it really needs to go.

Katrina: The availability of money does influence educators in almost every state; now even the schools in suburbia are affected. I have to give standardized tests. It is very inappropriate for my students; we know that, but we have to take children's valuable time to test them when they should be engaged in real reading and writing. As a teacher, I think it is very hard to balance the ethics of what you feel is developmentally appropriate with what is being mandated. Janesse really feels this pressure. People who are not classroom teachers developed all the mandates. The scripted reading programs and testing instruments are being pushed by the federal government. Many times these programs are developed by psychologists and special education educators and not reading educators who understand how children really learn to read. The bad programs I know about are coming down from the feds to the state departments of education, who are then pushing them down to the school systems. It is a battle, but it seems like Janesse is really winning that battle.

Danielle: Too many teachers are being forced to teach in ways that they know are not good for students because they need their jobs or they don't think they can convince administrators to let them develop what they know is best for students. I think if I were told to use a certain assessment, I would have a very serious ethical dilemma using it because I think some are built on faulty assumptions about the reading process. So many of those assessments send the message to children that they shouldn't be focused on meaning when they read.

Cedrick: I think Janesse has some of the same ethical concerns that we have. She is concerned about how to meet the needs of her students when administrators would like for her to use canned programs. Two concerns that struck me that I struggle with all year long are time and the influx of new students during the school year. As I was reading that part, I wanted to shout because I was thinking, "Sister, tell me about it."

Nara: I could identify with Janesse because she wants to teach her children and we all know that their needs are often challenging to say the least. She knows that there is a great value when you mainstream students for reading and writing. Janesse wants her students to have a meaning-centered curriculum. I also admire her for having her students work in collaborative groups because that can be very difficult when you don't have a 90-minute block. She had such a limited time to meet the needs of so many students.

Katrina: Janesse proves that you can have small groups even in large classes of older children. You can just see in your mind what a crowded classroom Janesse has. She pulls it off and shows other teachers that it is possible.

Cedrick: You could tell that the children felt the need for more time because they were still hanging around after the

CASE 4: JANESSE

                     bell. That is the biggest compliment to her teaching because the students didn't want to leave.

Nara: Another challenge that caused me stress just reading it was the administrative end. With all the different changes in philosophies, the different agendas of administrators, and materials purchased, the reality of the situation is they could use that money to support a teacher like Janesse to build a classroom library with more books. There are some administrators that just want power and want to use federal dollars for the flavor of the month in direct instruction materials. It's as though they don't trust their teachers.

I thought it was interesting where they divided the boys and girls because I've read about this. Janesse said it seemed to be positive and it shows that this experiment is an effort to make a difference. The school is exploring every possible avenue.

Cedrick: I especially liked how she wrote in her journal and left it out for the students to read. I appreciate how she is a writer herself and that comes through in her teaching.

Danielle: I was surprised that as much as she seems informed about best practices that she said she wanted to learn about miscue analysis. I would have thought that would have been part of her repertoire.

Nara: I'm only a first-year teacher, but I thought maybe she could try a wider variety of pre - and post reading strategies so she could build more comprehension. She could try guided imagery with that age because many children are very visually oriented. She knows that it is really important to connect with her students and, at that adolescent level, her students really need to know that someone cares about them.

Bea: Janesse has the ability to meet her students at many other levels. I can tell that they sense that she truly cares about what they think is important.

Katrina: I like how the kids are so interested in the articles she chooses for them to read. Wouldn't it be wonderful if they could become politically active at their ages? I want them to realize their political power. I want them

	to write letters to the editors because they are so impassioned about their topics. I wonder what would happen if they wrote letters to the newspapers about the flooding. They might actually see results, and they might feel some of the power of words.
Maryann:	What do you think the students are learning?
Danielle:	The students are learning that their experiences are valid and that their ideas have worth. They believe that what is going on in the classroom is relevant to them. They are establishing habits of mind that will go with them forever.
Cedrick:	What she is teaching is beyond a standardized achievement test, beyond a reading level or score, even beyond being a better reader. She is helping them be the best person they can be. She is at a much higher level in her expectations.
Denise:	What she is doing may help change them for the rest of their lives. She has given them a love for learning that goes way beyond the classroom and school.
Cedrick:	Fifth grade is the highest grade I've ever worked with and I'm intrigued by her ability to teach *anything* to adolescents. The exemplary teachers you so often hear about teach younger grades. Many middle school teachers who do a phenomenal job often aren't recognized for what they do.
Linda:	She has provided authentic experiences that are meaningful, and most importantly she has shown respect for her students. It is really wonderful when students encounter teachers like Janesse, particularly because it is harder to show caring to middle school students and Janesse is doing that so well.
Denise:	She seems to have a deep calling as a teacher, and I'm hoping there are others in that school who are catching the same spirit that Janesse is demonstrating.
Bea:	Sixth grade is such a hard age. Janesse goes the extra mile for the students she teaches. I wonder what the other teachers at her school think about the way she teaches.
Danielle:	Reading can be such a transcendent experience. It can take you away from where you are and help you con-

nect with another world. When you read some of the authors her students read, you see what real hardship is in real lives. Kids who live in very dire circumstances could see hope for themselves when they read such texts, especially when Janesse talks with them at the depths she reaches.

Cedrick: Maya Angelou and Walter Dean Meyers have helped a lot of students see that there are opportunities out there, and I applaud her for connecting her students with the best of authors. I'm so glad she has chosen to ignore the basal readers and scripted programs with text written to make it on grade level.

Denise: When her students read the books that Janesse uses, they think that this may be my today but it doesn't have to be my tomorrow.

READER REACTIONS TO THE EDUCATORS' DIALOGUE ABOUT CASE 4

SUMMARY AND ADDITIONAL QUESTIONS

The role of standards in teaching middle school children, as measured on standardized tests, is not an issue that has been resolved in the literature on teaching (Ohanian, 2001). Often, standards are written by individuals far from the students and by individuals influenced by test-makers. Ohanian refers to "standardistos" as individuals committed to standards-driven curriculum and the high-stakes testing from which those standards seem to grow. Others argue that we need standards to ensure that all students reach the same level, as a minimum, during each year that they are in school. Janesse, and teachers like her, are living increasingly in a standards-based environment with mounting pressures to conform to the standards-based curriculum that *guarantees* that students will perform well on standards-based high-stakes tests.

Yet poverty consistently remains one of the most accurate predictors of poor school performance (Darling-Hammond, 2004), particularly when that performance is measured by standardized tests. Karp (2004) suggests that instead of putting pressure on schools to perform up to standards, the pressure should be placed on the economy. He notes that in the present educational landscape, tests are administered and acceptable scores are determined. Students and schools not achieving acceptable scores are receiving sanctions reflective of the No Child Left Behind law. Karp suggests that we identify the median income and then demand that anyone's income below that median be raised to it. This raise would occur over a period of years with citizens required to have an increasing income (up to the median), which could be referred to as adequate yearly progress in economic growth. Failure to meet adequate yearly progress in economic growth could result in sanctions for the wealthy, for businesses, and others. Eliminating poverty, Karp suggests, is the key to eliminating the reading problem.

Street (1995) points this out as well; he asserts that the expectation that increasing reading scores will help the economy is wrongheaded. Instead, increasing the health of the economy creates conditions under which more children are better served by their parents (with better health benefits, time to read to children, access to owning books, etc.) and their teachers (in adequately funded schools). The case of Janesse and her students brings many political issues to mind. Consider using the questions on page 1 and the following additional questions to help clarify your thinking about the many issues in this case.

1. Imagine yourself as a teacher in Janesse's school. You would have to make decisions about the teaching of reading and writing. You would have to decide how much you could do "against the grain" and how much you would conform to the climate of the school. How would you choose to teach reading and writing? How would the students be served by your decision? How would you deal with questions from colleagues and the administration?

2. Some members of this dialogue discuss how much Janesse cares about her students. How does caring, both about literature and more broadly (such as culturally), influence children's learning to read?

3. Think about the children's identities in Janesse's classroom. Then, consider your own cultural identity. How can teachers with cultural identities different from their students ensure their students' successful learning of reading? How does a teacher's cultural identity make a difference in what occurs within the classroom? What does a prescribed program do with teachers' and students' cultural identities? How does culture matter in the teaching and learning of reading?

4. Suppose a school or district likes what a particular teacher is doing with her reading program. What are the pros and cons for encouraging such a teacher to become an administrator?

5. One of the reactors to Janesse's case suggested that Janesse engage her students in some sort of political activity to expose conditions at the school. What sort of activities might a teacher use to initiate such work with her students? What are the risks of such activity? What positive outcomes might emerge from such activity?

6. Janesse's classroom seems to be a safe place for students to read, write, think, challenge, study, inquire, and decide. What conditions do you think you might work to establish in your own classroom so that your students feel the same way about their literacy lives?

II

PUBLIC ARGUMENTS: THREE VIEWS OF THE READING PROCESS AND INSTRUCTION

Many teachers and preservice teachers feel tension about the teaching of reading. The teachers presented in the four cases in this book felt that tension, too. The tension is rooted in the sense that there are "reading wars" and that every teacher must choose or default to a particular side in this war. In this section, we explain three of these factions and why they exist. However, rather than calling them factions and perpetuating a war metaphor, we refer to these differing ideas as *views*. We want teachers to understand the views and to initiate a decision-making process about their own teaching based on that understanding. Of course, each of the groups of reading researchers and teachers (and sometimes legislators) that subscribe to the various views seems to think that their view is the right one. They offer research, experiences with children, experiences teaching, and opinion to support their view. Although they may suggest that no two children learn to read in the same way, they typically also state in implicit or explicit terms that their view is the right view. Tension about the views often leaves teachers and the public not only feeling confused, but caught in the middle and, at times, exasperated by legislative actions, changing standards, and the popular press' representations of teachers, children, and schools.

TEACHERS OF READING AS DECISION MAKERS

The teachers presented in the cases in this book are all struggling to teach children to read as best they can. Each has her own reasons and explanations for her view of reading. A common theme that runs through the four cases is teacher decision making. Each one of the teachers in these cases is a professional because of her educational background and willingness to learn, her ongoing desire to learn about effective reading instruction, and her dedication to her students. Each one also made decisions about how to teach, the materials she would use, the nature of her relationships with her students and her students' families, and the nature of the demands she places on her students each day that they are in school. Their decisions as teachers of reading are usually quite conscious as they actively think and act on how to teach phonics, how to assess comprehension, and the nature of the texts their children will read. Penny chose a phonics program, demanding that the school purchase it as a condition of employment. She also chose to leave her first job to pursue one with different children and, as part of that decision, abandoned the phonics program she chose. Kendra and Janesse are very secure in what they think about reading instruction and organized their programs reflective of those beliefs. They are confident that they do not need the systematic and sequential instruction offered by a basal program, even though some teachers at their schools use such a programs. Sylvia is committed to three of the four components of her reading program, yet she seems to have a broad view of teaching that involves cultural, emotional, and linguistic issues very much in the forefront of her writing program, although she hasn't figured out how to integrate that into reading. Sylvia's students have come to respond to her reading program more positively because of the ways she relates to them. Each teacher, as a professional decision maker, lives a reading program with her students reflective of her decisions.

The remainder of this chapter is an explanation of three views of reading with the goal of helping you make informed decisions about reading instruction in your classroom. Your decisions about instruction should be based on a well-articulated understanding of reading. As we explained in the preface, reading **process** refers to what we believe occurs in the mind as a reader reads. Reading **instruction** is the way that a teacher teaches reading, which reflects a view of the reading process. Throughout the following sections, "reading" refers to both process and instruction unless specifically noted otherwise. Keep in mind that some teachers may not be able to explicitly state what they think occurs in a reader's mind as she or he reads; however, the nature of instruction in their classrooms often reveals their view of the reading process. Furthermore, few teachers live within one view, even though it may appear that there are strict boundaries between the views. We return to the idea of teachers holding multiple and even contradictory views after we explain each of the views.

We use the following list of questions to explain three views of the reading process and instruction that appear in the cases we've presented. The questions will also help you uncover and make decisions about your views of the reading process and instruction.

1. What is the definition of reading to which this view subscribes?
2. What is the implied or explicit nature of teaching reading that the view expects or demands?
3. What is the role of the teacher within this view?
4. What is the implied or explicit nature of learning reading that the view expects or demands?
5. What is the role of the learner within this view?
6. How is reading assessed within this view?
7. What is the nature of the curriculum to which this view subscribes?
8. How does the view of reading take issues such as culture and social context into consideration?
9. What research supports this view of the reading process and instruction?

Each of the questions is related to the other questions. The first is more of a focus on the reading process, but that is directly connected to the teaching processes enacted (instruction). We cannot consider what teaching is without a consideration of the learner. And, we cannot explain a view of teaching and learning without a consideration of the curriculum that is being presented to or used by those teachers and learners. We also have to decide if we want to consider the source of the curriculum and the social contexts and cultures in which it is enacted. And, as reading consumers and users of programs and approaches, we cannot consider the aforementioned without also considering the research (or lack of research) on the curriculum. The overarching question typically reduces to the very basic question: What is the reading process? A teacher's deepest views about the reading process are what typically drive the way she or he teaches reading.

DIRECT INSTRUCTION VIEW OF THE READING PROCESS AND INSTRUCTION

Although this and other views have "instruction" in their names, the name is a reflection of a view of the reading process as well as how reading should be taught. The first view is often referred to as the direct instruction (DI) view of reading. You might see this view referred to as bottom-up, atomistic, interactional (or interactionist), or associationist. Some direct instruction views of reading refer to themselves as "balanced literacy," such as the *Four Blocks* program that Sylvia used. Balanced literacy is a form of DI because of its typically strong focus on sounds and words. Some school districts are using the term "balanced literacy" to refer to the use of a basal program; others use it to refer to a program that is more literature-based, meaning the children read more books (rather than an anthology). Balanced literacy, then, is a confusing term and should be interpreted based on what one sees at a school site. Of course, comprehension matters in the DI view; comprehension questions are asked and comprehension skills are taught. Comprehension is typically a check for the reader's understanding of what the author intended the reader to get from the piece.

Some DI views of the reading process focus more on sounds, whereas others focus more on words. The distinction depends on whether one believes that reading is based on the blending of sounds (strongly phonics-based approaches) or the learning of words (whole word approaches). The more phonics-oriented believers of this view argue that readers need to begin with the smallest unit of speech (phoneme) and move progressively to larger chunks (words) and ultimately to whole texts. The reader is expected to master each skill before moving on to the next prerequisite skill. Thus, readers are expected to synthesize sounds (which is why the view is sometimes referred to as a synthetic approach) to make words. Although the ultimate goal is comprehension of what is read, the focus on sounds and words for beginning readers uses most of the reading instruction time.

The whole word view, another type of DI, focuses on starting with words to teach reading. Some of us may recall learning to read by learning words on flash cards, a large chart, or a chalkboard. The teacher presented new words to us and we were expected to learn them. Some teachers had stacks of flash cards with words on them, and we practiced those daily prior to reading stories in the basal reader. The teacher would also take specific words and demonstrate how they were made. For example, she might take the word *dog* and write it on the board. She might stretch it out into its individual sounds saying, "dddd-ooooo-gggg." Perhaps she wrote *dog* on the board and erased the *d* and replaced it with an *l*, asking the class to read the new word (log). The teacher used words to help the children study sounds, analyzing those words by phoneme (sound) and grapheme (letter). Sometimes the whole word view of reading is referred to as the analytic view because larger chunks of language (words) are used to study (analyze) smaller chunks (sounds) in order to help readers learn sounds. The assumption is that the learning will generalize to new words that the reader meets in other texts. If you think that *dog* and *log* don't rhyme, like many people in the northeast United States, then you've found that dialect creates a flaw in some phonics lessons. Teachers must decide if the lesson needs to be adjusted to local pronunciations.

Goodman (1996) refers to DI views of reading as "common sense" views because, well, they just seem to make so much sense! If students learn the sounds or words of the language, then surely they are on the road to becoming readers. The DI approach is appealing because of its commonsense view; it is also a view that is easily explained to parents and other stakeholders in reading instruction. Let's consider the questions teachers should ask about this view and the responses that lie at or below the surface of the view.

What Is the Definition of Reading to Which This View Subscribes?

In this view, reading is the act of making words by associating a speech sound with a letter or group of letters. It may also be the learning and calling of words that readers are expected to commit to memory. Therefore, reading is considered a process in which the reader makes correspondences between letters and sounds and recalls words (often referred to as *sight words* because they are to be said instantly on being viewed). Furthermore, it is expected that readers will engage in this process fluently, which means that readers efficiently blend sounds and say words without long pauses, hesitations, or going back to reread what they've already read. From a DI view, in order to read, students must have phonemic awareness, be able to use phonics, have a growing list of vocabulary words in their mind, be fluent in their reading, and comprehend the text. We explain these terms as we get deeper into this view.

Comprehension is always discussed when definitions of reading are being considered. Subscribers to the DI view believe that the meanings of the words follow the saying of them, so the text is understood by saying it or, eventually, reading it silently (hearing it in your head). The view assumes that a child that is learning to read uses what they already know about language, so all they need to do is learn the sounds and words and comprehension will follow quite naturally. This is referred to as comprehension being "caught, not taught" (Pearson, Roehler, Dole, & Duffy, 1992). Comprehension is emphasized much more after students are able to read more words and longer texts. Comprehension is *interactional* in this view, meaning that the text contains all the answers a reader will need and skills are taught to locate those answers. Comprehension is a relationship—an interaction—between the reader and the text in which the reader delves into the text to find specific answers to questions. A teacher may ask children to predict what the story is going to be about prior to reading, perhaps by walking the children through the text and looking at illustrations. After the children have read, comprehension questions focus on the plot, theme, setting, characters, and main idea. Teachers might also ask children what they thought, how they felt, and what other things the story made them think of. A more strict interactional view focuses on the facts, both explicit and implied, within the story.

What Is the Implied or Explicit Nature of Teaching That the View Expects or Demands?

Teaching from a DI view involves direct and systematic instruction that follows a specific scope and sequence, much the way Penny did in her second-grade classroom. Similarly, the *Four Block* guide that Sylvia used provided directions for her lessons. Teachers are expected to follow a teacher's guide that accompanies the published reading program. The founder and president of the National Right to Read Foundation (NRRF), a strong advocate of the DI view, lists on the NRRF website seven principles and steps for children learning to read (http://www.nrrf.org/):

> 1. Teach phonemic awareness [sounds of letters] directly in kindergarten. This is instruction in the sounds children hear and does not require that they see letters. A teacher might say, "Which of these words starts like 'cat,'" and then offer the children some words that they must consider. The children might say "car" starts like "cat," but "truck" does not. Phonemic awareness work is done orally.

2. Teach each sound–spelling correspondence explicitly. This is the point at which children see letters and learn the correspondences between what a letter looks like and its possible sound(s).

3. Teach frequent, highly regular sound–spelling relationships systematically. Teachers might teach the *at* family, teaching words that end with those letters, such as *sat*, *rat*, etc.

4. Teach students directly how to sound out words.

5. Teach students sound–spelling relationships using connected, decodable text.

6. Teach reading comprehension using interesting teacher-read stories.

7. Teach decoding and comprehension skills separately until reading becomes fluent. (Teachers are often advised to teach sounds and sounding out and worry about comprehension later.)

Subscribers to the Direct Instruction view believe that children must know the names of all the letters of the alphabet, sometimes requiring them to know this before learning sounds or words. They also believe that the importance of knowing the sounds of each letter while learning to read is supported by the fact that good readers know the sounds that letters may make.

Teaching from this view often requires the presentation of phonics rules that children must commit to memory, such as the rules Penny's children recited during the phonics lesson. For example, in some classrooms, children are taught the three sounds for *oo* (as in *blood, moon,* and *book*). When the class comes to a new word with those letters in it, the teacher asks the children for the three possible sounds the vowels might have in the word. Or a teacher might say, "Long <a>," and children will recite different ways that sound is spelled (a-consonant-e, ay, eigh, etc.). Teaching reading from the DI view involves the presentation of the preset curriculum in a specific sequence by the teacher. Each DI lesson builds on the one before, and the texts the children read, as well as the concepts about words that they are taught, increase in complexity over time. Children might begin with the consonant sounds, learn short vowel sounds, then consonant blends, and more in the predetermined sequence.

The goal of having children master a large number of high frequency sight words is a common thread among educators with a DI view of the reading process. Sight words are practiced until they are committed to memory. The practice is often accomplished through games such as *Bingo* and *Go Fish*. Penny's children responded positively to the large stack of sight words she required them to read as she smiled and complimented them for the achievement.

DI teaching also involves demonstrations of fluency, during which the teacher has children read lists of letters, say sounds, or read words as quickly as they can. Children are sometimes expected to echo after the teacher, reading with the same fluency and expression, as practice. The assumption here, as is borne out by some of the research DI proponents present, is that comprehension increases with fluency; the faster a reader can blend the sounds and letters, the better his or her comprehension will be. Fluency is defined as the number of words (or sometimes isolated sounds or names of letters, for younger readers) read in a minute.

Teaching materials are provided by DI-based companies. As we mentioned, these programs are called *basal reading systems* or *programs*. The word basal refers to a baseline, such as a basal temperature being 98.6 degrees. In reading programs, basal refers to a baseline of expectations of what children are expected to learn during a specific period of time (from a given lesson, to a school year, and across school years) and how they are supposed to learn it. In addition to a teacher's guide, a classroom may be provided with a main text or texts, reproducible worksheets, workbooks, and even small classroom libraries. The textbooks and libraries for beginning readers are often discussed as "decodable" texts for beginning readers. Decodable texts contain, almost exclusively, words that follow the phonic patterns that the children have been taught. If a program begins by teaching some consonant sounds and the sound of <a> in "cat," then a decodable text might include a story like this:

Tad had a cat.

That cat is fat.

That cat had a nap.

A nap on a mat.

A nap on a pad.

A nap on a cap.

A nap in a hat. [*is, a, on,* and *in* are taught as sight words] (Koss, 1995)

Many children, their teachers, and even their families are quite proud when children read these seemingly simple texts. Although they may not seem to make a lot of sense, the argument is that comprehension comes later, when children are involved with more complex texts (having mastered the sound system of the language). In addition to being presented as decodable, the vocabulary in many DI programs is controlled. Controlled vocabulary means that any word that cannot be read by blending the sounds that have been taught is a word taught separately as a sight word (such as *is, on,* and *in* in the example story). Controlled vocabulary and decodable texts are expected to provide children with the fluency they need to comprehend more sophisticated texts.

The belief in this view is that it is necessary to directly teach all skills because even if a child comes to school reading, the skills that are considered prerequisite for reading must be learned in order to master unknown words. They also need the work with phonics and sight words to support their spelling once they move into writing. Penny realized this when she explained that she originally felt guilty teaching children things she thought they already knew. Then, after hearing the consultant from the basal program and talking to the study group, she decided that even though all the children are present for the same lesson, each child may be gaining something different and appropriate to them from the lesson.

What Is the Role of the Teacher Within This View?

Direction Instruction teachers typically deliver the published curriculum in the proper order. Many teachers appreciate the way that DI programs are organized. They believe in carefully following curriculum materials and place trust in the developers of the commercial products. The programs arrive with scripted teacher's guides, meaning the language that the teacher should use is provided by the publisher. This is often quite specific in that teachers are expected to use the exact language provided. For example, a guide might read, "Say this to the students: 'Yesterday we read about a monkey. What do you remember about the trouble the monkey got into?'" The correct answers are usually provided. Penny appreciated this because she wasn't sure what language her students needed to hear to learn to read; she delivered instruction in English, but she worried about talking above or below the level they might understand. She didn't want to insult her students by speaking too simply, nor did she wish to have them not understand her because she was using language that was over their heads. The language in the guide helped her deal with that. One of the teachers in the dialogue about Penny's case stopped using the guide after the first year, a decision that probably would make sense to Penny because that teacher had lived a full year with her grade level and learned enough about the children to use language they would understand.

Teachers in DI classrooms spend much time practicing sounds and words with students. The students are required to practice these skills in workbooks and on worksheets. The bulk of the reading that students do in DI classrooms is assigned to them. Students are most often homogenously grouped, typically into three reading levels because many teachers can balance their time and independent student work to teach three groups each day. Penny, and other teachers like her, decided that smaller groups serve the children even better. Each group works with the teacher for a while as the others work independently on practice and drill work. Recently, some publishers suggested that grouping is not equitable, and they suggest that teachers teach their whole class at once. These same publishers do provide soft cover storybooks at different levels, so higher performing readers do get to read more challenging texts. Struggling readers also have supplementary reading at their levels. Other programs suggest that having children leave their classrooms to be in homogenous groups within a grade or even across grade levels serves them best.

The order of each lesson is also provided, including the expected length of time that the lesson should take. The supplementary workbooks and worksheets are graded by the teacher, and sometimes reteaching lessons are provided so that skills may be retaught if students do not perform at a certain criteria level. The DI view of reading is prevalent in many classrooms in the United States and around the world. Because of governmental support (discussed later) for the DI view, there has been an increase in national and state mandates for its use. Reflective of those mandates, teachers are held accountable for using district-adopted programs explicitly as written. Some legislators have proposed linking salary increases to student performance as an incentive to have schools and teachers commit to DI basal programs. In the NCLB climate, the accountability issue is increasingly present for all teachers, regardless of their view of reading process and instruction.

What Is the Implied or Explicit Nature of Learning That the View Expects or Demands?

The view of learning in Direct Instruction reading programs is that children learn sequentially. Furthermore, the view suggests that learning is a fairly consistent, ever-increasing line on which a teacher is expected to map a child's reading progress by following the program. Learning is also something that occurs in small pieces, as children are expected to learn sounds, words, longer words, and concepts about words (rhyming, syllabication) in the prescribed order. All of these pieces of information add up to the child as a reader, and each piece is built on the piece that precedes it. Learning occurs best when teachers (and publishers) make choices about which selections children are to read, which skills they are to learn, and the order in which texts and skills are presented. Choices for the reader in these programs are typically very limited. Penny addressed this concern by starting each day with DEAR, during which her students chose texts to read. In *Four Blocks,* Sylvia had her children read books during the sustained silent reading block (SSR).

What Is the Role of the Learner Within This View?

In terms of reading, learners are viewed as being expected to pay attention to what the teacher presents and to assent and comply to the decisions about teaching that the teacher and publisher have made. Because educators with a DI view believe that reading is a decoding process, students should learn how to decode all words correctly. Readers are expected to strive for accuracy when reading and often will correct each other when they make a mistake. An interesting facet of the push toward 100% accuracy is the use of nonwords. Some DI programs demand that students learn to read nonwords (kam, kem, kom) as a way of demonstrating that they can blend sounds. The belief is that if students can say or blend any combination of letters presented to them, then unknown words (including words they may have heard but not yet seen in print) will not be a problem for them to read.

The learner must also read with automaticity and fluency. Automaticity is the uttering of words without hesitation, usually in a list such as the flash cards Penny used. Fluency involves the reading of sustained text without hesitation at a rapid rate and can also refer to the rapid calling of nonwords or letter names when the letters are presented in random order. It also entails reading with expression and with appropriate phrasing. Again, the importance of fluency is based on the belief that readers who comprehend well are fluent. The learner must be fluent, exhibit an automatic recognition of words, and recall facts and details as evidence of comprehension.

How Is Reading Assessed Within This View?

Standardized tests are relied on as the gold standard in DI programs. The tests are considered reliable, based on state standards, and scientific and provide the teacher and the greater public with performance and grade level scores that are often used for comparisons across classrooms and districts. Recently, in response to the federal No Child Left Behind (NCLB) legislation, states have been required to develop criterion referenced tests. Whereas some standardized tests are norm-referenced and based on a distribution of scores that fit into the bell curve, criterion referenced tests (CRTs) are based on state standards and have certain levels at which students must perform. Theoretically, it is possible for all students to pass CRTs, something that is not true when scores have to be normally distributed. The goal of everyone passing is at the heart of NCLB assessment. There is much assessment of words and parts of words on CRTs in the primary grades, so words and parts of words are the focus of many DI programs. Lists of nonwords are also used for some testing to determine if phonics rules are mastered, so students are often taught to say nonwords. Timed tests with stopwatches are used to check automaticity and fluency.

Because specific benchmarks are established for each grade level in each state, the teacher uses criterion-referenced tests, standardized tests, and other assessments to determine which students are in need of intervention. Often groups are formed based on the results of the test. One popular test with school administrators and other educators with a DI view of the reading process is the Dynamic Indicators of Basic Early Literacy Skills (DIBELS, 2005). The test begins in kindergarten with the letters of the alphabet (in random order, to determine fluency), phonemic awareness (hearing the sameness or difference of letter sounds), phonemic segmentation (being able to say the individual sounds of a word that is said by the teacher), and blending (being able to listen to a teacher say the sounds of a word and being asked to say the word). In the upper grades, there are tests on specific skills and comprehension is measured via multiple choice questions following a reading selection that is fairly short. Results of these tests often identify a student as needing to be in a particular reading level. Some of the programs suggest that teachers not allow students to select library or other free-reading books that are at a level higher than the one at which the students tested.

What Is the Nature of the Curriculum to Which This View Subscribes?

In DI classrooms, the curriculum is planned by publishers who claim to rely on scientifically based research to produce programs that meet the needs of all students. The year's curriculum is carefully mapped out, and supplementary materials are available for slower or faster readers. Supporters of a DI view of reading advocate a particular sequence for the presentation of phonics rules, but there is no general agreement across publishers about any specific order. Most supporters of this view believe rules should be taught early in the primary grades to aid decoding. Phonics instruction must be explicit and direct because, they believe, that is what the scientific studies of reading demand.

Many teachers who teach from the DI view follow the guides carefully and meticulously. Most decision making is deferred to the guide and publisher, and it is because of this deferral process that many teachers feel relieved of planning some specifics of their reading program. The decision of whether or not to use the guide is usually made in the privacy of the teacher's classroom. One drawback to a carefully designed and prescribed reading curriculum is that it does not always leave room for student choice. One of the controversial criticisms of this view of the reading process is that not allowing children to have choices in their reading may predispose them to not read independently, outside of school. Another criticism is that by limiting students to the responses provided by the basal, they are not being taught to discuss texts from multiple perspectives. Penny addresses the latter point during her oral reading when she encourages a broad range of responses to the text the children have heard. Thus, even though DI seems rigid to some critics, teachers like Penny, Sylvia, and many others find ways to express, in practice, some of the decisions they make about the program's efficacy by augmenting their use of it.

How Does the View of Reading Take Issues Such as Culture and Social Context Into Consideration?

Because most of the programs are published far from the sites at which they are used and it would be too expensive to produce site-specific programs, it is virtually impossible for publishers to take local social and cultural issues into account. In recent years, the number of fiction and nonfiction pieces from diverse cultures that are included in the textbooks has increased. Some publishers have gained access to entire books and offer those as parts of their anthologies. A student in an upper grade might read excerpts from a variety of books, whereas younger students might read entire stories that have been collated into a volume for them. Publishers, then, have responded to the call for greater cultural inclusion in their texts.

Teachers such as Penny and Sylvia are becoming more and more sensitive to issues of culture and context, each departing from the required curriculum in different ways in order to meet the needs and interests of their students. Penny works to find read- alouds in which her students recognize facets of their own cultures and contexts. Sylvia's use of oral language practices and her shift away from the prescribed way to teach writing in *Four Blocks* are efforts to do this as well. As Janesse pointed out, the more poorly a school performs, the greater the demand seems to be to have teachers use the program as it is written.

What Research Supports This View of the Reading Process and Instruction?

We could write an entire book—indeed, entire books have been written—about the research that supports DI. Much of the research on the Direct Instruction view of the reading process and instruction (Adams, 1990, is one review of the research) supports the idea that children should read good literature. Yet, many such programs spend significantly more time instructing in skills than in reading sustained texts, such as stories. Children spend much time working in workbooks and on worksheets. Some teachers are recognizing this and are adjusting their use of the programs so that students read more frequently. Some DI programs are also responding by having children read stories multiple times during a week. The children might hear the story one day, read it round robin the next, with it with a friend the next, and read it alone. The anthologies would become too large if students read different stories each day. The DI research on comprehension is referred to as *text comprehension* (another word for interactional) because the view asserts that a reader's goal is to understand a text exactly as it is written. Text comprehension refers to being able to report specifically what the text presented. This is important to understand because it is an area of extreme controversy, as becomes clearer in the presentation of the next view. A recent publication that received much attention was the National Reading Panel Report (2000a). The National Reading Panel was created by congressional mandate to the National Institutes for Child Health and Human Development (NICHD). The NICHD formed the reading panel with the goal of determining the most effective way to teach reading. This was an effort by the government to settle the reading debates once and for all. The document was not successful in that task, but it certainly stirred the research and teaching communities into heated debates. The panel purported setting "rigorous scientific standards" in an effort to evaluate the research regarding the teaching of reading. The conclusions of the panel were that there was no one best way to teach reading; they recommended a combination of methods. However, the executive summary of the report (just over 30 pages compared to more than 400 in the full report; National Reading Panel, 2000b) suggested that intense phonics instruction was good for all readers, from prekindergarten through sixth grade. The actual report made no such claim. The five reading skills always mentioned when speaking about the NRP are: phonemic awareness, phonics (relationships between sounds and letters), fluency, vocabulary development, and text comprehension because those were the topics for the subcommittees. Reading in the DI research is operationally defined as the orchestration of these five parts.

The panel's report led to the *Reading First* sections in the No Child Left Behind Legislation. *Reading First* requires that federal funding only be given to programs that teach the five reading skills as outlined in the report of the National Reading Panel and using programs that have been systematically researched. Sometimes this requirement is interpreted as meaning that the full report found intensive phonics as the only way to teach reading; this assertion, made by some publishers, is not accurate.

One of the major effects of the National Reading Panel was the development of the phrase *scientifically based reading research.* The Panel suggested that all reading instruction must be based on research that is experimental or quasiexperimental in design. This marginalized the reading research that relies on psycholinguistic, sociolinguistic, and anthropological strategies for studying reading. Thus, the debates continue. But the debates are not new. Chall (1967) wrote *Learning to Read: The Great Debate* to "settle" the reading debates over the use of phonics and its relationship to comprehension. Adams (1990) tried again, and 8 years later, Snow, Burns, and Griffin (1998) tried one more time to put to rest the national tension about the best view of the reading process and instruction. And while the tension mounts in legislatures and at state and federal education departments, some teachers report DI materials are working for their students; others use the materials as a point of origin for instruction that they enhance; still others find the materials limiting to the point of uselessness. The tension lies in fundamentally different views of the reading process, the nature of the child as a learner, and the roles of the teacher and curriculum. This leads to our next view of reading.

WHOLE LANGUAGE VIEW OF THE READING PROCESS AND INSTRUCTION

In this section, we use the term *whole language view of reading* because Kendra describes herself as a teacher who subscribes to this view and because *sociopsycholinguistic transactional approach* seems a bit lengthy. Goodman (personal communication) estimates that when Whole Language was at its peak, only 10% to 15% of U. S. classrooms represented this very controversial view. Whole Language (WL) views of reading suggest that the sound system of a language and the collection of words that comprise a language are superficial structures that we use to convey meaning. Meaning is understood as a deeper structure of language, one that is the goal of all oral or written language. Readers who are the most proficient use the least amount of visual information to make meaning, according to the WL view. For a teacher to teach from that view means that she approaches each text and child differently, with no script. This is one reason that many new teachers do not like Whole Language instruction; they feel unsure of what the teacher–child–text relationship should look and sound like. Whole Language has its roots in progressive education (Dewey, 1938; Shannon, 1990) and research done on the reading process (Goodman & Gollasch, 1982). WL teachers believe that reading is social (Bloome & Dail, 1997) (socio), psychological (psycho), linguistic, and transactional, hence the term *sociopsycholinguistic transactional approach*. Transactional (Rosenblatt, 1978) refers to the belief that comprehension has to do with an individual's experiences, so each person has a unique understanding of the text, an understanding that they create in their own minds. This belief about comprehension helped lead to research on the reading process through miscue analysis (which is explained later in the *assessment* question).

What Is the Definition of Reading to Which This View Subscribes?

The Whole Language view of the reading process and of reading instruction is rooted in the idea that the goal of reading is the making of meaning. Furthermore, meaning resides in the relationship between the reader and the text; meaning does not reside solely on the pages of a book. Readers bring certain experiences to a text, and those experiences matter in this view. When we say "experiences that a reader brings to a text," we mean that knowledge of the sounds of the language (phonics), words that are in the language (lexicon or vocabulary), grammatical structures, semantics, and meaning and feelings from events in one's life are reflected in that reader's understanding of the text. Reading involves the orchestration of all of this knowledge (Weaver, Gillmeister-Krause, & Vento-Zogby, 1997), usually into a unique and individualized understanding of what the text means.

This view of reading as transactional (Rosenblatt, 1978) means that a reader's experiences are considered an important facet of the sense that a reader makes of a text. If a reader reads a book about trucks, for example, that reader brings to the text experiences with trucks, both firsthand and vicarious experiences (perhaps from watching TV or a movie or hearing family stories about trucks). Each reader who looks at the text has a unique experience with that text because each reader comes to the text with the uniqueness of her or his own prior experiences and knowledge. This is true of a reader reading a book about trucks or reading a novel or reading an advanced organic chemistry text. Sense making (another way of saying meaning making) is at the heart of this view of reading. A reader might be able to say all these words: *woods, adz, cabin, built, she, an, used, build, to,* and *a,* but might not know how to make complete sense of this sentence: *She used an adz to build a cabin in the woods.* Not knowing that an adz is a type of ax, a reader would be left unsure of exactly what was used. However, in the Whole Language view of the reading process, a reader's meaning making is acknowledged. A reader might still know what was built, where it was built, and whether it was built by a woman or a man by reading the sentence. There might be a gap in meaning making if the reader didn't know what an adz is, but each time it is used in the text, discussed by the teacher and other students, or looked up in a reference resource, the reader's understanding will be enhanced. The Whole Language view involves a consideration of what the reader knows and what she or he may need to learn in order to understand a particular text. By comparison, in a DI classroom, the teacher would introduce the word "adz" prior to the selection being read. She might also provide the definition. Although Whole Language teachers sometimes introduce words prior to reading, they also believe that a text will teach a reader what a word means within the contexts of the reader's lived experiences and growing knowledge base. If we want children to be independent readers, we must, according to Whole Language theory, teach them strategies that do not rely on teachers for dealing with new words.

Subscribers to this view consider fluency as more complex than counting the number of words or letters a reader says per minute. As you look at this sentence again—*She used an adz to build a cabin in the woods*—you might predict that a reader's fluency is interrupted at *adz* because that's an unfamiliar word. Flurkey (1997) explains that fluency is more like the flow of a river. As readers negotiate text, they might move along fine until they come to something they don't know (like a rock in the way of a flowing river). This causes things to change, meaning to shift, and questions to be raised in the mind of the reader. The "rock" is the part of the text the reader does not know and is usually identifiable if the reader is reading aloud because they slow down, regress and reread, or skip the word. All of these factors affect the number of words read per minute.

Reading *flow*, which WL teachers see as a more accurate description of the process than *fluency*, is also affected by unknown structures or uses of words. A child might read the word *run* quite easily in *He can run fast*, but might not read *He can run a computer* as quickly if that child is not familiar with the use of the word *run* as something associated with a computer. A teacher might think the child is struggling with the word *computer* if the child pauses after the word *run*, when in reality the child has read *computer* in his mind but is rereading the sentence silently to figure out the use of the word *run*. Whole Language teachers know that the child's experiences with language and text contribute to her or his reading flow and understanding of what has been read. Recent work on eye movements (Paulson & Freeman, 2003) supports this as researchers can now track the position of the eyes in relation to what a reader is reading.

Quite often, the Whole Language view is explained as the view that is against phonics. This is not accurate. This view is one that acknowledges four systems (called cueing systems) that readers use to make sense. The systems are graphophonics (sound–symbol relationships or phonics), lexicogrammatics (vocabulary and grammar), semantics (meaning), and pragmatics (relationships and contexts). Teachers from this view teach phonics, vocabulary, grammar, and semantics with a constant focus on meaning and meaning making. Sometimes a cueing system that is being studied is scrutinized closely by the teacher and the students, such as, for example, a study of prefixes. However, the lessons almost always originate from and return to sense and meaning making. In a Direct Instruction classroom, children might read this list of rhyming words: fin, pin, win, bin, din. Once they're read, the teacher usually moves on, as instructed by the guide. Whole Language teachers would only use such a list if the meanings of the words were known or soon-to-be learned. WL teachers would argue that many children don't know what *bin* or *din* mean when they're in a list. These teachers would use a list if it reflected an authentic use of a list, such as writing a shopping list or working as a group to find the rhyming words in a text they've read. Kendra's students are involved with text as meaning making, whether it is the text on a box of clay, a photograph, a big book, or other texts they read or write.

Whole Language teachers argue that everything they teach children influences the children's understanding of reading. They do not teach children to say nonwords because they believe that teaches children that reading does not need to make sense. A child who is told that saying "kam kem kom" is reading may extend the idea that text does not have to make sense into his or her reading of books. The concern is that the reader may sound out something and continue reading even when the sounded-out word or words do not make sense. Whole Language teachers do not want children to be taught to expect written text to not make sense, and these teachers believe that is one of the less apparent lessons being taught when teachers ask children to read nonwords.

What Is the Implied or Explicit Nature of Teaching That the View Expects or Demands?

The Whole Language view of the reading process relies on reading instructional practices that reflect the needs and interests of the children. Teaching is an ongoing process of decision making based in a teacher's constant use of assessments that inform instruction. Teaching is not the enactment of a prescribed program; rather, it is a process in which goals and standards are addressed. Children's understanding of what they've read, the strategies they use to understand, and the ways in which an individual's understanding may differ from (and contribute to) a group's understanding of text are important parts of the Whole Language view. Children's choices are integrated into teaching.

In Whole Language classrooms, children are often involved in *grand conversations* (Peterson & Eeds, 1990). These are times when children transact with texts by discussing the things they notice about a text and the ways in which those salient features of the text intersect and interact with what they already know. In one Whole Language classroom, the first graders listened to *The Hungry Giant* (Cowley, 1990) At the end of her reading, the teacher asked, "What did you notice or think about?" One child noticed that *hungry* starts like *Henry*, a boy in the class. Another noticed the word *bommyknocker*, which the author uses to describe and name a club that the giant bangs a lot. As the teacher listens, she decides things to teach at the moment or later. Eventually, one of the children points out that the giant is mean, sort of a bully. The class initiates a conversation about bullies, and many stories are told. The teacher suggests that the children write some of their bully stories later in the morning. This grand conversation involved the cueing systems (phonics, grammar, and semantics) and the connections that the readers made to their own lives. The teacher could also determine the children's comprehension, but not through explicit questioning. Instead, she listened to what they noticed and discussed as a window into their understanding. The discussion could also lead the teacher to read more books about bullies and suggest readings to specific children that seemed particularly interested in the topic. With no basal to rely on, the teacher is constantly searching for interesting and appropriate texts to read with the students and ones that they might read independently, much the way Kendra and Janesse did in their classrooms.

What Is the Role of the Teacher Within This View?

Teaching from a Whole Language perspective involves teachers in ongoing decision making about texts, strategies to teach, and assessment. Students are constantly making connections within and beyond texts, and their teachers guide them in using those connections to demonstrate comprehension. Keene and Zimmerman (1997) suggest that teachers ask students to make connections to other texts they've read (text to text), to their own experiences (text to self), and to what they know about the world beyond school (text to world). These connections reveal the sense that the readers have made of a text. When a class of third graders discusses different versions of the Cinderella story, they talk about: the way the stepsisters treated the main character (who sometimes is not named *Cinderella*), the charming prince, the events that led up to the appearance of the fairy godmother, the different endings, and more. During these conversations, the teacher discerns that her students have learned about the characters, setting, plot, themes, and other literary elements of the stories. The teacher does not have to ask the children a strict list of comprehension questions because the conversation reveals what they've learned and what the teacher might teach.

Self-selection is a vital part of the Whole Language classroom. Teachers work to set up classrooms as environments in which students have many choices, all of which are educative. Children are invited to read extensively (many different books that are interesting) and intensively (texts that may be more challenging; Peterson & Eeds, 1990). Students in these classrooms read individually, in small groups, and sometimes with the entire class. For example, one sixth-grade teacher invited children to read a letter to *Dear Abby* one morning. The letter was about sixth graders using drugs. After the reading, the class discussed the ways in which they thought Abby should respond, leading to a deep discussion about choices, friends, and peer pressure. In that same classroom, some children are reading longer chapter books together. Others are reading books individually. All of the groups or individuals write in response journals daily, in which they discuss their thoughts, connections, and feelings about the books they are reading.

Response journals are one way that teachers in Whole Language classrooms connect reading and writing. Teachers in these classrooms understand that children need to be receptive to language (by listening and reading) and they need to engage in language use in expressive ways (by speaking and writing). The classrooms are active places in which different children may engage in different reading and writing activities. Writers' workshops (Graves, 1983) are also an integral part of Whole Language classrooms because Whole Language teachers view reading and writing as intimately related. A writer is the first reader of his or her piece.

Children choose topics, and teaching is focused on responding to the teacher- and student-identified needs that writers and readers in the room have. Teaching takes place in homogenous and heterogeneous groups, which vary over the course of the year. A group of students interested in death in one classroom read a variety of stories; some read long novels while others read shorter illustrated books. They could all join together for conversations rooted in their reading. No one was excluded because of reading level.

Beginning reading instruction in Whole Language classrooms is focused on whole texts and the lessons that readers may learn from relationships with those texts. When a teacher reads a big book to the class (*big* meaning that the text and illustrations are oversized so that all can see the words and pictures), that is a reading lesson. Then, the teacher chooses specific skills and strategies to teach based on what she notices within the text and within her class of children learning to read. In contrast to phonetically regular books (decodable texts) used in Direct Instruction classrooms, Whole Language teaching involves the use of predictable texts (in which the grammar, vocabulary, and semantics are predictable).

Decodable texts, discussed in the Direct Instruction section, are often presented as phonetically regular words. Predictable texts use all the cueing systems to make the text accessible to readers. For example, Goss and

Harste (1985) wrote a children's book, *It Didn't Frighten Me*, in which each page begins, "One pitch black night, right after my mother turned out the light, I looked out my window only to see a _____ _____ up in my tree!" On each page, a different color and thing appear in place of the lines. It might be a white unicorn on one page or a silver tiger on the next. After teachers read the first few pages, the children understand the pattern and can predict what comes next (One pitch black, very dark night…). They begin to read along with the teacher. Books like this yield wonderfully rich grand conversations about fear, made-up animals (unicorns), and more. The refrain from the children after the book is concluded is, "Read it again!" The teacher shows the children that they can read it. Children move from reading the whole text (some reading without actually looking at the words because they know the pattern and can use the illustrations to predict the color and animal) to recognizing parts such as words, phrases, and the sounds of individual letters. This whole-to-part (meaning leads to learning words and sounds) view of learning to read stands in contrast to the DI part-to-whole (sounds and words lead to learning meaning) view and is one of the biggest areas of contention between the two views.

Many critics of this approach suggest that the children are memorizing the book. Supporters of this view explain that they aren't memorizing as much as they are understanding the language and finding it so predictable as to be easy to read. This is a subtle but crucial distinction because it is based in meaning. It's the meaning that makes the book easy to predict and read. The meaning is based in children's own sense of being afraid in the dark, their understanding of real and imagined animals, the rhythm of the words, and the clues provided by the pictures on each page that show the green goblin or other creature. Predictable books use all the cueing systems, not just phonics, so they sound more like language that children experience every day in oral language and in texts. When a child reads *It Didn't Frighten Me*, she or he feels like a real reader and is a real reader, according to this view, because the child is making meaning from printed text.

Whole Language classrooms keep two ideas very close together in teaching children to read: children need to learn to read and children need to read to learn. Books like *It Didn't Frighten Me* help them do both because the children engage in all the processes that real readers use. The children predict, confirm their predictions, stop and go back to reconsider if something seems to not make sense, and make decisions about when their reading is complete. Teaching reading in Whole Language classrooms involves understanding children's predictions, confirmations, and decisions as they work to comprehend. Thus, teachers in Whole Language classrooms need to be well informed about the reading process and instructional strategies. They need to understand the cueing systems and the ways in which readers orchestrate those systems to make meaning. They often want to read professional books and converse in teacher study groups (Meyer et al., 1998), and they want to discuss their classroom and students with other teachers. This is not to suggest that DI teachers do not want to meet and discuss; however, historically, Whole Language teachers have been social in their learning as evidenced by the number of Teachers Applying Whole Language (TAWL) groups that existed around the country as forums for professional development.

Teachers in Whole Language classrooms use formal and informal assessment of their students, make decisions about skills and strategies to be taught, and have a vast knowledge of books and other reading materials, including Web sites, that would be of interest or use to the readers in the classroom. The teachers know about children's literature, but not limited to fiction; these teachers are aware of a variety of genres, fiction and nonfiction, and are constantly expanding their classroom libraries (usually with their own money). Their commitment to a variety of reading material, so that students may choose what to read, makes all this necessary.

Students' interests, their own agency as learners (Short & Harste, with Burke, 1996), and their transactions with texts drive the teaching and learning in a Whole Language classroom. When a child in one first-grade classroom told the rest of the class that there are spiders in the basement of the school (Meyer, 1999) and that those spiders could pee on you and you'd freeze and never move again, the teacher brought the question to the entire class. Some didn't know there was a basement in the school; others didn't know spider pee was so powerful. The teacher explained to the children that this was a problem that they all needed to figure out how to face. After a long silence, someone suggested that a group go down the basement and find out. Another silence ensued. Then one child said he'd go check it out, if the principal would go with him. A few others said they'd go with the principal, too. The teacher wove reading and writing into this activity as notes were sent to the principal to find a time to meet and go and, once they returned, a book was written about NO spiders in the basement (the school uses an exterminator). That book, the result of research by the children and weeks of writing and editing by a group dedicated to sharing important information, was placed in the school library so, as one first grader put it, "everyone would know that we are safe from spiders here." Other children in the class studied spiders and their bites and webs. Much information was learned and shared from this spontaneous, yet very important, inquiry.

Whole Language teachers are typically articulate about their view of reading instruction and use that understanding to justify studies such as the spider pee inquiry. They want their students engaged in texts (both to read and to write), and they speak against enforced district-wide adoptions of particular texts or programs because they are committed to choice as an integral part of their students' success. They can present their students' growth in the form of portfolios and other qualitative and quantitative data.

What Is the Implied or Explicit Nature of Learning That the View Expects or Demands?

The view of learning in Whole Language programs is that children are curious and responsive individuals who learn as individuals and socially. WL teachers believe that there are conditions under which children learn best and when these conditions are honored, learning is important to the learners (we've found out about spiders) and evident (we have shared our findings). Cambourne (1995) suggests seven conditions for learning: immersion, demonstration, expectations, responsibility, use, approximation, and response. Immersion means that children should live in classrooms where they are surrounded by language in use in important and relevant ways. Demonstrations are subtle (Smith, 1983) and ongoing; when teachers read a book with expression and then wonder aloud about it, they are demonstrating what readers do. In Whole Language classrooms, children are expected to learn and to participate as active citizens within the classroom. They also assume responsibility for their learning and are encouraged and supported to use what they are learning by being active readers and writers. Approximations are important in learning to read or write. No reader is expected to read every text perfectly, nor are they expected to write without misspellings or other nonconventional (and temporary) features appearing in their work. It is those nonconventions that provide specific ideas for teachers developing literacy lessons.

The teacher's goal is that each member of the WL classroom learns that she or he is a member of the literacy club (Smith, 1988), a club that involves readers and writers actively making meaning in texts they read and compose. Children are encouraged to learn from each other as they plan, read, write, talk, listen, view, and perform (Schwartz & Pollishuke, 1991) with and for each other. The relational features of learning—the idea that learning is a social affair—is honored and supported so that children learn from children, the teacher learns from children, and children learn from the teacher.

What Is the Role of the Learner Within This View?

Learners in Whole Language classrooms are expected to engage in their learning. This means that the teacher and learner come to specific agreements about the substance and nature of the learning. During reading instructional time, learners may be involved individually or in small or large groups. They may be expected to make choices from a variety of texts and genres, to keep track of what they've read (in literature logs or other record-keeping devices), and to present evidence of their understanding of those texts. That evidence might be in the form of conversations, projects, graphic organizers, semantic webs, songs, posters, paintings or drawings, performances with puppets or through readers' theater, and more. Children are expected to make connections across texts and cueing systems.

Learners in Whole Language classrooms learn phonics. If a teacher determines that the learner needs a more intense study of the relationships between letters and sounds, that teacher selects phonic elements and concepts to teach, all based on what the learner is doing—his or her actual performance. Learners also study the structure of words, the use of language across texts, grammar, and many other facets of the cueing systems—almost exclusively by beginning with an authentic text (like *It Didn't Frighten Me*), extracting the element to be studied, and eventually returning to the text (and other texts) to practice and confirm the learning. Learners learn that reading is supposed to sound like language and make sense (Goodman & Marek, 1996).

How Is Reading Assessed Within This View?

The Whole Language view of reading is rooted in the idea that children must learn that the goal of reading is sense making. With that in mind, all assessments must include "windows" (Goodman, Watson, & Burke, 1987) into what the child is doing as a meaning maker. In one classroom, a teacher listens as a child reads this text: "Come, Boy," she whispered, "come and play" (Silverstein, 1964). However, instead of saying *whispered*, the child says *said*. In a Direct Instruction classroom, the teacher might demand that the child return to the selection and read it exactly as written. The Whole Language teacher considers the substitution of *said* for *whispered* a high quality miscue. Rather than consider a child's misreading as a mistake, it is considered an indication of the child's making of meaning, hence the use of *miscue*, rather than *mistake* (Davenport, 2002). In the case of this reader, *said* and *whispered* are very close in meaning, especially in the context of the story. They are the same tense (past) and both are dialogue carriers, indicating the child predicted and confirmed dialogue. DI teachers that learn WL strategies might decide to do what the WL teacher did, an idea we return to later.

Every reader makes miscues. The teacher decides which miscues are important to study, usually because they are low quality. If the *whispered/said* miscue was the only miscue the child made in the entire book, a teacher might say, "I noticed something that I want to ask you about. When you read this sentence, you said *said* for this word [teacher points to *whispered*]. Let's look at that word. It starts with a letter that *said* doesn't start with." Usually, by this point, the child self-corrects. It's important to note that the teacher would not have this discussion until after she and the child have discussed the content of the story. Meaning comes first. Studies in miscue analysis (Brown et al., 1996) have revealed that many readers make more meaning than some would have imagined, but that meaning is often marginalized when a teacher asks too many questions and does not let the reader explain the sense she or he made from the text. WL teachers believe that readers' retellings of what they've read reveal more about comprehension than responses to teacher-directed questions. Running records (Clay, 1985) are another tool that provides information on the quality of miscues.

The connection between reading and writing is a cornerstone of the Whole Language classroom. Much information about a learner's knowledge of letter–sound relationships, grammar, story grammar, language structure, and genre is gleaned from their writing. Writing portfolios are systematic collections of children's work over time, often constructed in partnership with their teacher. In Whole Language classrooms, teachers and students use portfolios as evidence of what reader-writers are doing. Indeed, these teachers often say that their children read like writers and write like readers (Hansen, 2001).

What Is the Nature of the Curriculum to Which This View Subscribes?

Whole Language classroom teachers construct curriculum with standards and their children's interests and needs in mind. Based on that understanding of their children, they make choices about areas of study, types of texts, written language activity, and the way time is used in their classroom. Curriculum, then, is a local affair that keeps in mind state and national standards. It reflects children's development and age and is construed with appropriate materials. It is very rare that teachers in such classrooms would teach the same thing in the same way from year to year.

A teacher with an interest in astronomy might have her children study the stars one year, inviting the children into one of their teacher's passions. However, if interest wanes, the teacher knows that children learn more when their interests are piqued and addressed, and may choose to abandon the study. Other years, the children might spend considerable time studying stars, planets, galaxies, telescopes, and more. State and national standards may be reached in a variety of ways and with a variety of texts and activities. These teachers work to create curriculum (Short & Burke, 1991) that will reach those standards while teaching children the important lessons that: reading is important; it helps us get information; it brings us joy; it is social; it is a way of sharing, knowing, and understanding; and it helps us escape and return.

How Does the View of Reading Take Issues Such as Culture and Social Context Into Consideration?

Whole Language teaching demands knowledge of the contexts in which children live. Culturally responsive (Au, 1993) and relevant teaching (Ladson-Billings, 1994) are parts of this view of teaching reading because teachers subscribing to this view believe that a child learns to read more easily when linguistic, social, and cultural norms of the community are integrated into the school. Sylvia learned this intuitively as she initiated platicas in her classroom. When children see characters and events in books that look like themselves and their community, the children's lived experiences inform the sense they make of the texts. Specific cultural and linguistic features of a text will make it more accessible to some children. It falls to the teacher and the school to develop curriculum that is relevant to the lives and needs of the children—a very local affair from a Whole Language view.

What Research Supports This View of the Reading Process and Instruction?

There have been many studies on miscue analysis and its influence on understanding the reading process and on informing instruction (Brown et al., 1996). Teachers with a WL view of reading may engage in the systematic study of their classrooms and write books (Whitmore & Crowell, 1994) or articles. The National Council of Teachers of English has published a significant amount of this research, most notably in journals such as *Language Arts* and *Primary Voices* (no longer in print). Anthropologists (Anderson, Herr, & Nihlen, 1994) have suggested that teachers are students of the cultures that emerge and grow within their classrooms. With the support of anthropologists and others, teachers study their classrooms to inform their teaching and the field. There have been studies of language in classrooms (Cazden, 1992) and the development of written language from before school (Harste, Woodward, & Burke, 1984) and through the first few years of school (Wells, 1986). Most of these studies have been specific to particular classrooms, schools, and communities.

Since the publication of the report of the National Reading Panel, research on Whole Language classrooms has been considered by some to be problematic. The problem rests in the notion of *reliable replicable research*, which means statistical studies. Statistical studies are considered by some researchers to be of a higher caliber than other types of research on reading because statistical studies are said to be replicable. Studies of classroom cultures are not considered replicable because each classroom culture is unique. Therein lies a huge tension in the reading research community at the present time. Some believe that understanding specific classrooms supports other teachers' understanding of issues in their own classrooms and may also influence how we educate future teachers. Others believe that large population studies provide more accurate implications for what should be done in classrooms. The February 2005 Phi Delta Kappan provides multiple perspectives on this issue as researchers argue about the National Reading Panel Report's usefulness and applicability. Allington (2005), in that same issue, asserts:

> I know of no evidence that following the tightly scripted lessons from any reading program has ever succeeded in building local capacity or even building teacher expertise. However, there is much evidence that mandating a "scientific" instructional package will fail to provide teaching or learning if local capacity is limited or wholly lacking... It is only by fostering 1) teacher expertise about how readers develop and how teachers can help and 2) personal professional accountability for the reading development of each child under our watch that we might hope to ever leave no child behind. (p. 467)

As the debates between WL and DI continue, as researchers disagree with each other and teachers make decisions about what to teach and how to teach it, teaching reading becomes increasingly political. Teachers like Kendra are sometimes quiet, retreating to their classrooms to avoid the debates, yet continuing to teach from a WL perspective. Some WL teachers comply with the demands that they use scientifically based reading instruction (basal programs) to compensate for not meeting adequate yearly progress. The tension grows, frustrations build, and yet, in the past 10 years, another view of reading has emerged. We suggest that it began in WL and the dedication that WL teachers have to culturally relevant and responsive curriculum; it arose from a growing commitment to addressing issues of social justice. The discussion of "spider pee" suggests that growth. The students used literacy as a tool to act on their world to address an issue that they perceived related to their safety. The event was political because the students felt fear and somewhat helpless. Then they developed and acted on a plan not just to study the topic of spiders, but also to exert understanding in order to alleviate their discomfort and the discomfort of others (or potential discomfort). Their use of literacy to reposition themselves from fearful and helpless to informed and safe is an example of the critical literacy view of reading. We turn now to that view.

CRITICAL LITERACY VIEW OF THE READING PROCESS AND INSTRUCTION

The Critical Literacy (CL) view of the reading process and reading instruction is composed of four dimensions: "disrupting the commonplace, interrogating multiple viewpoints, focusing on sociopolitical issues, and taking action and promoting social justice" (Lewison, Flint, & Van Sluys, 2002, p. 382). These four dimensions are aimed at the transformational teaching and learning of reading. Transformational teaching has as its goals: the awakening of awareness of, disrupting, and acting on inequities and injustice. For example, in the cases of Sylvia and Janesse, we saw teachers responding to the cultural lives of their students. Sylvia disrupted her own and her students' commonplace view of what they thought school should sound like. Her anxieties and angst about her students' lives resolved to some degree when she engaged with her students in some of the oral language practices of their community, a way of welcoming multiple viewpoints. Janesse responded to her students as cultural beings as evidenced by the books and other texts she read with and to them, their writing, and their discussions about their personal and family lives and the broader community. This is sociopolitical work as students consider social and economic issues, justice, and the quality of their lives. If 10% of teachers are WL teachers, as Goodman suggested in the previous section, we'd estimate that less than 1% of teachers are CL teachers. However, this view is gaining momentum as teachers and students face an increasingly complex world and schools are becoming the forums in which that complexity is discussed, studied, and addressed.

CL teachers move from the awareness of cultural relevance that WL teachers have to an active involvement with cultural issues. Culturally responsive teaching (Ladson-Billings, 1994) is rooted in the idea that children learn best when cultural and linguistic familiarity and sensitivity are integrated into the reading curriculum. CL teachers prefer *culturally responsive* over Au's (1993) "culturally relevant" because the former is a more accurate indicator of the enactment of teaching that takes into consideration and acts on the idea that students' lives have cultural foundations that influence their learning in school. For some students, the presence of their cultures in the classroom is a disruption of their understanding of their concept of school. Culturally responsive teaching fits into the dimensions of Critical Literacy that Lewison et al. (2002) outlined.

Teachers who teach from a Critical Literacy perspective do not limit curriculum to welcoming and respecting children's diversity. These teachers build their reading curriculum around the belief that learning a language cannot be separated from the culture in which a student lives. Gutiérrez and Larson (1994) describe the sense of isolation that some children feel when their cultural and linguistic identities are marginalized or bracketed in the classroom:

> I came to kindergarten so excited and ready to learn. I came prepared with my *maleta* (suitcase) full of so many wonderful things, my Spanish language, my beautiful culture, and many other treasures. When I got there, though, not only did they not let me use anything from my *maleta*, they did not even let me bring it into the classroom. (p. 33)

Teachers committed to the Critical Literacy view welcome, include, and embrace diversity and support students in becoming active within and upon their worlds.

At this point, it might seem that learning to teach reading is developmental. Perhaps all teachers begin as DI teachers because it's a comfort zone that resonates with how they went to school, how they imagined teaching, and the expectations at many school sites. Then, some (but not all, by any means) learned about WL and changed their views to that. Finally, a tiny number learned of Critical Literacy and are moving in that direction. Although such a developmental scheme is quite possible, it's also possible that a teacher begins her career as a CL teacher or as a WL teacher. It's also true that many teachers subscribe to the DI view for their entire careers. And, as we demonstrate after explaining CL further, many teachers seem to draw on all the views.

Some Critical Literacy teachers engage their students in issues specific to the students' community by having the children work to find multiple viewpoints and consider sociopolitical issues. Three teachers (Craviotto, Heras, & Espindola, 2004) had their middle school students interview community members, something that led to the writing of immigration stories that went deeper than the brief vignettes in the social studies text. Others have their children understand and then act on their worlds, such as Kolbe's (1999) work with his middle school students to understand why, during the 1960s, a house was burned down to maintain segregation in their community. His students interviewed community members, learned that Martin Luther King, Jr. visited and marched in their community, catalogued songs of the civil rights period, and gained insights into their own identities. The students were considered extremely "low" readers and writers (according to state tests), yet they composed poetry and expository text, combined it with video and voice data they collected, and burned a CD as a compilation of their learning. The students learned all of the state-mandated material about civil rights and much more as their study focused on who and what they knew, where they lived, and the use of literacy skills to access, extend, and present their learning. Kolbe and his students disrupted the commonplace view of civil rights as something that is not necessarily local. They also heard from a variety of speakers and reported their interview data as ways that strove to present and analyze different points of view. The students eventually took social action as they succeeded in putting two important local African Americans' homes on the national register of historic places. The Critical Literacy view of reading grows out of the belief that reading is intimately involved with being an informed citizen in a democracy, committed to the idea of "literacy and justice for all" (Edelsky, 1991).

What Is the Definition of Reading to Which This View Subscribes?

Critical literacy teachers and researchers believe that we cannot consider a definition of "reading" without considering the purposes of schools. They argue that most schools reproduce the inequities that exist in our society (hooks, 2003). The "critical" part of critical literacy is focused on gaining knowledge of and responding to inequitable distributions of power, prestige, and wealth. Wealth is not simply a reference to economics, although that is certainly one facet of it. Wealth also includes studying whose cultures and languages seem to be "worth more," meaning they allow access to various kinds of success. The idea that one's culture has value leads to discussions of cultural capital (Bourdieu & Wacquant, 1992). Some children's cultural capital predisposes them to success, suggesting that their social capital is turned to social profit, whereas others' social capital does not lead to such profit (Lareau, 2000). Profit, in this sense, refers to jobs, wealth, power, prestige, and privilege.

Within this broad sociopolitical landscape, reading is much more than the saying of words. Critical Literacy involves comprehension, of course, but all comprehension is rooted in power and position, thus it is political. The way a teacher asks questions, the answers the teacher accepts or rejects, and the way that language is used to repress certain ideas and groups and value others are all taken into consideration in every literacy lesson when teaching from a CL view. The cueing systems are integrated into multidimensional lessons.

Luke (1999) suggests that each individual is involved in learning different things as she or he reads a text. Readers learn the conventions of the way texts are written and read, including phonics and grammar. Readers also learn that reading involves the making of meaning by comprehending what a text says within the language and culture in which the reader lives. At the same time, a reader learns to use texts that are part of various social and cultural settings. And, along with the other three, a reader learns that texts are politically charged and that they, as readers, are involved in making sense of and responding to the political positions that texts occupy. CL teachers teach all four of Luke's facets of being a reader. Wolpert (1994) presents a good example of this in a primary classroom in which children are listening to the story of *The Three Pigs*. The children can see the text, so they are learning about print. They discuss the pigs and the wolf and the ways in which the story makes sense to them, connecting it to their own experiences in a variety of ways. They are hearing the story in school, so they are learning about the types of texts that teachers find important and relevant. And, the children discuss the values of different types of homes. The teacher and children discuss that straw or wood houses are not always flawed and that there are cultures that do build durable and functional homes of wood or straw. The children are disrupting some of the commonplace views of the straw house because they look at the house from multiple viewpoints and consider when such a house serves the occupant well and when it does not. They might even discuss the differences between houses in their neighborhoods. CL is not the same as critical thinking or higher order thinking skills. Those skills are not systematically and intentionally politically charged the way CL is.

The CL definition of reading involves understanding that reading—all reading—is a political activity. The selection of curriculum by the teacher is a political act, the way in which children are asked to use or respond to the text is a political act, and any actions that emerge from a relationship with the text are political acts. CL teachers understand that reading situates the reader in a political context (Stuckey, 1991) and that teaching a child to read a word cannot be separated from teaching the child to read the world (Freire & Macedo, 1987). Stuckey goes on to explain that reading is intimately tied to access to knowledge and power, but not in the simplistic belief that if we taught the poor to read, they wouldn't be poor anymore. She points out the ways in which texts and access to texts are regulated, keeping the rich wealthy and confining the poor to poverty. She explains that poor and minority children typically are assigned reading programs that are skills-based with little time for in-depth discussions. Stuckey believes that "literacy is a weapon, the knife that severs the society and slices the opportunities and rights of its poorest people" (p. 118). Kozol (2005) saw this in high schools and elementary schools that he visited over many years. He observed poor children in the younger grades required to experience scripted programs while more affluent children read real books and engaged in conversations; he reported the dismal conditions of many inner city, mostly nondominant-culture schools. CL teachers work to understand this, disrupt it, and provide all children access to texts that are meaningful, authentic, and culturally responsive, and that stimulate conversation, reflection, and action.

Critical Literacy teachers are committed to helping to develop thoughtful citizens, an idea that they discuss often with each other and their students. When Janesse's students discussed the effects of unemployment on their families, she guided one group to think about what they need to have better jobs. She had the children consider what it means to have a "better job," the obstacles to obtaining that job, and ways in which citizens can overcome those obstacles. Janesse was helping her students interrogate multiple points of view as they looked at social issues; this is political work and Janesse understands it as such. It is *critical* work in two ways: critical meaning extremely important and critical meaning involved in criticisms of the status quo (Bomer & Bomer, 1999). The goal is for children to begin to understand the complexity of social justice so that they might feel a sense of agency in their lives, meaning that they believe that they can influence some of the issues that they face now, as children, as well as those they will face as adults.

Some teachers might feel hesitant to engage in such political work because they are not political themselves; others might think that such work is not appropriate for schools because it seems that the students are being used as pawns for the teacher's political agenda. Critical Literacy teachers explain that they rarely disclose their own points of view on an issue because they want their students to explore the issue themselves, not merely parrot the teacher in order to gain acceptance or a good grade. Freire (1985) believes that children are too often involved in a banking or transmission model of education in which the teacher makes loans to children's minds but also expects the children to return the information (on a test or in a written paper). He argues that students are too often taught to "become passive before the text" (p. 31), rather than engage with it, argue with it, and make decisions about how they position themselves in relation to it.

CL teachers and researchers are extremely critical of the view of reading presented in the report of the National Reading Panel (National Reading

Panel, 2000a). They argue that in that report, reading is described as the adding together of: phonemic awareness, phonics, fluency, vocabulary, and text comprehension. Their criticism is that by reducing reading to these five elements, the political and cultural natures of reading have been systematically teased out, thus committing "culturalectomies" (Barrera, cited in Florio-Ruane, 2001) on reading that result in perpetuating the historically marginalized status of specific groups of people. This process of marginalization serves to perpetuate the existing power structures in our society, keeping the poor in disempowered and minoritized positions (McCarty, 2002).

Some Whole Language teachers are, in reality, Critical Literacy teachers because they engage with texts and students in ways discussed in this section. If a teacher works with students' identities by asking for personal reactions and thoughts regarding a text, that teacher is helping the students understand their position, the power they have or don't have, different perspectives, and political issues. As students' question texts, make connections, and gain deeper understanding of texts, the position of texts in relation to other texts, and the ways in which texts are open to interpretation, they are assuming a critical stance. Critical Literacy teachers believe that all teachers make political decisions in their teaching; some do so by default if they use a program without considering the political implications of the program and others do so because of more conscious decisions. CL teachers know that the idea of reading being politicized makes others feel uncomfortable and that most teachers did not enter teaching thinking that it is a political arena. CL teachers respond that any view of reading is political; they contend that their view is the most honest because it takes into account the multiple perspectives and many layers that are inherent in any text. They argue that Direct Instruction is quite political in that it involves compliance, also a political act.

What Is the Implied or Explicit Nature of Teaching That the View Expects or Demands?

CL teachers explain that teaching is successive acts of consciousness raising in which the teacher works with students to shed light on the ways in which texts affect our thinking. Teaching typically involves going against the grain, but doing so carefully so that the teacher is not fired. CL teaching involves much decision making as teachers assess their current understanding of their students and decide what to offer students as ways of interacting with and responding to texts. The conversations in CL classrooms are focused on bringing issues of difference, justice, equity, fairness, cultural diversity, wealth, and power to the floor for discussion. Teaching also involves helping students uncover ways in which they might act on their worlds as decision makers.

When Rick was teaching second grade, one of his students brought an empty box of cereal to school. On the front of the box was an illustration of a volcano with a Tyrannosaurus Rex walking in front of it. "FREE VOLCANO INSIDE" was written across the box, below the name of the cereal. The child who brought the box to school wanted to discuss it at the class meeting. "Look at this," he begged his second-grade colleagues. "I was so excited about this, and I don't even like this cereal. It doesn't have enough sugar in it. But I made my mom buy it because I wanted the volcano." The children watched quietly as the child spoke. "Well, look at the volcano!" He reached into his pocket and pulled out a 2- inch piece of green plastic shaped like an upside down "V" with an indentation (the crater) in the top. "You put a drop of red food dye in here with some vinegar and baking soda and it's supposed to erupt." "

"Wow, can we do it?" one of the other children asks?

"Well," the child continued, "It's not so great. It just sort of bubbles. Not like the fire and lava on the box." He shows the box again and points out the bright red fire, the hot orange lava, and the black smoke pouring from the crater behind the head of the T. Rex.

Rick provided the necessary chemicals and the class watched the fizzing volcano "erupt." There were moans of disapproval. "What should we do about this?" Rick asked his class.

"What can we do?" one of the children asked.

"We could write to the company and tell them that it's a big phony," suggested one of the other children.

"Let's not buy that cereal," suggested another.

"We could write and tell them we won't buy it!" another said with much zeal.

During writers workshop, the letter was drafted and, in subsequent days, perfected and sent. After the letter was sent, one of the children asked, "Can they do that? Can they just advertise like that so we buy the cereal and then you get a piece of junk?"

Many children responded: "They do it a lot." "It's not fair." "We should do something." "Kids can't do anything." "Yeah, like with Cheerios!"

CRITICAL LITERACY VIEW 145

"Wait a minute," Rick interrupted the flow of complaints to address the Cheerios remark. "Who said that? What do you mean?"

One of the children explained that Cheerios advertises itself as "unsinkable" and that just can't be true. Over the next few days, the children tested Cheerios and recorded their findings in their journals, even leaving Cheerios in a bowl of milk over night. They didn't sink.

"Now this is interesting," Rick began at a class meeting. "This company seems to have told the truth."

"We should write to them," one of the children suggested. The class still hadn't received a response from the volcano letter, but hopes were running high. A small group perfected a letter that was sent a few days later. About a week later, the class received a package from the company with coloring books, small boxes of Cheerios, and letters on bright yellow paper thanking them for their "research." The children learned about consumer research and wanted to do it on many products, which they did over the course of the year. They tested paper towel strength and absorbency, the flavors of various cookies, and more. Discussions got very serious in late November and early December when advertisements for toys appeared everywhere as the holidays approached. The children studied toys, discussed their quality, and changed their holiday wish lists after these discussions. Reports of other CL teachers with their students, from kindergarten through high school, are becoming available (Comber & Simpson, 2001; Christensen, 2000).

What Is the Role of the Teacher Within This View?

Teaching, in a CL class, is focused on the four dimensions we explained earlier. The teacher works to match texts to her students, much the way the Whole Language teacher does. She helps the children learn the cueing systems (phonics, syntax, and semantics) and she also helps them make connections to themselves, texts, and the world beyond the school (Keene & Zimmerman, 1997). The added piece from the CL view is that the teacher explores the political nature of texts and their contents and contexts with the class. In the WL public argument, we talked about Cinderella stories; the CL teacher would include a version of the story such as *The Paper Bag Princess* (Munsch, 1980) in which the girl in the story rejects the prince. The teacher then facilitates the discussion by helping the students consider the "commonplace," such as whether or not a princess needs a prince and the notion of "happily ever after." She might ask the children, "What does 'happily ever after' mean? What do you imagine Cinderella's life is like 5 years or 10 years after the marriage if she does marry a prince?"

Again, paralleling the public argument on Whole Language, let's suppose the CL teacher asks her students about a Dear Abby column in which sixth-grade children are using drugs. The conversation might flow into many of the same areas that the WL teacher led her class. The CL teacher has certain issues in mind to push her students' thinking about drugs and drug use. They might discuss ways in which drug use affects their community, ways in which drug users can get help, whose responsibility it is to clean up a drug-infested community, where the money comes from to do that cleaning, who profits from the addiction, which communities have drug problems that are very apparent and which ones have hidden drug problems, and things that children can do to address the problem locally and nationally. CL teachers help children uncover ways in which they might respond: letter writing, phone calls, interviews with legislators, discussions with the police department, opinion surveys of the neighborhood, photographic essays (perhaps even called exposés), or the development of a classroom newspaper that contains stories about the neighborhood. CL teachers teach children about ways that their voices can be heard within and beyond the school in order to teach them that they can enact all four dimensions discussed earlier.

Vasquez (2000) led her kindergarten children into investigations about products that were earmarked for their age group. The children studied toys and games, discussed TV advertisements, and developed what they considered to be more accurate advertisements of some products. CL teachers do not limit themselves to engagements with upper grade students. They believe that every child can and should develop his or her voice and sense of agency.

In CL classrooms, beginning reading instruction looks a lot like WL instruction. Children make choices about their reading and writing, the connections between reading and writing are part of the instructional setting, and texts that are predictable form a cornerstone of the curriculum. The teacher might work with the whole group, small groups, or individuals over the course of a typical day. Like WL teachers, CL teachers know that learning is social, students must participate in evaluating their progress, and prior experiences influence learning. The children are encouraged to bring their worlds into their writing (Bomer & Bomer, 1999). Bomer and Bomer report that CL teachers help children consider (in their reading and writing lives): groups they belong to and ones they repel; studies of power, both financial and political; things taken for granted, such as "commonsense" ideas; fairness and justice; voice and silence; ways in which people or groups are portrayed; gender; race; class; money; labor, including why we work, who works where, and attitudes about jobs; language; familial and other relationships, including nontraditional families such as gay/lesbian relationships; peace and violence; and beliefs about individual versus collective actions (pp. 30-37).

What Is the Implied or Explicit Nature of Learning That the View Expects or Demands?

Learning in the CL classroom has an explicit focus on the element of critique (from a political perspective). Learning in the Critical Literacy classroom is always rooted in becoming a citizen, finding voice, understanding the commonplace in order to disrupt it if it is not democratic, understanding multiple points of view, gaining insights into sociopolitical issues, and taking action. One facet of learning in the CL classroom that is often overlooked in other classrooms (or perhaps simply assumed to be present) is the acceptance of multiple perspectives. Students are not only expected to learn about different points of view; they are expected to develop tolerance. Learning to be tolerant demands that children and their teacher engage in conversations about critical issues with which they are faced each day. Learning is conversation-based in the CL classroom, and those conversations become points of origin for inquiry and action.

Learning typically begins in the CL classroom with discussions of beliefs about the commonplace. Beliefs are discussed as tentative and in a constant state of development, even when students argue that they are committed to their points of view. Students become sociologists, linguists, and anthropologists as they dig into their beliefs by finding people and resources that seem to agree with them as well as those that do not agree with them. Learning is a commitment to intense searching, data collection, data analysis, arguments about what data seem to say, and presentation of the data in a manner that reflects the content and intent of the data. Learning in the CL classroom is active and may involve individuals working alone, in pairs, in small groups, or with the entire class.

What Is the Role of the Learner Within This View?

Learners in Critical Literacy classrooms are treated as and expected to be productive and thoughtful members of a democratic community. They are expected to participate in class meetings, suggest topics for those meetings, and explore their own feelings and beliefs. In their reading and writing, the children are expected to respond to and create texts that are honest and probing. Christensen (2000) explains that simply expecting students to be critical, aware, and responsive is not sufficient for the difficult task of forming a CL community in the classroom. The teacher supports learners in engaging with the important texts that surround and influence their lives. She also encourages them to be honest; Christensen found that students will write the truth about gangs, drugs, and some of the real pains in their lives. CL Learners are part of an authentic community when it is a place in which they can be safe to delve into themselves and the issues in their lives willingly, with the sense of urgency and reality that such a setting can provide. Christensen learned that:

> ...the key to reaching my students and building community was helping students excavate and reflect on their personal experiences, and connecting them to the world of language, literature and society. We moved from ideas to action, perhaps the most elusive objective in any classroom. (p. 9)

Learners in CL classrooms learn strategies for agency (actions they can take) by studying others who have been activists before them, both well-known individuals and local heroes known only in their own neighborhoods. They look into their own identities, their families, and the many groups to which they belong and they look out, from themselves, to the worlds in which they live. They study those worlds, their and others' places within those worlds, and the powers and forces that affect them. They learn that they can influence their worlds, have their voices heard, and understand what it means to be an active member of many communities within and beyond the school walls.

How Is Reading Assessed Within This View?

Many of the assessment strategies that are used in Whole Language classrooms are used in Critical Literacy classrooms. We do not review those here. Additionally, from a critical perspective, teachers listen to conversations, thoughts students have about their reading, and their students' writing with a different sort of ear—a political one. CL teachers rely on strategies like retelling, in which the student works to recall the contents of a story, to see how the student uses literary elements (plot, theme, setting, time, etc.) to understand a text. They also listen for the critical perspectives that students might have appropriated from ongoing demonstrations of such criticism by the teacher and colleagues in the class. Here is one example of this type of assessment so that readers may gain insights into the thinking of the CL teacher.

Imagine a group of sixth graders in which the students are overheard making disparaging remarks across gender lines. "Boys can't do anything right…girls stink at sports…girls have to be so primped all the time…" and more. The teacher, Ms. P., gathers the class together for their daily read-aloud. She holds up a book saying, "Many of you know this book, but I'd like to read it to the class today and then talk about it." Ms. P. shows the students *The Giving Tree* (Silverstein, 1964). "I know that book," one student says. "We read it in second grade," another says.

"I know some of you think this book might be too simple for sixth grade, but I want to talk about it with you because I've been thinking about some of the things that happen in it."

"I love this book," a girl shyly admits.

"Ohhhh, how cute," one of the boys says. The girl gives him a sharp look.

Ms. P. begins the story. Most readers know it is the story of a boy who plays in a tree as a youth, sells her apples to make money as he grows and wants money, uses her branches for a house, and eventually cuts down her trunk to make a boat. Each time the boy approaches the tree, the tree is thrilled to see him and offers him whatever she can to help him in his life. At the end, the tree is a stump and says she has nothing left to offer the boy (now a very old man). He says he doesn't need much, just a place to sit, and she straightens herself up, as much as a stump can, and he sits on her. Ms. P. finishes the story and looks around the room. The students know her and expect her to initiate a conversation as she typically does, showing them the depth of her scrutiny of texts and inviting them to present their views. Instead, she says, "We're going to break into groups. The names of the people in each group are on the board. Each group takes one of these index cards [she holds them up] and reads it. Then, the group works together to make a poster about the book, but the poster must respond to what is on the card." The children look at the board and most seem pleased with the group to which they've been assigned. Most don't recognize and no one says that the groups are gender specific, all girls in some groups, all boys in others. After the children are in their groups, seated around tables with markers and chart paper already on them, Ms. P. hands each group a card. The contents of each card follows.

Card # 1: Each member of this group is a relationship counselor. You need to talk with your group about the relationship between the tree and the boy and then draw something that shows what you think about the relationship. You'll present your poster to the entire class. Please make sure that everyone in your group gets a turn to speak during the presentation. Remember that different points of view are welcome and, if they come up in your discussion, must be on the poster, too.

Card # 2: You are a group of feminists. Feminists believe that men and women are entitled to equal treatment and should act equally responsible in just about every situation. You need to talk with your group about the relationship between the tree and the boy and then draw something that shows what feminists think about the relationship. Please make sure that everyone in your group gets a turn to speak during the presentation. Remember that different points of view are welcome and, if they come up in your discussion, must be on the poster, too.

Card # 3: Think about the book that you just heard. You need to talk with your group about the relationship between the tree and the boy and then draw something that shows what your group thinks about the relationship. Please make sure that everyone in your group gets a turn to speak during the presentation. Remember that different points of view are welcome and, if they come up in your discussion, must be on the poster, too.

There are two copies of each card so that two groups get the same card, one a group of boys and the other a group of girls. Ms. P. collects important assessment data as she circulates around the room. Anticipating that the groups would want to see the book, she found five other copies and gives each group a copy of the book. She listens and writes what the children say, noticing who talks and who does not, and what the talkers say. She'll compare these notes to other notes about the children's oral language, their writing, and their responses to reading they do independently. After about 15 minutes of discussion in the small groups, Ms. P. asks the groups to do the drawing part of the assignment. Again, she circulates and takes notes on what the children say and do. She'll use some of these quotes in the discussions that occur during the poster presentations.

As the groups complete their posters, Ms. P. tapes them to the chalkboard at the front of the room. She asks them to quietly rehearse what each person in the group will say during the presentation. Each group presents their poster, and each child in every group says at least one thing. Ms. P. takes notes again. She's accumulated a lot of data from this one literacy activity, noting who presents alternative views, who seems strong and confident, who seems tentative, and which students are dominant or withdrawn. Ms. P.

CRITICAL LITERACY VIEW   151

thinks that the presentations reveal quite a bit of sexism as boys don't see, for the most part, the giving as a negative thing. Some of the girls don't either, explaining that giving is what women and girls do and they do it much better than boys.

The conversation about the posters lasts well into the afternoon, and Ms. P. culminates the activity by asking the students to write in their journals about their thoughts, feelings, and things they learned during this activity. The room falls to silence as the children settle into their journals. Some write intensively, some stare at the ceiling or out the window, some write a bit and erase it to start again, and some observe their colleagues. The students expressed a broad range of thoughts, orally and on the posters. They discussed their families and the gender-based roles they experience there. Others couldn't find gender biases in their homes, but did find them at school, on the playground, and in some texts, including TV and magazines. They talked about the differences between army action figure dolls that some of the boys played with and compared them to the types of dolls that many of the girls played with. They discussed what boys and men expect from women and what girls and women expect from men. One girl said, "If a girl acts like that [referring to something a boy said that men should do], how come she's called...well, she's called the b-word?" Now, as the intensity of the conversation settles, Ms. P. writes in her journal too. Later in the day or early in the morning, with the posters still on the wall, she'll read her thoughts and invite students to read theirs.

Ms. P. will look at all the journals and her notes and write anecdotal records about her students. Her notes will include spelling and punctuation concepts that children need to learn, grammatical and structural weaknesses and strengths, the depth and intensity of the students' feelings and their voices, and the political nature of their writing. She keeps track of how they make arguments for and against their positions. She will help each one of her students, in groups or individually, to address all of these facets of their writing. Ms. P. will do the same with their responses to reading and other writing that they do over the course of the year. Later in the year, when they are discussing environmental issues, a student will remind the class of *The Giving Tree*, making a connection between the book and the way some companies seem to be treating the environment. The class will look at it again from an environmental perspective, referring to it and many other texts to inform their views on the purposes of the resources on our planet. Assessment in the CL class is, consistent with the ideas and ideals behind Critical Literacy, multidimensional. It is quite possible that DI and WL teachers reading this may decide to use *The Giving Tree* in their classrooms for reasons similar to Ms. P.'s. DI and WL teachers, indeed most teachers, relish moments in which their students engage thoughtfully. For CL teachers, that thoughtfulness is always political, and articulated as such, during literacy activity within their classrooms.

What Is the Nature of the Curriculum to Which This View Subscribes?

The Critical Literacy view of the curriculum is quite similar to the WL view in that teachers from these two views believe that they and their students need much control over what happens in their classrooms, what texts they use, and how they use them. Some CL teachers do not want to use standards because they see those as texts that control their classrooms and limit their students' and their own decision making. Curriculum for CL teachers is always a very local affair, one that is generated with the students present or in mind. CL teachers work to understand the contexts in which their students live, typically relying on the students to be participants that inform the teachers about those contexts. Curricular activities are built from that understanding, starting with the individual and the local and building to broader levels, such as national and international. CL teachers have goals for their students, particularly about citizenship and the literacy skills and strategies that informed and reflective citizens need to be participating members of society. Within that curriculum, "participating members of society" always includes sensitivity and response to situations of injustice.

How Does the View of Reading Take Issues Such as Culture and Social Context Into Consideration?

We've covered this question in considerable depth throughout this section. Culture and social context drive the reading and writing curriculum in CL classrooms. Relying on the four dimensions, culture and social contexts are studied from multiple perspectives, understood from different points of view, and "interrogated," all with the goals of understanding and responding to inequity and injustice and leading to the promoting of social justice and action. The teacher carefully considers the reliance on conversation in the CL classroom so that she or he will honor the diverse cultures present in the room. CL teachers work to know the structures of participation (Philips, 1971) of their students so that they do not dismiss students from a cultural group as quiet (for example), when in reality they are responding to the rules for speaking within their cultural and social groups. CL teachers work to know their students, the communities in which their students live, and the various cultural norms that their students bring to the classroom. They learn these in order to cultivate a context in which all voices and multiple perspectives can be heard, much the way Sylvia and Janesse did in their classrooms.

What Research Supports This View of the Reading Process and Instruction?

Almost all of the research we cited in the Whole Language section also applies to Critical Literacy, supporting the ideas that children and teachers need choice, students read for meaning first and foremost, and that all the cueing systems contribute to the making of meaning. We've already cited works by Au (1993) and Ladson-Billings (1994) that support culturally responsive teaching. Work is being done in the United States and in Australia that focuses on Critical Literacy. Virtually all of the research on CL is qualitative, including teacher narratives of students' and teachers' experiences in classrooms, ethnographies, and case studies. There are different perspectives to this work. For example, a group of teachers started an organization called *Rethinking Schools*. They have a Web site and a journal that deal with critical issues in teaching and learning. One of the founders, Linda Christensen, was discussed earlier. The *Rethinking Schools* group has published two volumes (Bigelow, Christensen, & Karp, 1994; Bigelow, Harvey, Karp, & Miller, 2001) in which teacher-tested ideas using CL are presented. In the current political climate, with a focus on quantitative research, the work of the many teachers in the *Rethinking Schools* network is dismissed. CL teachers find it difficult to dismiss the work of their colleagues, particularly when they read children's writing or see other documentation of the actions in which they've engaged.

Comber and Simpson (2001) and Ayers, Hunt, and Quinn (1998) have collated work by researchers and practitioners from around the world. They consistently find that students are willing to address, think about, and respond to critical issues. For example, Martino (2001) works with students to confront homophobia, a critical issue that is represented (often negatively) in texts that children see each day, including books, magazines, movies, and TV shows.

The study of discourse, the ways in which language influences and controls lives, is at the center of many of the studies of CL because the power of language and the language of power are constantly at work in ways that tend to perpetuate power structures as they exist (Gee, 1990). Rogers (2003) studied the ways in which texts produced by schools, including committees on special education, define students' lives and limit the efficacy of students and their families in the school setting. She followed one sixth-grade student through the entire "labeling" process and critically analyzed ways in which the student's poverty and her family's position because of that poverty left the child and her mother helpless and hopeless regarding the school situation. In the home, Rogers found a very different scenario, one in which the mom and daughter are active and confident readers and writers. The mom even started a petition in the neighborhood to have a traffic light installed at a hazardous corner. Taylor (1996) followed homeless people, the poor and other individuals whose lives were in a constant state of crisis because of official texts (such as rules for public assistance and hospital records) that dominated their lives and left them powerless. Compton-Lilly (2003) showed the inequities between poor and privileged families in the teaching and learning of reading. She documented ways in which poor children are blamed for their own illiteracy (p. 53). Carger (1996) also followed the literacy life of a family, this one with Mexican roots arriving in the United States to fulfill dreams about success but met with a system that did not work for them as the strengths of the family were not valued by the school. CL teachers read these studies and respond to them by working to help their students empower themselves as literate and active souls. As we close these public arguments, we are convinced that teachers' beliefs about reading are the greatest influence on what occurs as reading instruction in their classrooms.

AFTERTHOUGHTS ON THE THREE VIEWS

("Can't I be some of each?")

One night, as the study group of new teachers was about to leave Rick's house, one of the members (Ann) lamented, "Teaching reading is so messy." The group was gathering their things to go home and they all stopped.

"What do you mean?" Rick asked.

She folded her coat over a chair and leaned on it and said, "I listen to our discussions about the views of reading and I think I know where I stand and what my view is; I think I'm a Whole Language teacher, but I'm considering some of the Critical Literacy ideas we've discussed tonight...like *The Giving Tree* idea. I could see doing something like that in my class. And it would be a political discussion with my girls and boys. But tomorrow a kid will get stuck on a word and I can just hear myself saying 'sound it out, sound it out,' like that's the only strategy that I know. I just slip into the use of sounds sounds sounds. I'm confused about all these views. Can't I be some of each?"

Like many teachers learning about the different views of reading, this teacher is trying to figure out the relationships between her thinking and her practice. She feels overwhelmed by what she thinks are contradictions between the two. The group of new teachers spends another half hour together trying to make sense of the contradictions they feel. They decide that teachers have to understand what they think reading is and what it is for. Once they know that, or at least have a temporary understanding of it, they can work to build their practice toward that understanding. Any teacher might have a child sound out a word because that fits with all the views. All teachers should use the sound system of English (phonics) to help children read. Yet, if the teacher believes that reading is sounding out word to find what the author intended to mean, asking a child to sound out a word is very different from saying the exact same words ("sound it out") if the teacher believes that reading is about transactions with text or reading is about social justice. The same teacher talk can mean different things, reflective of what the teacher believes. To make matters more confusing, there are times when all teachers want their students to be able to understand or have insights into an author's intention. Teachers of any view may feel this way because there are times when that intention matters (such as following science experiment directions).

Teachers who spend time thinking about their view of reading are making an important investment that will ultimately pay off in their practice. Based on what you've read in this book, you decide which view of reading matches what you think should happen in school and how you think it should happen. You decide the view you might want to draw on as you compose a reading program for the children you teach. As you engage in that important work in an ongoing and reflective fashion, you will probably find, as Sylvia did, that your own identity plays an important role in the process. Your understanding of yourself, your lived experiences, your beliefs about what reading is for, and the cultures that are represented in your class all influence your view of reading and what should happen in school. Teaching reading is also about a teacher's view of children, which we discuss in the next section.

In reality, teaching reading *is* messy. Teachers have to deal with complex behavioral issues and an ever-growing curriculum. Making a commitment to one view of reading does not mean that every lesson and every moment of every day in your classroom reflects that commitment. Human beings don't function at such a simple level. The view of reading that you hold is a frame of reference that you use to reflect on what unfolds in your classroom. It is a frame that may change, open wider, get smaller, or be disregarded or replaced. Teachers live with the constant tension between what they are doing, what they might do, who they are, and who their students are. That tension makes teaching reading messy, but it is the kind of mess from which organized, thoughtful, and effective reading instruction may arise.

"So," Ann begins after we discuss the points Rick has summarized, "I can be a little of everything in practice…it might look like I'm all three views throughout the day. The important thing seems to be to understand who I want to be and what I believe reading is. I have to keep the next minute in mind and the goals I have for children in the long run. I can live with that. It means I don't have multiple personalities [the others laugh]; I'm just growing and thinking and changing to better serve my kids."

III

A FINAL ARGUMENT AND SOME SUGGESTIONS AND RESOURCES FOR FURTHER REFLECTION

In this final chapter, we present some of our thinking about the complexity of reading, both the process as it occurs in the human mind and the choices you'll make about instruction reflective of your understanding of the process. In the previous chapters, you met four teachers as they taught in their classrooms and other educators as they responded to them. You also had the opportunity to respond to those teachers and the responding educators. Through this process of reading, responding, reading responses, and responding further, you initiated two thought processes: You increased your understanding of the complexity of the reading process, and you saw how that understanding informs the instructional decisions teachers make.

DECISION MAKING AND TEACHER DEVELOPMENT

All teachers make decisions. Teachers have the opportunity to know their students' literacy lives better than anyone else. If teachers are informed about the reading process and the possibilities for instruction and act on that knowledge, they can make decisions that support students' development as readers. All four cases presented earlier in this book are descriptions of reflective teachers at different points in their professional development. Some are quite involved in the school-provided programs (Penny and Sylvia), but all of them are increasingly aware of and responsive to their students' unique needs. It is this awareness and responsiveness that constitute the essence of a reflective teacher. Some teachers may want to move further away from DI programs as they grow in confidence, understanding of their students, and understanding of the reading process and instructional options. However, they might feel too much administrative or even collegial pressure to make that move. Their decisions will directly affect their teaching. Reflective teachers' decisions are responsive to any factors that might erode or undermine their students' success. Janesse would not comply with the district's DI materials because she was conscious of her students' needs and, in responding to those needs, she needed to use processes, teach strategies, and engage her students with materials and ideas not provided by her school or the district. Other teachers may decide that DI programs are well organized and meet their students' needs. The important idea is that teachers reflect and make decisions about reading instruction.

Cultivation of relationships with students and colleagues is another facet of reflective teacher development. Increasingly, each school year, all four of the case teachers lived teaching as relational work, responding to the cognitive and emotional needs of their students and cultivating ever-deepening relationships with them. Reflective teachers live the idea that teaching is about relationships, as well as content, by making content responsive to their students. They thrive on relationships with other teachers, too, such as the student teacher–cooperating teacher relationship prior to entering their own classroom and sustained mentoring once they are licensed teachers. Sylvia would have benefited from such a relationship as she struggled with her identity during student teaching and her first semester in her own classroom. Janesse and Kendra's student teachers, and student teachers who experienced teachers like them for sustained periods of time (such as a full semester), typically arrive at their first teaching position confident in their understanding of curriculum, decision making, reading process and instruction, and relationships. They arrive more inclined to be reflective teachers. Good mentors help novice teachers explore their identities, gain deeper understandings of the relationships between language, culture, and learning, and enhance the relational nature of teaching reading. Sustained relationships with mentors, well into their first few years of teaching, may help novices become reflective. Reflective teaching is a political stance because it involves studying and possibly working around mandates, rather than complying. Our commitment to reflective teaching is based in one idea: Students' needs must be met in school. In order for that to happen, teachers must be informed and supported in making decisions to serve their students.

In the next part of this chapter, we take a brief trip into a first-grade teacher's dilemma (Lampert, 1985) about teaching reading when she is forced to use a phonics program. The teacher has grown into being a confident decision maker about reading in her classroom, but the mandate from her district forces her into being a technician who is not free to make decisions. Many experienced teachers, teachers who have developed into reflective decision makers, are being told that they may no longer rely on their professional decision making if they want to remain employed. We include this brief case because it represents a scenario that is unfolding across our country and provides readers with an opportunity to consider how they will respond to some of the political pressures on teachers. We are not saying that every teacher who is asked to implement a new program should balk. We are saying that reflective teachers should be supported in making decisions about reading activities that they incorporate or decline to incorporate into their classrooms.

TEACHERS FACE DILEMMAS AND MAKE DECISIONS

In one of Rick's earlier books (Meyer, 2001), he described a classroom in which the teacher was required to use a phonics program as the cornerstone of the reading instruction she delivered to children. The children sat for 60 to 90 minutes each day as their teacher read from a scripted teacher's guide that provided: the exact words she was to say to her first graders, what materials to use (all of which were provided by the program), and what sequence she was to follow. The teacher, Karen, is a veteran teacher who was told by her district that all children were to experience the program, regardless of their reading level, proficiency in English (she had English language learners in her classroom), or other specific learning needs. Rick documented the children's behaviors during the phonics lessons: rocking back and forth, sucking on their clothing, tearing at the rug, rubbing their ears, braiding each other's hair, picking their noses, making noises like bombs dropping, and more. During other parts of the day, when Karen was allowed to make informed instructional decisions, these behaviors were noticeably absent.

Rick, consistent with the work of others (Durand, 1990), concluded that the children, as social beings, communicated their need to be engaged in cognitively stimulating activity through the messages their bodies sent. During the phonics lesson, the children's thirst for meaningful engagement as learners collapsed on itself, and that collapse manifested itself into physical activity that provided some (minimal) stimulation and communicated their boredom.

Karen's principal regularly appeared in her classroom with a publisher-provided checklist to ensure that she was following the scripted lessons that were provided to her. Her district reading consultant told her that teachers were not to create curriculum, they were to deliver it. He also told Karen that she was "not self-employed" and was required to follow the scripted lesson verbatim or would risk losing her job for insubordination. As authors of this book and researchers, we know that many teachers face Karen's dilemma: follow the script or find a different job. We empathize with teachers and children who are held hostage by a scripted reading program that massages away individual differences, interests, talents, and needs—those of teachers and children. Many such programs emerged after the passage of the No Child Left Behind Act in 2002. The *Reading First* portion of that act articulates very specific guidelines for spending federal dollars. This often leads to the purchase of programs like the one that Karen was required to use.

Many arguments have been made against the use of such programs (Allington, 2005; Coles, 2003; Garan, 2005), some suggesting that our schools are being used by profiteers (Poynor & Wolfe, 2005) and need to be saved (Goodman, Shannon, Goodman, & Rappoport, 2004). Others (McCardle & Chhabra, 2004; Shanahan, 2005) argue that the report of the National Reading Panel (2002a) settled this issue, and the need to teach phonics intensively and systematically has been clearly decided. In the middle of these arguments, in the midst of the heated passionate debates in journals, at professional conferences, and even in the press, lie classrooms with teachers and children. They arrive each day faced with increasing pressures to perform well on tests that often do not portray the students accurately.

Many teachers teach from a place of tension between complying with what is required of them and their beliefs. Karen's compliance to teaching a strongly phonics based program to her whole class, although she knew only a very few would benefit, caused her to have headaches, feel sad about her job, and consider leaving the profession. She felt coerced into behaving like a technician rather than the informed reflective professional she knows she is. The tension grew until she decided, in the second year of being required to use the program, to find ways to abbreviate many of the lessons with the whole class. As her principal became less present in her room (trusting that the teachers "got" the program), she deviated from the prescribed curriculum.

Karen carefully considered her knowledge and beliefs about her teaching life. She made decisions based on those considerations. She considered her thoughts about the pressure the district was under to perform well on standardized tests. She considered her knowledge of her students' experiences with written language and the experiences she wanted to offer them based on her knowledge. She considered the published program and what it offered her as a decision maker. She considered what she was told about curriculum and whether or not she thought she should or should not be someone who creates curriculum (Short & Burke, 1991). Each consideration involved a deeply reflective process and Karen kept returning to her view of herself as a teacher. She knew she was informed about the reading process and instruction; she knew her students; she knew the mandated program was not meeting many of her students' needs. She reflected and made decisions about deviating from the mandate in order to serve her students. She quietly, at first, and then more vocally (as she collected evidence of her students' successes as readers and writers) chose not to comply.

CONSIDERATIONS FOR READING AND TEACHING

Karen's decision-making process was described as *considerations*. The rest of this section is organized around considerations. Considerations are issues that we invite you to ponder as you make decisions about yourself as a teacher of reading. Each of the considerations is intended to be a vehicle to help you understand and respond to the complexity of reading. Each may have implications for the nature of your teaching and your students' learning, depending on your understanding of and commitment to its relevance to the teaching of reading.

Our leaning in these considerations tends toward Critical Literacy because we believe it brings teaching back to this important basic: The purpose of school is to live democratically in school in order for students to become effective and participating citizens in the greater democracy in which they will eventually live. After you read each consideration, think about and discuss with colleagues your position on and response to what we've presented.

Consideration 1: Decision Making Involves Responsibilities

Reflective teachers of reading assume the responsibilities inherent in sound decision making. That means they work to remain informed and current about issues facing the field. They always consider the needs and interests of their students and juxtapose those with the demands of local, state, and federal education agencies. They know that researchers often present conflicting evidence about best practices for reading instruction, so these teachers read the research. They study the participants and methods of the research in order to decide for themselves if the research resonates with the children they face each day in their classrooms. They consider sources of information, such as publishers claiming they have the tools and materials teachers need for success for all their students, and they ask questions of such publishers in order to clarify the validity of the publishers' claims.

Consideration 2: It's Important to Understand How Children Learn

In teaching reading, it is important to consider how children learn in areas beyond reading. Children learn how to relate to other children, how to relate to different genders, cultures, language groups, and cultural and ethnic groups, and they learn how to play alone as well as with others. Children are constantly learning and learning how to learn. Children are busy constructing their worlds (and their words) long before they arrive at school. Teachers should know whom their students live with, how they get to school, what they do before and after school, what matters to them, and what they are curious about. They should know what their students are passionate about so they can construct curriculum with their students in ways that build on their students' lives. Sylvia found that children's learning becomes enhanced and her own teaching is more effective when children's identities are welcome, even embraced, in the classroom. Kendra, Janesse, and Sylvia understand that conversations are an essential part of the curriculum (Applebee, 1996) because through talk, children can present, consider, and reconstruct ideas and concepts. Lewis (2001) studied students in a classroom in which the teacher led discussions and also encouraged children to engage in peer-led discussions. She describes the complexity and richness of these discussions:

> The social drama that exists in any classroom will surface during peer-led discussions, creating opportunities for students to negotiate social positions.

(p. 176)... if classrooms are going to function—at least some of the time—as sites for social negotiation and change, conflict and difference need to be visible rather than hidden dimensions of the classroom. (p. 177)

In other words, learning is not a clean, teacher-directed process imposed on children. It is complicated, social, emotional, and constantly in flux as positions within the learning context are negotiated and renegotiated.

Montessori (1966) wanted teachers to honor the spirit of the child in order to cultivate what children brought with them to the school experience. A child's spirit includes things such as temperament, interests, physical needs, curiosity, and passions. Each child brings those things to the classroom and expresses them in the social context in the zone of proximal development (Vygotsky, 1978). The zone is not just a cognitive place; it is saturated with emotions and, as Goldstein (1999) pointed out, love makes a difference in children's learning in school. Children need to talk, act, wonder, wander, listen, write, be loved, love, plan, enact, perform, live as social beings, invest time and energy, commit, engage, and feel safe in order to learn anything—especially to read. Their identities and cultures matter (see Consideration 5) as they learn to read. They also need to have a sense of agency, meaning a belief that they can act on and affect their worlds.

Consideration 3: Teachers Do Not Need to Feel Isolated and Lonely

Sarason's (1971) now classic study of teachers led to his conclusion of teaching as cellular, as though teachers are in separate cells with walls that are almost impervious to communication with other teachers. Years after his study, many teachers of reading in our graduate courses express a sense of isolation because they rarely have sustained conversations with other teachers and are not able to visit other teachers' classrooms to see how they teach reading. The loneliness that some teachers feel contributes to their compliance to mandated programs for teaching reading. Such teachers are convinced that "everyone is doing it this way" so they should, too. Teachers communicating and studying their own classrooms (Cochran-Smith & Lytle, 1993) has been shown to enhance teaching and learning. Kendra was fortunate to be in a long-term teacher study group with colleagues at her school; the group served as a thought collective in which she could present ideas, be safely challenged, and challenge the ideas and practices of others. Janesse had colleagues through the National Writing Project. But Sylvia often felt alone and unsafe to the point of not trusting her intuition until she could not tolerate her pain any longer. Penny was so excluded by the teachers at her school that their actions contributed significantly to her decision to leave.

Teachers may work to end their isolation and loneliness. One of the ways that the oppression of teachers is perpetuated is through acts that extend isolation. One teacher recently pointed out to Rick that the staff development at her school is "one way," meaning that it is a model in which an outsider arrives at the school with "the latest answer" to the school's falling reading scores. Such staff development sessions do not allow conversation and admonish teachers who question the efficacy of what is being presented. This type of staff development disenfranchises teachers who want to build their reading curriculum based on the specificities of the local school and the children in it. In these sessions, conversation is not allowed as part of the official discussion of curriculum.

Teachers respond to isolation by reading and talking to construct a zone of reflective development that allows them to be thoughtful. They teach against the grain and do so carefully in order to keep their jobs and serve their students. They fight the loneliness that seems inherent in the profession by being with colleagues through conversations in person or through books. They may choose to be involved in study groups, take graduate courses, join national organizations, and partake in local discussion groups as vehicles for undermining the isolation and loneliness that has historically been instrumental in keeping teachers intimidated, isolated, and afraid to trust their ever-growing knowledge of children, reading, teaching, and learning.

Consideration 4: Teachers Need to Know About the Reading Process and Reading Instruction

Many teachers learned to read using the very programs on which they want to turn their backs. We suggest that they learned to read in spite of the programs, not because of them. Basal programs do not work to uncover the literacy possibilities within a classroom because the programs treat everyone the same. If a child brought in a box of clay to present to her first-grade friends, the way Maria did in Kendra's classroom, such a connection may be treated as a diversion in the basal classroom because of the pressure to cover material. We're not saying that such teachers don't care; it's the urgency of time to cover things that exerts huge pressure on such classrooms. In Kendra's classroom, the important connections between a book and the home where the child composed the box of clay were viewed as a teachable moment. Kendra made decisions about how to use the moment to learn about the child's thinking, to make connections to other texts, and to offer other opportunities for reading and writing.

Teachers of reading should consider the physical structure of the text. When teachers look at first graders balancing a basal anthology on their laps, they think of themselves balancing a hardcover copy of the phonebook from a large urban area on their own laps. These are unwieldy, to say the least. A 6-year-old child who needs to find page 175 to read the first page of *The Day Jimmy's Boa Ate the Wash* (Noble, 1980) has a different experience with the concept of "book" than a child who gets to read the same story as a self-contained text. In older grades, publishers provide students with anthologies that typically have excerpts of full-length books. One sixth grade teacher asked Rick, "Why would we read one chapter of *The Phantom Tollbooth* (Juster, 1988), when we could read the whole thing?" Anthologies may be acceptable to some teachers, but we'd rather schools spend money on real books so that children can have the full and visceral experience of holding the whole book and reading the whole story as a self-contained unit.

Consideration 5: Culturally Responsive Teaching Is a Teacher's Responsibility

Teachers using basal programs typically do not have the time to consider the specific cultural groups they teach during reading instruction. These teachers might consider cultural groups at other times during the school day, but subscribing to a specific reading program rarely allows teachers to engage in pedagogical decisions that are sensitive to the specific diversities in their classrooms. Simply representing a variety of cultures within a book is a relatively superficial way of attempting to include diversity.

Published programs usually provide the teacher with lists of questions to check for comprehension, but such lists may not address the connections children make as they read. The children's ways of relating to the stories are at risk of becoming secondary to the teacher's goal of having the children provide responses as they are listed in the teacher's guide. "Using" stories with characters and events that represent different cultures in order to teach a set of specific skills may reduce the importance of the literacy event. Teachers need to consider ways to include cultural issues at the center, not as an add-on. Students need books in their classrooms that represent the cultures of the students in their classrooms and a variety of other cultures, as well, so that children may draw connections between and understand the differences and similarities that exist across cultures.

There is a rich and growing research base demonstrating the importance of the teachers' understanding of the cultures of their students. For example, in some Hawaiian communities young children engaged more in oral language activities when those activities reflected communicative practices (particularly the use of stories) that were common in the community (Au, 1981). Sylvia learned this as well when she found her students engaging more in every aspect of classroom activity when she allowed some time for them to talk in school in ways that reflected the community's cultural and linguistic practices. For example, Goodman (1985) describes a situation in which a child is told by the teacher not to "waste" any milk. The child opens a milk container at snack time, takes one sip, closes it carefully and carries it to the garbage pail, placing it in the pail very gently. The teacher is annoyed that the child did not finish the milk and asks why the child wasted it. The child, thinking that *waste* means *to spill*, does not comprehend the teacher's anger, having been very careful to not spill a drop. The understanding (or lack of it) of differences in the uses of language and cultural practices can support (or undermine) a teacher's teaching and children's learning of reading.

One of the most poignant examples of a strong commitment to culturally and linguistically responsive teaching is McCarty's (2002) description of a Navajo community, Rough Rock, taking control of their school in order to develop a curriculum in which children can succeed within and beyond their community. As McCarty finishes her story, she writes about the pressures facing the teachers at Rough Rock as state standards and testing force teachers to sacrifice the goals with which they started the school. She explains that the Navajo students are not minorities; rather, they have been *minoritized* (p. 198), meaning they've been forced into a devalued position:

> The very existence of Indigenous community schools depends on their compliance with standards that not only devalue Indigenous knowledge, but jeopardizes children's life chances by threatening to deny them a high school degree. That children are subjected to these pressures in preschool is among the more perverse manifestations of a national education that, while masquerading as an equalizing force, in fact begins to stratify and segregate the moment children enter school. (p. 198)

McCarty's description of the connections between language, culture, learning, and teaching resonates with teachers who know that these things are connected to each other and are at the root of learning to read.

Reflective teachers, even if they are not bilingual, support bilingual programs because of the overwhelming evidence that such programs lead to proficient reading performance in both languages (Thomas & Collier, 2002). When many language groups are represented in a single classroom, bilingual programs are not always viable. In such situations, sound English language learner programs support children's learning to read in English. Nieto (2002) explains that "[g]iven the increasing number of students who enter schools speaking native languages other than English, it is clear that attending to the unique condition of language minority students is the responsibility of all educators" (pp. 96-97). Kohl (1991) explains that responsiveness to our students' cultural and linguistic identities encourages them to "assent" or agree to learn. As a teacher of many years, he's learned that "not-learning to read can be confused with failing to learn to read if the rejection of learning is overlooked as a significant factor" (p. 13).

Reading is a social act (Bloome, 1983) involving relationships between a reader and a text, the text and the author, the reader and the author, the reader and other readers, the text as having a place within a larger canon, the text as having a position relative to other texts the reader has read, and the ways in which the reader connects the text to his or her existing relationships (including the relationship with the teacher). This was true for Maria when she arrived with a mystery box in Kendra's first-grade classroom, and it is true for students studying Langston Hughes' poems in Janesse's classroom. Such classroom activity can only occur if a teacher makes decisions specific to her classroom and her students—specific to their cultural, linguistic, economic, social, and spiritual identities.

Consideration 6: Teaching Is Political

Most teachers never imagined that being a teacher who teaches reading (or any other subject, we would add) would involve us in a tangled web of politics. The reality is that every act of teaching, from the most compliant to the most radical, is a political act. Most teachers are not politically active or articulate about political issues, yet everything we do as teachers is a political act. If you use a basal reading program, you are involved in political work for a number of reasons. For example, compliance is a political act. When you agree to use the basal as it is written, you become complicit with the methods, inherent beliefs, and goals of that published program. Perhaps you agree when a program states its goals of having children be fluent readers (most of us would), using skills to decode new words (most of us agree there, too), and reading for understanding (who could argue with that?). It's when we dig a little deeper that we see some of the political stances to which we've complied if we use such a program. We comply with the publisher's definition of reading; we comply with the way they want us to teach; we comply with materials selection; we comply with scope and sequence; we comply with who is represented and who is left out of the text; and we comply with the measures provided that are to be used as evidence of our students' learning. Our hope is that if you use such a program, that you do agree with the publisher's position on these issues.

Reading programs and, more broadly, schooling in general, rest on views of the child. Some schools, programs, and teachers portend that children are born basically evil and training them to be compliant is one way of ensuring that they will become good citizens (Lakoff, 2004). Lakoff refers to this view as the *strict father* view of the child. In school, the view translates into the strict teacher who demands compliance even when things do not make sense or have meaning because the underlying belief is that students must learn to comply and that complying is being good. The *nurturing parent* view of the child sees her or him as curious, fundamentally good, and eager to learn as long as nurturing conditions are operating. This view considers school to be a forum for honoring and responding to cultural and linguistic differences. Such honoring is considered necessary for good citizenship, a citizenship that will question inequities. The view of the child that teachers have shows itself in the nature of the activities and relationships that occur within a reading program. We know that this is not easy to digest, but it is an idea that is very much at hand. The NCLB law is, according to Lakoff, rooted in the strict father view of the child. This helps to explain the repressive climate that many teachers feel in school. Thus, the view of the child is a political position that shows up in our teaching. It is another issue that appears operationally in that the way we teach reading rests on our view not only of reading but of the child as well.

The idea that texts are open to interpretation (Rosenblatt, 1976) is a political stance. It suggests that a publisher's questions with predetermined responses may not serve some students very well. Students are thoughtful, and their responses to texts matter, are unique, are measures of comprehension, and are opportunities to teach about multiple perspectives. The idea of literature as exploration surfaced in one class when students and their teacher questioned the way that civil rights were presented in their social studies text. It surfaced in another class when children read about a giant and engaged in a discussion of bullies. Reflective teachers of reading use these moments to engage children, encourage them to read and write more, work with them to help them articulate their own points of view, and help them make a connection to writing. We are suggesting that your decisions about your view of reading instruction influence more than the results on a standardized test. Your decisions are political because they ultimately influence children's thinking.

In today's world, when children can see in the media the results of extremely upset individuals and groups, we want schools to be places where children are safe to think and discuss to the fullest depth necessary to learn to support a safe and democratic way of life. We worry about many students who are forced to be compliant because when the "dam breaks" they may drop out, act out, or engage in other intense behaviors. They are truly at risk, or, perhaps more accurately, they may put us at risk. The potentials that rest in children (both positive and negative) suggest the importance and political nature of the teaching of reading.

Consideration 7: Reflective Teachers Invent Spaces in Which They and Their Students Can Thrive

The reality is that teachers have to live in that precarious and sometimes tentative space between their ideals of teaching and the realities of the demands of their districts. Presently, many states are feeling the increased pressure from the accountability parts of the No Child Left Behind Act. Standards and standards-based measures are used to control, assess, and often publicly embarrass schools, teachers, and children. Teachers like Penny, Sylvia, Janesse, and Kendra work to find spaces in which they can enact reading programs consistent with their views of reading while, at the same time, balancing the demands of their schools, districts, and states.

Gutierrez, Rymes, and Larson (1995) posit that teachers using published programs mandated by their districts offer their students a "monologic script" (p. 447), meaning that the students only hear a single voice, the voice of the publishers through their teacher. In such classrooms, "the relevance of students' counterscripts to the processes or topics discussed in this classroom has little influence on the teacher's script" (p. 447). When a teacher's script and students' counterscripts become mutually valued and informative, a "third space" opens up in which "it becomes possible for both teacher and students to redefine what counts as knowledge" (p. 467). Sylvia and her students invented a third space in which she could and would address her students' identities.

Sylvia's conflicted feelings and responses to the presence of culture in her classroom related to her own past as she described family events at which she felt the need to choose between her mother, cast as an outsider because she did not speak Spanish, and her father's family, which was at-hand and constant. Sylvia's family sent subtle messages to Sylvia and her mom that it was not acceptable for Mom to be the way she was. Being excluded at family gatherings is a subtle form of aggression. These "microaggressions" (Solorzano, Ceja, & Yosso, 2000) affected Sylvia deeply. Microaggressions are "subtle, stunning, often automatic, and non-verbal exchanges which are 'put downs'" (Pierce, Carew, Pierce-Gonzalez, & Willis, 1978, p. 66, cited in Solorzano et al., 2000, p. 60). Davis (1989, cited in Solorzano et al., 2000, p. 60) explained microaggressions as "stunning, automatic acts of disregard that stem from unconscious attitudes of white superiority and constitute a verification of black inferiority" (p. 60 in Solorzano et al., 2000).

Although the cited work on microaggressions refers to work within Black populations, virtually any power dynamic is a potential context for such actions. The subtle messages sent repeatedly that suggest what a teacher should be, what a teacher should do, and what a child should be and do may serve as "put-downs" of language groups, cultures, and the individual identities of teachers or children. These are microaggressions. Sylvia received such messages as a child in school, learning by daily example which cultural groups and languages had power and prestige. Penny felt microaggressions from her colleagues as she was excluded.

Grumet (1988) relates microaggressions to the tension between motherhood and teaching:

> We need to acknowledge that, even as we celebrated their maternal gifts, we have required women to draw children out of the intimacy and knowledge of the family into the categorical and public world. We have burdened the teaching profession with contradictions and betrayals that have alienated teachers from our own experience, from our bodies, our memories, our dreams, from each other, from children, and from our sisters who are mothers to those children. (p. 57)

Sylvia figured out that the "contradictions" she felt as a student teacher and first-year teacher were evidence of betrayals that she was taught to perpetuate. Her belief that school could only be one right way and her commitment to "learning to do this" were the result of years of microaggressions committed on her. The dismissal of her students' language and culture, essentially the perpetuation of the belief that their cultural capital would yield little cultural profit (Lareau, 2000), hurt her deeply because it perpetuated acts of microaggressions against herself and her students.

Sylvia's exhaustion by January of her first year was not so much a first-year teacher's fatigue, although that was certainly part of it, as it was her coming to feel that she was an aggressor with the goal of making her children compliant and mainstream. She concomitantly came to understand her own cultural roots and those of her students because of the growing sense that the walls between the school and the community were impenetrable in ways that were not serving her students well. In other words, Sylvia's original sense was that her students (in student teaching and her first group of first graders) were in some ways pathologized (Walkerdine, 1990). Their "ways with words" (Heath, 1983) were viewed by the system at large as deficient at best and most probably defective.

Yet Sylvia learned that by honoring her students' language and culture, they achieved more in a traditional sense and they formed a community that was consistent with their neighborhood. She helped them to learn to live in two worlds. The changes that occurred were not dramatic to the point of disrupting anyone's world. In that sense, they were microtransformations (Wolfe, 2003) that involved a teacher facing and changing the pattern to interrupt years of microaggressions that convinced her that she and children like her were defective. Sylvia's ultimate struggle was to invent a linguistic and cultural space that supported her students' learning.

Consideration 8: Finding a Community of Reflective Teachers Is Not Easy, but It's Worth the Effort

One very hopeful forum for such teachers is the site of the National Writing Project (http://www.writingproject.org/). This organization hosts summer institutes at which teachers learn about reading and writing processes by living those processes in a reflective way. They read, write, talk, present, argue, and care about each other's literacy lives, taking the lessons from the summer institute back to their own classrooms (Brooke, 2003). Another forum is a teacher study group, like the one that Kendra was a member of for so many years. Teachers who actively seek or carve out places in which they can talk and think are working at being informed, reflective, and responsive. We hope that teachers find that increasingly rare principal who is willing to support each teacher in his or her professional endeavors—a principal brave enough to support reflective teachers during this period in time, when so many forces seem to be at work to deprofessionalize teaching by defining it as adherence to a curriculum and compliance to a script. Sometimes a graduate course can help you find the group that will support your thinking. We hope that you find others to think with because we believe that within a community of thinkers, we can grow the same hope that Dewey (1904) offered over a century ago: "If teachers were possessed by the spirit of an abiding student of education, this spirit would find some way of breaking through the mesh and coil of circumstance and would find expression for itself" (p. 28).

SOME SUGGESTIONS

In this section, we offer some suggestions for actively enhancing your understanding of the reading process and reading instruction. These activities require that you spend time collecting data with teachers, families, and in classrooms and communities where you might observe, ask questions, and take notes on what you see. Use your data and analysis as a way of thinking further alone and with colleagues about what should occur in the teaching of reading. Try to find classrooms that are unlike the classrooms that you attended as a child. You already know a lot about those classrooms; see if you can find classrooms that have diverse groups, different from groups with whom you may have attended school. As you enter classrooms, think about the literacy world outside of the school (something we'll help you consider), and compare that to what you see occurring in the classroom. For example, at home a child might write e-mails, play video games, play games on the Web with people around the world, instant-message friends and family, and read on the Web about a variety of interests. How many of these activities also belong or appear in schools? Consistent with our view that reading is individual, cultural, linguistic, psychological, transactional, political, and more, we've composed activities to help you understand those many facets of literacy lives.

Write Your Literacy Autobiography

Your literacy life will undoubtedly influence the way you teach children to read and write. If you look at reading as *work* that you have to do, you'll probably teach children that same thing. This is consistent with our idea that "you are who you teach and you teach who you are" (Meyer, 1996). There are many ways to study your literacy life. We'll offer one that you might elaborate on as much as you like and time permits.

Begin by drawing a line on the middle of a piece of paper, like a time-line. On this line, put points that represent literacy events from your life. These include texts that you read or heard and remember as being important to you, experiences from which you learned about reading (for example, if your mom read to you in the evening), and teachers who influenced your attitude about reading. Put both positive and negative points on the line. You only need to put a word or two to remind you of the story behind the point.

Enter points on your time-line that represent the various events in your literacy learning life. Share these stories with others and try to extract from yours and theirs the themes that dominate your literacy life. If learning to read was worksheet after worksheet, what's your theme of learning to read? How will that influence your teaching of reading? How can you decide to change that influence? Do you love, hate, or have no feelings about reading? Why? Where are the events that shaped your feeling? How might those feelings affect your views of reading process and instruction? Studying your own reading past and present is an important tool for helping you to clarify you view of reading.

Interviews

There are many people you can interview to learn about your literacy life and the literacy lives of others. Begin with interviews of people with whom you grew up or family members who raised you. Here are some questions we used with our siblings and family members (because we didn't remember the answers!):

- Who read to us? How often?
- What other literacy activities were we involved in at home, at church or temple, outside of the home?
- Who influenced us as readers when we were growing up?
- Who read in our home? In what language? Who couldn't read? How come?

You might also interview teachers, principals, and family members about the literacy they recall from your past. Ask if you might audiotape the interviews so that you may study the data closely and make decisions about the views of reading and reading instruction that these individuals have. Think about how each interviewee influenced you as a reader.

Observations in a Classroom

Find a teacher who would be willing to have you observe during the teaching of reading in his or her classroom. Take copious notes during your observation and also try to capture some direct quotes that are said by the teacher and the children. Notice things such as: how children are grouped; what children are asked to do; who gets to talk (look at gender, ethnicity, etc.); who is silent or silenced; who gets to read; how comprehension is checked; how reading is taught; what cueing systems are relied on most frequently; what children do when they are "stuck" while reading; what strategies teachers offer; who chooses what is read; how differences in performance are addressed; how interests are addressed; how long children get to read books; and what types of texts they get to read. You want to address the question: "What is reading in this classroom?"

Observations in a School

These activities of interviewing teachers and other stakeholders about reading and observing in classrooms is further enriched if you and others observe throughout an entire school. By viewing and comparing what is occurring across grade levels, you gain insights into the definition of reading throughout the school.

Observations in a Community

Reading is something we learn for use outside of school. It is not merely a skill that we learn to perform so that we can move from grade level to grade level; it is something that we learn in order to function in our world. Print is virtually everywhere and children are constantly learning what it's for. When we live in a community, we take for granted much of the reading information around us (environmental print). Engage in a literacy dig in your neighborhood or in a neighborhood in which you are teaching or student teaching. Find every bit of written language that you can as you, for example, walk from the school to the nearest main street. You may notice signs, sewer covers, meters, writing on houses, litter, billboards, and more. Next, choose a store that your students frequent and study the literacy there. What languages do you notice? What cultures are represented by different foods, clothing, or other items for sale in different stores? Study the literacy of the neighborhood and try to make comparisons to the literacy that is lived out in the school.

Observations in a Family Setting

Now that you have some insights into classrooms and the community, see if you can find a home of a student to visit to study the literacy activity within a family. We strongly recommend that you do this with a partner, not alone. The first few times we did this, students who visited children in high poverty areas reported no reading material in the homes. When we inquired further, our students reported that the children had no books. Then we asked: What about junk mail? What about writing on clothing? What about writing on cans and boxes in cupboards, the refrigerator, and in the garage? Then our students looked more closely and found many things that students read daily, beginning with the toothpaste tube in the morning and the box or bag of cereal at breakfast. During your visit, find out about the languages spoken in the home, levels of education, length of time in the United States, types of written materials in the home (not just books), TV viewing, and reading activity.

A Case Study of One Reader

Now that you understand the community, classroom, and family settings, you may want to study one reader very closely. Of course, you may do this without the contextualizing that the previous activities provide. Again, we ask for family permission before beginning the study of any child. If the child is in the family that was already visited for the home visit, you'll have a lot of information on this one child. Observe a child's reading life in school over the course of a few days. Collect evidence in the form of notes you take and copies of what they read. Remember that children are the first readers of their own writing, so collect writing samples as well. Look for the official curriculum of reading and the unofficial (Dyson, 1993) or underground curriculum that children create, such as writing notes, instant-messaging, sharing books that are not part of the school's reading program, and reading magazines that are contraband at school (Finders, 1997).

Use some of the questions Burke (in Goodman, Watson, & Burke, 1987, p. 219) suggests we ask readers:

> When you are reading and come to something you don't know, what do you do? (This question helps get at the child's view of the reading process. If the child says, "I sound it out," you may suspect she's committed to seeing reading as using sounds to say words.) Do you ever do anything else? (To see if she uses other strategies.) Who is a good reader you know? (To get at the

child's understanding of what good readers do.) What does that person do when they come to something they don't know? (to see if she thinks other/proficient readers do things she does not do).

Refer to Goodman et al. (1987) for more questions to gain insights into what readers think about their own reading process.

Learn More About the Phonics

Take any sentence from a book that a child is reading and study each word. How many rules can you recite to account for the sounds of the letters? How many of these rules should be systematically taught? Begin with just one letter in small words. What are the rules for the sounds that <a> makes in these words: was, war, car, stair, saw, cat, ham, create, great, hall?

Learn About School Funding for Reading Instruction

Find out how schools in your district are funded. How much of that money is spent on reading? Who decides how the money is spent? Where else does money come from for reading programs? (*Reading First* is a popular funding source at the present time but has severe restrictions on how the money may be used.) How much is spent on each child for reading? How much, per child, is allocated for the purchase of library books at the school?

Learn About Professional Development Opportunities for Teachers

Study teacher professional development in a school. How is it conducted? Who decides the focus or topic? Who gets to speak? How are questions and challenges addressed? Is it sustained over time or a "single program? Are there teacher study groups? If so, how often do they meet? How are topics selected? Can you attend professional development offered to teachers to learn more about them? If so, take notes to discuss with colleagues and try to address some of the questions we've posed here. Check out the Web sites of literacy organizations such as the International Reading Association (reading.org) or National Council of Teachers of English (ncte.org). Learn what they offer for professional development.

CONCLUSION

We are committed to sustained conversations about reading process and reading instruction. Any group or individual who attempts to silence dissent is, from our perspective, antidemocratic. We believe that classrooms and any professional forums (conferences, staff development sessions, graduate courses, etc.) must be open to multiple perspectives. We also are convinced that a meaning-based view of reading allows a teacher to compose a reading program that addresses the students in the classroom. No teacher, from our perspective, should subscribe to a one-size-fits-all curriculum that ignores children and brackets a teacher's reflective decision making. We know that novice and experienced teachers have to be supported in thinking about practice, trying new ideas, and developing an ever-deepening understanding of reading as a process and the instructional possibilities that may emerge from that understanding. We hope that you, as a teacher of reading, will use reading as a tool with your students to help them unlock the mysteries of the world and to help them make sense of who they are, their relationships with others, and their responsibilities in a democratic society.

REFERENCES

Adams, M. (1990). *Beginning to read: Thinking and learning about print.* Cambridge, MA: MIT Press.
Allington, R. (2005, February). Ideology is still trumping evidence. *Phi Delta Kappan, 86*(6), 462–468.
Altwerger, B. (Ed.). (2005). *Reading for profit: How the bottom line leaves kids behind.* Portsmouth: Heinemann.
Anderson, G., Herr, K., & Nihlen, A. (1994). *Studying your own school: An educator's guide to qualitative practitioner research.* Thousand Oaks, CA: Corwin Press.
Angelou, M. (2002). *I know why the caged bird sings.* New York: Random House.
Applebee, A. (1996). *Curriculum as conversation: Transforming traditions of teaching and learning.* Chicago: University of Chicago Press.
Atwell, N. (1998). *In the middle: New understanding about writing, reading, and learning.* Portsmouth, NH: Boynton/Cook.
Au, K. (1981). Participations structures in a reading lesson with Hawaiian children: Analysis of a culturally appropriate instructional event. *Anthropology and Education Quarterly, XI*(2), 91–115.
Au, K. (1993). *Literacy instruction in multicultural settings.* Fort Worth: Harcourt Brace Janovich.
Ayers, W., Hunt, J. A., & Quinn, T. (Eds.). (1998). *Teaching for social justice.* New York: Teachers College Press.
Berliner, D., & Biddle, B. (1995). *The manufactured crisis: Myths, frauds, and the attack on America's schools.* Reading, MA: Addison-Wesley.
Bigelow, B., Christensen, L., & Karp, S. (1994). *Rethinking our classrooms: Teaching for equity and social justice* (Vol. 1). Milwaukee, WI: Rethinking Schools.
Bigelow, B., Harvey, B., Karp, S., & Miller, L. (Eds.) (2001). *Rethinking our classrooms: Teaching for equity and social justice* (Vol. 2). Williston, VT: Rethinking Schools.

Bloome, D. (1983). Reading as a social process. *Advances in Reading/Language Research, 2,* 165–195.

Bloome, D., & Dail, A. (1997). Toward (re)defining miscue analysis: Reading as a social and cultural process. *Language Arts, 74*(8), 610–617.

Bomer, R., & Bomer, K. (1999). *Reading and writing for social justice.* Portsmouth: Heinemann.

Bourdieu, P., & Wacquant, L. (1992). *An invitation to reflexive sociology.* Chicago: University of Chicago Press.

Brooke, R. (Ed.). (2003). *Rural voices: Place consciousness education and the teaching of writing.* New York: Teachers College Press.

Brown, J., Goodman, Y., & Marek, A. (Eds.). (1996). *Studies in miscue analysis: An annotated bibliography.* Newark, DE: International Reading Association.

Cambourne, Brian. (1995). Toward an educationally relevant theory of literacy learning: Twenty years of inquiry. *Reading Teacher, 49*(3), 182–190.

Carger, C. (1996). *Of borders and dreams: A Mexican-American experience in urban education.* New York: Teachers College Press.

Cazden, C. (1992). *Whole language plus: Essays on literacy in the United States and New Zealand.* New York: Teachers College Press.

Chall, J. (1967). *Learning to read: the great debate: An inquiry into the science, art, and ideology of old and new methods of teaching children to read.* New York: McGraw-Hill.

Carlson, N. (1988). *I like me.* New York: Viking Penguin.

Christensen, L. (2000). *Reading, writing, and rising up: Teaching about social justice and the power of the written word.* Milwaukee: Rethinking Schools.

Clay, M. (1985). *The early detection of reading difficulties.* Portsmouth, NH: Heinemann.

Cochran-Smith, M., & Lytle, S. (1993). *Inside outside: Teachers research and knowledge.* New York: Teachers College Press.

Cochran-Smith, M., & Lytle, S. (2000). Relationships of knowledge and practice: Teacher learning in communities. In A. Iran-Nudged & P. D. Pearson (Eds.), *Review of research in education* (Vol. 24, pp. 249–306). Washington, DC: American Educational Research Association.

Coles, G. (2003). *Reading the naked truth: Literacy, legislation and lies.* Portsmouth: Heinemann.

Comber, B., & Simpson, A. (Eds.). (2001). *Negotiating critical literacies in classrooms.* Mahwah, NJ: Lawrence Erlbaum Associates.

Compton-Lilly, C. (2003). *Reading families: The literate lives of urban children.* New York: Teachers College Press.

Cowley, J. (1990). *The hungry giant.* Bothell, WA: The Wright Group.

Craviotto, E., Heras, A., & Espindola, J. (2004). Cultures of the fourth-grade bilingual classroom. In V. Vasquez, K. Egawa, J. Harste, & R. Thompson (Eds.), *Literacy as social practice: Primary voices K–6* (pp. 91–106). Urbana, IL: National Council of Teachers of English.

Darling-Hammond, L.(2004). From "separate but equal" to "No Child Left Behind": The collision of new standards and old equalities. In D. Meier, A. Kohn, L. Darling-Hammond, T. Sizer, & G. Wood (Eds.), *Many children left behind: How the No Child Left Behind Act is damaging our children and our schools* (pp. 3–32). Boston: Beacon Press.

REFERENCES

Davenport, R. (2002). *Miscues not mistakes: Reading assessment in classrooms.* Portsmouth, NH: Heinemann.

Delpit, L., & Dowdy, J. K. (2002). *Skin that we speak: thoughts on language and culture in the classroom.* New York: New Press.

Delpit, L. (1995). *Other peoples' children: Cultural conflict in the classroom.* New York: New Press. Distributed by W. W. Norton.

Dewey, J. (1904). The relation of theory to practice in education. In C. McMurry (Ed.), *The third yearbook of the National Society for the Scientific Study of Education* (pp. 9–30). Chicago: University of Chicago Press.

Dewey, J. (1938). *Experience and education.* New York: Macmillan.

DIBELS (2005). Information downloaded from http://dibels.uoregon.edu/ on April 27, 2005.

Durand, V. M. (1990). *Severe behavior problems: A functional communication training approach.* New York: Guilford Press.

Dyson, A. (1993). *Social worlds of children learning to write in an urban primary school.* New York: Teachers College Press.

Edelsky, C. (1991). *With literacy and justice for all: Rethinking the social in language and education.* London: Falmer Press.

Finders, M. (1997). *Just girls: Hidden literacies and life in junior high.* New York: Teachers College Press.

Flesch, R. (1955). *Why Johnny can't read and what you can do about it.* New York: Harper.

Florio-Ruane, S. (2001). *Teacher education and the cultural imagination.* Mahwah, NJ: Lawrence Erlbaum Associates.

Flurkey, A. (1997). *Reading as flow: A linguistic alternative to fluency.* Unpublished doctoral dissertation, University of Arizona, Tuscon.

Freire, P. (1985). *The politics of education: Culture, power, and liberation.* Hadley, MA: Bergin & Garvey.

Freire, P., & Macedo, D. (1987). *Literacy: Reading the word and the world.* Westport, CT: Bergin & Garvey.

Gannett, R. (1948). *My father's dragon.* New York: Random House.

Garan, E. (2005, February). Murder your darlings: A scientific response to *Evidence in reading research. Phi Delta Kappan, 86*(6), 438–443.

Gee, J. (1990). *Social linguistics and literacies: Ideology in discourses.* London, England: Falmer Press.

Goldstein, L. (1999, Fall). The relational zone: The role of caring relationships in the co-construction of mind. *American Educational Research Journal, 36*(3), 647–673.

Goodman, K. (1996). *On reading: A common-sense look at the nature of language and the science of reading.* Portsmouth, NH: Heinemann.

Goodman, K. & Gollasch, F. (1982). *Language & literacy: The selected writings of Kenneth S. Goodman, Volume 1.* Boston: Routledge & Kegan Paul.

Goodman, K., Shannon, P., Goodman, Y., & Rappoport, R. (2004). *Saving our schools: The case for public education saying no to "No Child Left Behind."* Berkeley, CA: RDR Books.

Goodman, Y., & Marek, A. (1996). *Retrospective miscue analysis: Revaluing readers and reading.* Katonah, NY: Richard C. Owen.

Goodman, Y. (1985). Kidwatching: Observing children in the classroom. In A. Jagger & M. T. Smith-Burke (Eds.), *Observing the language learner* (pp. 9–18). Newark, DE: International Reading Association.

Goodman, Y., Watson, D., & Burke, C. (1987). *Reading miscue inventory: Alternative procedures.* Katonah, NY: Richard C. Owen.
Goss, J., & Harste, J. (1985). *It didn't frighten me.* Worthington, OH: Willowisp Press.
Graves, D. (1983). *Writing: Teachers and children at work.* Portsmouth, NH: Heinemann.
Grumet, M. (1988). *Bitter milk: Women and teaching.* Amherst: University of Massachusetts.
Guerra, J. (1998). *Close to home: Oral and literate practices in a transnational Mexicano community.* New York: Teachers College Press.
Gutiérrez, K., & Larson, J. (1994). Language borders: Recitation as hegemonic discourse. *International Journal of Education Reform, 3(1),* 22–36.
Gutiérrez, K., Rymes, B., & Larson, J. (1995, Fall). Script, counterscript, and underlife in the classroom: James Brown versus *Brown v. Board of Education. Harvard Educational Review, 65*(3), 445–471.
Hansen, J. (2001). *When writers read* (2nd ed.). Portsmouth, NH: Heinemann.
Harste, J. (1989). The basalization of American reading instruction: One researcher responds. *Theory into Practice 28*(4), 265–273.
Harste, J., Woodward, V., & Burke, C. (1984). *Language stories and literacy lessons.* Portsmouth, NH: Heinemann.
Heath, S. B. (1983). *Ways with word: Language, life, and work in communities and classrooms.* New York: Cambridge University Press.
hooks, b. (2003). *Teaching community: A pedagogy of hope.* New York: Routledge.
Huey, E. (1908). *The psychology and pedagogy of reading.* Cambridge, MA: M. I. T. Press.
Jiménez, F. (1997). *The circuit: Stories from the life of a migrant child.* Albuquerque: University of New Mexico Press.
Juster, N. (1988). *The phantom tollbooth.* New York: Yearling.
Karp, S. (2004). NCLB's selective vision of equality: Some gaps count more than others. In D. Meier, A. Kohn, L Darling-Hammond, T. Sizer, & G. Wood (Eds.), *Many children left behind: How the No Child Left Behind Act is damaging our children and our schools* (pp. 53–65). Boston: Beacon Press.
Keene, E., & Zimmerman, S. (1997). *Mosaic of thought: Teaching comprehension in a reader's workshop.* Portsmouth, NH: Heinemann.
Kitchen, R., Velázquez, D., & Myers, J. (2000). *Dropouts in New Mexico: Native American and Hispanic students speak out.* Paper presented at the Annual Meeting of the American Educational Research Association, New Orleans, LA (ERIC Document Reproduction Service No. ED440795).
Kohl, H. (1991). *I won't learn from you! The role of assent in learning.* Minneapolis: Milkweed Editions.
Kolbe, T. (1999). *The civil rights movement in Lincoln, Nebraska.* Unpublished compact disk, Lincoln, NE.
Koss, A. (1995). *The cat.* New York: Open Court.
Kozol, J. (2005). *The shame of the nation: The restoration of apartheid schooling in America.* New York: Crown.
Ladson-Billings, G. (1994). *The dreamkeepers: Successful teachers of African American children.* San Francisco: Jossey-Bass.
Ladson-Billings, G. (2001). *Crossing over Canaan: The journey of new teachers in diverse classrooms.* San Francisco: Jossey-Bass.

REFERENCES

Lakoff, G. (2004). *Don't think of an elephant! Know your values and frame the debate.* White River Junction, VT: Chelsea Green.

Lampert, M. (1985). How do teachers manage to teach? Perspectives on problems in practice. *Harvard Educational Review, 55*(2), 178–194.

Lareau, A. (2000). *Home advantage: Social class and parental intervention in elementary education.* Lanham, MD: Rowman & Littlefield.

Lewis, C. (2001). *Literacy practices as social acts: Power, status, and cultural norms in the classroom.* Mahwah, NJ: Lawrence Erlbaum Associates.

Lewison, M., Flint, A., & Van Sluys, K. (2002) Taking on critical literacy: The journey of newcomers and novices. *Language Arts, 79*(5), 382–392.

Liston, D., & Zeichner, K. (1996). *Culture and teaching.* Mahwah, NJ: Lawrence Erlbaum Associates.

Luke, A. (1999, June). Further notes on the four resources model. *Practically Primary, 4*(2). Retrieved March 1, 2005 from http://www.alea.edu.au/freebody.htm.

Martino, W. (2001). "Dickheads, Wuses, and Faggots": Addressing issues of masculinity and homophobia in the critical literacy classroom. In B. Comber & A. Simpson (Eds.), *Negotiating critical literacies in classrooms* (pp. 171–180). Mahwah, NJ: Lawrence Erlbaum Associates.

McCardle, P., & Chhabra, V. (2004). *The voice of evidence in reading research.* Baltimore: P.H. Brookes.

McCarty, T. (2002). *A place to be Navajo: Rough Rock and the struggle for self-determination in indigenous schooling.* Mahwah, NJ: Lawrence Erlbaum Associates.

Meyer, R. (1996). *Stories from the heart: Teachers and students researching their literacy lives.* Mahwah, NJ: Lawrence Erlbaum Associates.

Meyer, R. (1999, October). Professional voices/theoretical framework: Spiders, rats, and transformation. *Primary Voices, 8*(2), 3–9.

Meyer, R. (2001). *Phonics exposed: Understanding and resisting systematic direct intense phonics instruction.* Mahwah, NJ: Lawrence Erlbaum Associates.

Meyer, R. , Brown, L., DeNino, E., Larson, K., McKenzie, M., Ridder, K., & Zetterman, K. (1998). *Composing a teacher study group: Learning about inquiry in primary classrooms.* Mahwah, NJ: Lawrence Erlbaum Associates.

Moats, L. (2000). *Speech to print: Language essentials for teachers.* Baltimore: Paul H. Brookes.

Moll, L., Amanti, C., Neff, D., & Gonzalez, N. (1992, Spring). Funds of knowledge for teachers: Using a qualitative approach to connect homes and classrooms. *Theory into Practice, 31*(1), 132–141.

Montessori, M. (1966). *The secret of childhood.* (M. Joseph Costelloe, Trans.). Notre Dame, IN: Fides Publishers.

Munsch, R. (1980). *The paper bag princess.* Toronto: Annick Press.

Myers, W. (2005). *Bad boy: A memoir.* Waterville, ME: Thorndike Press.

National Reading Panel (2000a). *Teaching children to read: An evidence-based assessment of the scientific research literature on reading and its implications for reading instruction. Report of the subgroups.* Washington, DC: National Institutes of Health.

National Reading Panel (2000b). *Teaching children to read: An evidence-based assessment of the scientific research literature on reading and its implications for reading instruction. [Summary Report].* Washington, DC: National Institutes of Health.

Nieto, S. (2002). *Language, culture, and teaching: Critical perspectives for a new century.* Mahwah, NJ: Lawrence Erlbaum Associates.

Noble, T. (1980). *The day Jimmy's boa ate the wash.* New York: Dial Books.

Ohanian, S. (1999). *One size fits few: The folly of educational standards.* Portsmouth, NH: Heinemann.

Ohanian, S. (2001). *Caught in the middle: Nonstandard kids and a killing curriculum.* Portsmouth, NH: Heinemann.

Paley, V. (1995). *Kwanzaa and me: A teacher's story.* Cambridge: Harvard University Press.

Paulson, E., & Freeman, A. (2003). *Insights from the eyes: The science of effective reading instruction.* Portsmouth: Heinemann.

Payne, R. (1998). *Framework for understanding poverty.* Baytown, TX: RFT Publishers.

Pearson, P.D., Roehler, L., Dole, J., & Duffy, G. (1992). Developing expertise in reading comprehension. In J. Samuels & A. Farstrup (Eds.), *What research has to say about reading instruction.* Newark, DE: International Reading Association.

Perry, T., & Delpit, L. (Eds.). (1998). *The real ebonics debate: power, language, and the education of African-American children.* Boston: Beacon Press.

Peterson, R., & Eeds, M. (1990). *Grand conversations: Literature groups in action.* New York: Scholastic.

Phi Delata Kappan, (2005, February). [Entire issue]. *Phi Delta Kappan,* 86(6).

Philips, S. (1971). Participant structures and communicative competence: Warm Springs children in community and classroom. In C. Cazden, V. John, & D. Hymes (Eds.), *Functions of language in the classroom* (pp. 370–393). New York: Teachers College Press.

Poynor, L., & Wolfe, P. (Eds.). (2005). *Marketing fear in America's public schools: The real war on literacy.* Mahwah, NJ: Lawrence Erlbaum Associates.

Rogers, R. (2003). *A critical discourse analysis of family literacy practices: Power in and out of print.* Mahwah, NJ: Lawrence Erlbaum Associates.

Rosenblatt, L. (1976). *Literature as exploration* (4th ed.). New York: Modern Language Association.

Rosenblatt, L. (1978). *The reader, the text, and the poem: The transactional theory of the literary work.* Carbondale and Edwardsville: Southern Illinois University Press.

Sarason, S. (1971). *The culture of school and the problem of change.* New York: McGraw-Hill.

Schwartz, A. (1984). *In a dark, dark room and other scary stories.* New York: Scholastic.

Schwartz, S., & Pollishuke, M. (1991). *Creating the child-centered classroom.* Katonah, NY: Richard C. Owen.

Shanahan, T. (2005, February). But does it really matter? *Phi Delta Kappan,* 86(6), 452–455.

Shannon, P. (1990). *The struggle to continue: Progressive reading instruction in the United States.* Portsmouth, NH: Heinemann.

Short, K., & Burke, C. (1991). *Creating curriculum: Teachers and students as a community of learners.* Portsmouth: Heinemann.

Short, K.,& Harste, J., with Burke, C. (1996). *Creating classrooms for authors and inquirers* (2nd ed.). Portsmouth, NH: Heinemann.

Silverstein, S. (1964). *The giving tree.* New York: Harper & Row.

Smith, F. (1983). Demonstrations, engagement, and sensitivity. In F. Smith (Ed.), *Essays into literacy* (pp. 95–106). Portsmouth, NH: Heinemann.

Smith, F. (1988). *Joining the literacy club: Further essays into education.* Portsmouth, NH: Heinemann.

REFERENCES

Snow, C., Burns, M., & Griffin, P. (1998). *Preventing reading difficulties in young children.* Washington, DC: National Academy Press.

Solorzano, D., Ceja, M., & Yosso, Y. (2000). Critical race theory, racial microaggressions, and campus racial climate: The experiences of African American college students. *Journal of Negro Education, 69*(1/2), 60–73.

Street, B. (1995). *Social literacies: Critical approaches to literacy development, ethnography, and education.* New York: Longman.

Stuckey, J. E. (1991). *The violence of literacy.* Portsmouth: Heinemann.

Taylor, D. (1996). *Toxic literacies: Exposing the injustice of bureaucratic texts.* Portsmouth: Heinemann.

Thomas, W., & Collier, V. (2002). A national study of school effectiveness for language minority students' long-term academic achievement. Santa Cruz, CA: Center for Research on Education, Diversity, & Excellence. (ERIC Document Reproduction Service No. ED475048)

Valdés, G., (1996). *Con respeto: Bridging and distance between culturally diverse families and schools.* New York: Teachers College Press.

Vasquez, V. (2000). Finding our way: Using the everyday to create a criticial literacy curriculum. *Primary Voices K-6, 9*(2), 8–13.

Vygotsky, L. (1978). *The development of higher psychological processes.* In M. Cole, V. John-Steiner, S. Scribner, & E. Souberman (Eds.), *Mind in society.* Cambridge: Harvard University Press.

Walkerdine, V. (1990). *Schoolgirl fictions.* London: Verso.

Weaver, C. (1988). *Reading process and practice: From socio-psycholinguistics to whole language.* Portsmouth, NH: Heinemann.

Weaver, C., Gillmeister-Krause, L., & Vento-Zogby, G. (1997). *Creating support for effective literacy education: Workshop materials and handouts.* Portsmouth, NH: Heinemann.

Wells, G. (1986). *The meaning makers: Children learning language and using language to learn.* Portsmouth: Heinemann.

Westcott, N.B. (n.d.) (Illustrator, no author cited). *Peanut butter and jelly: A play rhyme.* New York: Dutton Children's Books.

Whitmore, K., & Crowell, C. (1994). *Inventing a classroom: Life in a bilingual, whole language learning community.* Portland, ME: Stenhouse.

Wilson, L. (2002). *Reading to live: How to teach reading for today's world.* Portsmouth: Heinemann.

Wolfe, P. (2003). *"Transformational" responses, student identity, and ways of reading.* Paper presented at the annual convention of the National Council of Teachers of English, San Francisco, CA.

Wolpert, E. (1994). Rethinking "The Three Little Pigs." In B. Bigelow, L. Christensen, S. Karp, B. Miner, & B. Peterson, *Rethinking our classrooms: Teaching for equity and justice* (p. 11). Milwaukee, WI: Rethinking Schools.

AUTHOR INDEX

A

Adams, M., 122, 123
Allington, R., 160
Altwerger, B., xvi
Amanti, C., 32
Anderson, G., 136
Angelou, M., 91
Applebee, A., 162
Atwell, N., 84, 94
Au, K., 32, 66, 135, 138, 153, 166
Ayers, W., 153

B

Berliner, D., xvi
Biddle, B., xvi
Bigelow, B., 153
Bloome, D., 124, 167
Bomer, R., 142, 146
Bomer, K., 142, 146
Bourdieu, P., 140
Brooke, R., 171
Brown, J., 92
Brown, L., 131
Burke, C., 131, 135, 136, 161, 175
Burns, M., 123

C

Cambourne, B., 132
Carger, C., 154
Carlson, N., 64

Cazden, C., 136
Ceja, M., 170
Chall, J., 123
Chhabra, V., 160
Christensen, L., 153
Clay, M., 134
Cochran-Smith, M., 96, 163
Coles, G., 160
Collier, V., 167
Comber, B., 145, 153
Compton-Lilly, C., 154
Cowley, J., 63, 127
Craviotto, E., 139

D

Dail, A., 124
Darling-Hammond, L., 107
Davenport, R., 134
Delpit, L., 89, 90
DeNino, E., 131
Dewey, J., 124, 172
DIBELS, 120
Dole, J., 114
Dowdy, J. K., 89
Duffy, G., 114
Durand, V. M., 160
Dyson, A., 38, 175

E

Edelsky, C., 140

Eeds, M., 64, 66, 127, 128
Espindola, J., 139

F

Finders, M., 175
Flesch, R., xv
Flint, A., 138
Florio-Ruane, S., 143
Flurkey, A., 126
Freire, P., 141, 142
Freeman, A., 126

G

Gannett, R., 75
Garan, E., 160
Gee, J., 154
Gillmeister-Krause, L., 125
Goldstein, L., 97, 163
Gollasch, F., 124
Gonzalez, N., 32
Goodman, K., 113, 124, 160
Goodman, Y., 92, 133, 135, 160, 166, 175
Goss, J., 129
Graves, D., 129
Griffin, P., 123
Grumet, M., 170
Guerra, J., 38, 57
Gutiérrez, K., 139, 169

H

Hansen, J., 135
Harste, J., 129, 130, 131, 136
Harvey, B., 153
Heath, S. B., 171
Heras, A., 139
Herr, K., 136
hooks, b., 140
Huey, E., xv
Hunt, J., 153

J

Jiménez, F., 91
Juster, N., 165

K

Karp, S., 107, 153
Keene, E., 94, 128, 145
Kitchen, R., 97
Kohl, H., 167
Kolbe, T., 139
Koss, A., 116

Kozol, J., 142

L

Ladson-Billings, G., 32, 66, 83, 135, 138, 153
Lakoff, G., 168
Lampert, M., 159
Lareau, A., 140, 171
Larson, J., 139, 169
Larson, K., 131
Lewis, C., 162
Lewison, M., 138
Liston, D., ix, xiv, 96
Luke, A., 141
Lytle, S., 96, 163

M

Macedo, D., 141
Macedo, D., 141
Marek, A., 92, 133
Martino, W., 153
McCardle, P., 160
McCarty, T., 143, 166
McKenzie, M., 131
Meyer, R., 131, 159, 172
Miller, L., 153
Moats, L., xvi
Moll, L., 32
Montessori, M., 163
Munsch, R., 145
Myers, J., 97
Myers, W., 91

N

National Reading Panel 122, 142, 160
Neff, D., 32
Nieto, S., 167
Nihlen, A., 136
Noble, T., 165

O

Ohanian, S., 54, 83, 107

P

Paley, V., 36
Paulson, E., 126
Payne, R., 93
Pearson, P.D., 114
Perry, T., 90
Peterson, R., 64, 66, 127, 128
Phi Delta Kappan, 135
Philips, S., 152

AUTHOR INDEX

Pollishuke, M., 133
Poynor, L., 160

Q

Quinn, T., 153

R

Rappoport, R., 160
Ridder, K., 131
Roehler, L., 114
Rogers, R. 154
Rosenblatt, L., 124, 125, 168
Rymes, B., 169

S

Sarason, S., 163
Schwartz, A., 57
Schwartz, S., 133
Shanahan, T., xvi
Shannon, P., 124, 160
Short, K., 135, 161
Silverstein, S., 134, 149
Simpson, A., 145, 153
Smith, F., 94, 132
Snow, C., 123
Solorzano, D., 170
Street, B., xvi, 107
Stuckey, J.E., 141

T

Taylor, D., 154
Thomas, W., 167

V

Van Sluys, K., 138
Valdés, G., 39
Vasquez, V., xx, 146
Velázquez, D., 97
Vento-Zogby, G., 125
Vygotsky, L., 163

W

Wacquant, L., 140
Walkerdine, V., 171
Watson, D., 135
Weaver, C., 94, 125
Wells, G., 136
Westcott, N. B., 61
Whitmore, K., 136
Wilson, L., xx
Wolfe, P., 160, 171
Wolpert, E., 141
Woodward, V., 136

Y

Yosso, Y., 170

Z

Zeichner, K., ix, xiv, 96
Zetterman, K., 131
Zimmerman, S., 94, 128, 145

SUBJECT INDEX

A

Agency and learners, 131, 142, 146, 148, 163
Articles
    magazine, 151, 153, 175
    newspaper, 66, 91, 93, 103–104, 136
Assessing reading
    Critical Literacy, 148–152
    Direct Instruction, 119–121
    Whole Language, 133–135
Automaticity/automatic recognition, 119, 120, 170

B

Balanced literacy, 48, 71, 112
Basal reading program, 2, 4–8, 13–14, 16–24, 29–30, 48, 105, 110, 112, 116–118, 121, 128, 137, 164–165, 167
Best practice, 99, 103, 162
Big books, 127, 129
Bilingual children and teachers, 3–4, 44, 56–57, 167

C

Canned programs, *see* Basal reading program
Centers, 13–14, 56–59, 63, 101
Central administration, 84, 100
Chapter books (novels and longer texts), 22, 63, 66, 129
Children's lives outside of school, 14, 36, 38, 48, 93–94, 121, 174

Choice and instruction/learning, 3, 44, 52, 99–100, 119–121, 127–129, 132–133, 135, 146, 153, 157
Cinderella, 128, 145
Class size, 97
Classroom flooding, 85, 97–99, 104
Classroom management and discipline, 16–18, 35, 45, 77
Coding, 10–11, 14, 21, 29–30
Colleagues, 29, 32, 48, 55–57, 81, 84, 97, 108, 144, 149, 151, 153, 158, 161, 163–164, 170, 172, 176
Common sense view of reading, 113
Comprehension
    Critical Literacy classrooms, 134, 143
    Direct Instruction classrooms, 112–119
    text comprehension, 122, 123, 143
    Whole Language classrooms, 124, 128
Conditions for learning, 132
Connections
    to self, 128
    to texts, 128
    to world, 128
Consejos, 39
Context (and teaching reading), 39, 58, 68, 145, 152–153, 163, 170, 175
Contradictions, 155
Control
    controlled vocabulary, 117
    of teachers, 76, 99, 117, 152, 169
Conversations
    critical issues, 153
    reading instruction, 127–129, 133, 142, 146–148, 151–152, 162, 164, 177

191

Cooperating teacher, 2–3, 32–35, 42, 47–48, 158
Criterion referenced tests, 120
Critical Literacy
　activism, 146
　advertising, 145
　assessing reading in, 148–152
　culture and social context, 152
　critical work, 142
　curriculum, 152
　defined, 83, 137–156
　definition of reading, 140–143
　four dimensions, 152
　gender, 150, 151
　inquiry, 145
　kindergarteners, 146
　multiple points of view/perspectives, 142, 149
　nature of learning, 147
　reading assessment, 148
　role of the learner, 147–148
　role of the teacher, 145–147
　teaching, 143–145, 147
　view of the reading process, 153–154
Cueing systems, 92, 126, 128–131, 133, 140, 145, 153, 174
Culturally relevant teaching, 32, 40, 54, 66, 83, 137–138
Culturally responsive teaching, 33–34, 47, 50, 135, 138, 142, 153, 165
Curriculum
　administratively controlled, 90, 160, 171
　bilingual education, 51
　Critical Literacy, 141, 152
　culturally relevant, 137–138
　Direct Instruction, 120
　meaning-centered, 102
　official, 36, 38, 175
　one size fits all, 54, 177
　prescribed (*see also* Basal reading programs), 40, 96–97, 120–121
　standards driven, 107
　students, 25
　teachers making changes in, 78, 123, 162
　test driven, 101
　Whole Language, 135

D

Decision making, 49, 50–51, 90
Decodable books, 86, 115–116, 129
Definition of reading
　Critical Literacy, 140
　Direct Instruction, 112–114
　Whole Language, 124–127
DIBELS, 120
Direct Instruction
　assessing reading in, 119–120
　culture and social context as a consideration in, 121–122
　curriculum, 120–121
　definition of reading, 112–114
　learning in, 118–119
　research supporting, 122–123
　role of the learner, 119–120
　role of the teacher, 117–118
　teaching, 114–117
　view of the reading process, 120
Discourse, 77, 153
Diversity/diverse schools, 3, 14, 51, 55, 121, 152, 172
Drop Everything and Read (DEAR), 5
Dropouts, 169
Drugs 148

E

English as a second language (ESL)/English language learners, 4, 25, 56, 159, 167
Explorers' club, 57, 68
Extensive reading, 128

F

Families, 18, 21, 29, 38–39, 41, 44, 49, 51, 56, 85, 88–90, 94, 97, 110, 116, 142, 147, 151, 154, 172
Fear
　compliance, 79
　conversations with children, 130
　hurting exceptional teachers, 73
　losing instructional time, 37
　of being seen as incompetent, 76
　response to administration, 75
　students addressing, 137
First grade, 7–8, 16, 33, 35, 41, 55, 72, 131, 159
First year of teaching, 2, 5, 16–18, 20, 23, 25, 29, 35, 40, 70, 73, 77, 103, 117, 170
First-year teachers' study groups, 36
Flow, 126
Fluency (*see also* Flow)
　defined, 7, 116, 119, 123, 125
　writing and, 94
Four Blocks, 34–35, 37–38, 40, 45, 49, 112, 114, 119, 122
Free/reduced lunch, 2, 56, 85
Funds and school funding, 97, 101, 107, 123, 176
Funds of knowledge, 32–33, 39, 45–46, 48

G

Gangs, 148
Gender, 91, 97, 147, 149, 151, 162, 174

SUBJECT INDEX

Gender-specific classrooms, 87
Graphic organizers, 133
Grouping students, 3, 5, 7
Guided reading, 22, 34, 40, 45
Guiding questions, for dialogues, 1

H

High-frequency words, *see* Sight words
High-stakes testing
   teacher salaries, 118
   test scores, 90, 107

I

Identity
   child, 54
   cultural, 32–33, 44, 83, 96, 108, 155, 158
   teacher, 54
Immigrant children, 51
"ing" alert, 65
Intensive reading, 128
Isolation, 163

J

Justice and social action, 140

K

Karen, 159-160

L

Language in the home, Spanish, 3, 33, 37, 41, 44, 51, 57, 139, 170
Literacy autobiography, 33, 50, 172
Literature circles, 57, 66
Literature in classrooms,
   children's, 47–48, 74, 84, 98, 122
   civil rights, 168
   literature-based program, 90, 96, 112
   Spanish, 44
Loneliness, 163

M

Making meaning/meaning making, 58, 70, 92, 125, 127
Mentoring, 4, 44–45, 78, 158
Methods courses, 2, 26, 32–33, 40, 47, 55
Microaggressions, 170
Middle school
   standardized tests in, 179
   teachers work in, 83–84, 90
Miscue analysis, 32, 61, 65–66, 92, 103, 124, 134

Morale in school, 97
Moving the furniture, 49, 51, 78

N

National Institute of Child Health and Human Development (NICHD), 122
National Reading Panel (NRP)
   critical literacy critique, 143
   influences on instruction, 122–123, 136–137, 142, 160
National Writing Project, 84, 163, 171
No Child Left Behind (NCLB), 16, 19, 22, 85, 107, 120, 123, 160, 169

O

Observing
   a community, 174
   children reading, 175
   family, 175
   school, 174
Oral tradition, 91-92

P

Paintings, 133
Parent support, 19
Peanut butter and jelly, 61
Performance(s), 133
Personal reading, 56, 62
Phonemic awareness
   explained, 113–114, 120, 123, 143
   phonemic blending, 112, 117, 120
   phonemic segmentation, 120
Phonics
   Critical Literacy and, 141
   Direct Instruction phonics programs, 3, 9, 14, 18, 21, 29, 34, 112, 115
   instruction, 6, 8–12, 27, 68, 92, 123 159
   rules, 121
   scientifically based research, 123
   Whole Language, 124
Platica, 37
Poems, 45, 57, 60, 89, 93, 167
Politics and teaching reading, 189
Popular press representing teachers, 109
Posters, 41, 64, 86, 133, 149
Power structures, 154
Predictable texts, 129–130, 146
Predictions, and guessing, 59, 61, 114, 126, 129–130
Preservice teacher education, 33, 46, 109

Principals, 41, 48–49, 75, 160, 171
Professional development, 176

R

Reading
  assessment, Critical Literacy, 148–152
  assessment, Direct Instruction, 119–120
  assessment, Whole Language, 133
  comprehension,
    assessing, 110
    Critical Literacy, 140, 142
    Direct Instruction, 7, 112, 114, 116
    interactional, 114
    questions, 8, 13
    transactional, 124–125, 131, 155, 172
    Whole Language, 124, 128
  conference form, 67
  definitions of
    Critical Literacy, 141–143
    Direct Instruction, 112
    Whole Language, 124, 128
  groups, 5, 12–13, 16, 20, 24, 26, 29, 45, 51, 89, 118
  instruction, teachers' roles in, 117
  National Reading Panel, 123
  political activity and, 141
  purposes for reading, 93
  social act, as a, 167
  wars, 109
Relationships
  with children, 17, 48
  with colleagues, 48
  with families, 48
Reliable replicable research, 136
Research
  supporting Direct Instruction, 122
  supporting Whole Language, 136
Rethinking Schools, 153
Running record, 134

S

Schedules for teaching, 5, 24, 35, 56, 87
Scientifically based reading research (SBRR), *see* Reliable replicable research
Scripted lessons, 30, 160, 169, 171
Second grade, 2, 4, 16, 42, 44, 114, 144
Self-selection, 128
Semantic webs, 133
Shared reading, 45
Sight words, 9, 113, 115–116
Socioeconomic levels, 77, 87–90, 93, 99
Songs, 92

Spelling, 6, 13, 25, 41, 115, 117, 132, 151
Spiders, 131
Standardized tests, 3, 41, 83, 99, 101, 104, 107, 119–120, 161, 169
Standards
  Criterion referenced tests, 120
  Critical Literacy, 152
  curriculum driven by, 107
  Direct Instruction, 119
  high-stakes testing, 107
  middle school, 107
  states, 25
  used against children in schools, 169
  Whole Language, 127, 135
Strategies versus skills 81
Struggling readers, 5, 8, 13, 23, 29, 65, 92–93, 118
Student teaching, 2, 26, 32–34, 170
Students as activists/citizens, 139, 142
Study groups
  experienced teachers, 55, 131, 163, 171
  first-year teachers, 2, 4, 14, 36, 154
Symbolic violence, 170

T

Tasks during reading instruction, 6, 12
Teacher isolation, 4, 29, 52, 77, 139, 163–164
Teacher read alouds, 6, 13, 16, 23, 57, 63, 66, 75, 91–92, 122, 149
Teachers Applying Whole Language (TAWL), 131
Teaching reading
  across all four cases, 158
  addressing student needs, 81, 109
  Critical Literacy, 144
  culture in, *see* Culturally responsive or culturally relevant teaching
  deferred decision making, 121
  poverty and, 25, 31, 55–56, 85, 89, 97, 107, 141, 154, 175
  responsibilities, 152
  singing/songs, 24, 66, 93, 133, 139
  units, 26
  Whole Language, 127
Test scores and intervention, 85
Tests and testing
  criterion referenced, 120
  cultural relevance, 160
  Direct Instruction programs, 119–120
  end-of-year performance, 29, 41
  high-stakes, 90, 92, 99, 101, 104, 107
  intervention, 85
  preparation for, 20, 22
  referring special-needs students, 23

SUBJECT INDEX

relationship to standards, 107
spelling, 6
standardized, 3, 77, 83, 107, 161, 169
versus other measures, 139–140
The Three Pigs, 141
Tone with children, 20
Transactions and reading, *see* Comprehension

V

Vocabulary
  charts, 86
  controlled
    in Critical Literacy, 143
    in Direct Instruction, 117
    in Whole Language, 125
  Direct Instruction, 113
  in journals, 94

teaching specific words, 7

W

Whole Language
  assessing reading, 133–135
  culture and social context, 135–136
  curriculum in, 135
  definition of reading, 124–127
  learning, 132–133
  teaching, 127–128
  research supporting, 136–137
  role of the learner, 133
  role of the teacher, 128–132
  view of the reading process, 127
Workbooks, 6–7, 90, 116, 118, 122
Worksheets, 3, 5–8, 11, 90, 116, 118, 122, 173
Writing and teaching reading, 40